My Casting Couch Was Too Short

My Casting Couch Was Too Short

Marion Dougherty
with
Robert Roussel

Library of Congress Control Number:		2014922666
ISBN:	Hardcover	978-1-5035-2950-2
	Softcover	978-1-5035-2951-9
	eBook	978-1-5035-2952-6

To order additional copies of this book, contact:
Xlibris
1-888-795-4274
www.Xlibris.com
Orders@Xlibris.com
695714

Contents

It's really nice, you know. To be able to see the arc of your life . . . that it's all connected . . . and see how you got from there to here . . . to see the line, you know . . . it really has been an adventure.

The World According to Garp

Casting Away, Then and Now

Back in the heyday of the 1930s and 1940s Hollywood Studio system, the Golden Era as it is sometimes referred to, a movie studio was in its own world. Everything needed to make a movie was right there on the studio lot. There was no need to go on location and no need to have a worldwide search for the right actor. Actors, for parts large and small, were chosen from those many under contract to the studio. The supply was constantly nurtured and replenished by on-site studio schools with lessons provided in acting, voice, elocution, dance—whatever was needed—all designed to keep the talent pool thriving and performing. Actors were given the chance to appear first in small roles before moving onto featured supporting roles and finally, if the public responded to them, starring roles.

Clint Eastwood shared some stories with me about his early days while he was under contract at Universal. Clint was studying business administration at Los Angeles City College and wound up taking a few acting classes. He began to study Michael Chekhov's book titled *To the Actor* and attended some of George Shadanoff's lectures on the subject. Irving Glassberg, a known cinematographer at the time, managed to arrange a screen test for Clint at Universal. They liked what they saw and signed Clint as a contract player at the rate of seventy-eight dollars per week, which was pretty good money in those days. He began to show up at Universal and take the different classes offered each day in acting, dance, voice, physical education, horseback riding—whatever the schedule was on a particular day. He said some of the others under contract didn't always show up, but he thought it was so much fun that he went almost every day. It was during this time that he began to hone in on his craft and to better understand the filmmaking process. Universal kept him under contract for almost two years before they finally let him go. He managed to hang in there and, not too long afterward, was cast as Rowdy Yates in the television series *Rawhide*.

Actors under contract were cosseted by studio publicity departments, which handled press releases and magazine interviews, all of which flattered them and hid any revelatory details. They had their photos taken by studio photographers (rather than paparazzi), whose job was only to capture their images in the most flattering manner. Actors were guided in their choices of even the small details of their private life—which car to drive, which new hair color, who to be seen with—as part of the studio's master plan to keep them favorably in the audience's field of vision and, for the most part, constantly employed, moving from one production to the next. They may have had to suffer being typecast or punished by the studio for some indiscretion by being forced to appear in a movie that did not appeal to them, but they were more than taken care of by the studios that held their seven–plus-year contracts. Most of the studios also owned their movie houses across the country. As fast as they could turn out a movie, they booked it into their own nationwide theater chain and, hopefully, watched the money roll in.

That was until 1948 when an antitrust suit came to the United States Supreme Court, *United States v. Paramount Pictures et al.*, and the studios lost their theater chains, and all that assured income became considerably less. Movie studios had to begin to downsize, shedding their "systems" and shutting down sizable chunks of their back lots, which were sold to real estate developers. They ended their long-term contracts with actors and no longer provided them with the in-house publicity managers and other trainers. The studios had to find a new way to find the right talented and trained professionals to appear before the camera and to engage the public's emotions and affections. It was certainly the end of an era for many actors.

I started when this art (and I do think it's an important one) of casting was just beginning. I have often been asked, "How do you cast?" and can tell you truthfully, "I don't know." I did not know when I first began my career, and I still do not know today. At least I can't tell you, number one, do this; number two, do this; number three, do this; and—*voila!*—you have just cast a production. Much of my success as a casting director was, simply put, gut intuition.

Good casting results when the right actor is cast in a role and gives a performance that is highly credible, interesting, and involving. Great casting results when someone who has not previously had the chance gets cast in a role that produces a performance with the above-mentioned criteria or an actor is cast in a role that is so vastly different from anything they have done before as to be stunning in revealing a new side of the actor's unforeseen talents.

In old Hollywood, the selection of leading roles was done by producers and directors at a studio who went over their lists of performers who were under contract to that studio. At times, the studios would "trade" their stars. Many performers were from theater and many of the ingénues had gotten on the lists by providing social services to the big studio executives.

This led to cliché casting. If an actor had made a good butler, doctor, etc., they were apt to be considered only for the same type of roles over and over. In a different way today, cliché casting is still going strong. Pity the actor who was a hit in a blockbuster movie that pulled in big bucks for the studio whose producers were convinced that the audience would only want to see that actor in the same type of role in the future. This has made many actors very wealthy; but with so many sequels, so much sameness being dealt to the movie audience, cliché casting really does not serve the audience well.

There are actors who avoid this by carefully choosing roles based on material or directors and also those who refuse to keep repeating themselves in the "same" role over and over. The very beautiful Charlize Theron broke herself out of always being cast based on her physical appearance when she produced, starred in, and won an Academy Award for her terrific performance in *Monster*.

The role of a casting director is a preproduction process in film and television that involves the selection of actors and other talent to hire for a live or recorded performance. It really all begins with finding a good script and scheduling a meeting with the director to better understand their take on each individual role. You may not see the material as they do. I've been fortunate enough to be able to disagree with a director about how a part should be cast. Sometimes I'm right; sometimes I'm not. It's going to be the director's vision that will be on the screen, and if he or she cannot agree with you, fight, and then forget it. Nowadays, many directors will just want to see demo reels of an actor, a shame because what they see is a different part of someone else's interpretation of it. I have always thought it much better and more productive to just sit and have the actor read the part for the director.

It's also during this preproduction process with the producers and director that a casting budget is put together. Based on experience, I was able to help develop a budget that included the leading roles and how many days each of the other actors worked according to the script and production schedule. Of course, it depends on the amount of money the production company has to work with on the project. I was always very good with negotiating good deals for the company; it was always harder for me to make a deal for my salary. I finally asked a friend of mine, Bill Truesch, to take care of that.

I've always despised what is known in casting as a cattle call, literally to herd all possible comers for a part in a room and see them one after another. It's important to see films, television, and theater. After seeing a good actor's performance, I'll invite the actor in to see me and simply visit, not necessarily to audition for a specific role. I'll ask where they were born, if they have any pets, what their hobbies and interests are—seemingly idle chitchat to put the actor at ease. And in this organic way, I'll learn more about that actor's skills, their immediate personality and seriousness as an actor, and if they have a sense of humor. When a level of comfort is reached, I'll perhaps ask the actor to read a scene with me, and I'd read the other part so we can "act" together. I always made certain that I personally knew the scene well enough so that I could make eye contact and wouldn't emote so much that I'd drown the actor out but rather give them an energy that they could bounce off. When the actor left, I'd make up my own personal three-by-five index file card and detail my instinctive and intuitive feelings about the actor. *(See Appendix 1)*

I'm not fond of bringing in a slew of people for the same part. A good casting person should be able to present just a few people and see who fits the bill best. If no one seems right, then you must try again, but you will have learned more about the part and the director's thinking by then.

After many weeks, and sometimes months of work, the final casting decisions are made, and I'd work with the actors' agent and write up a deal memo and give it to the production company to let their managers or lawyers draw up the contracts to be signed. Occasionally, I'd have to find a replacement for an actor who couldn't seem to "fulfill" their contract during production.

Elia Kazan once stated that 90 percent of directing is casting.

Throughout my years in the business, the actor's contract has changed immensely. When I first started at *Kraft Television Theatre* in 1949, we were paying the lead actor for an appearance in a one-hour dramatic episode about seventy-five dollars. There were very few agents based in New York back then, and our contracts were rather simple. When I left *Kraft Television Theatre* in 1958, the lead actor was being paid in the neighborhood of $750 per episode, and there were now more agents, and the contracts began to include several new clauses for the actor. Today some agents do know talent, while others would sell you their grandmothers for an ingénue if they could. There are so many agents these days that it's hard to keep track of them. Some are interested in suggesting newcomers with budding talent, and some are only interested in those agency clients who can command the highest salaries. If you find one who has the same taste and dedication as yourself, it's a much happier relationship.

There are agents like Iris Burton who specialize in children and bring them along in their careers with loving care. There are some whose "eye" is very acute and can be trusted to recommend really talented actors who may or may not be right for a certain part but give them an interview anyway; they may be worthwhile to remember for other things. Susan Smith, who later moved onto managing, was such an agent. She was also very savvy about scripts and carefully guided her clients to the material that would be best for them.

The good agents would have researched the background and experience of their clients; would have gone to see them in the theater, however small, to check out their work, watched their film progress; and would have found out where their talent works best. These are the agents that you depend on for good suggestions.

You have to be honest with agents. If your budget is very low (as mine was at times), tell them. There is no sense in getting in an actor, having the director fall in love with that person, and then finding out that you can't afford them. It then is twice as hard to find someone who can replace them.

Usually, we know the qualities we're getting with well-known actors, or at least we should. There are times, though, when we're not positive, and then it's best to ask them to meet with us and the director and discuss the project and possibly read the material together. On more than one occasion, I've had agents refuse to let their client read for a part. And at times, a skillful director can override an agent saying, no, they will read. Agents usually hate that, but if you have a respected director and a good script, there are, surprisingly, very good actors who will understand and, for their own information, want to experiment with a meeting or reading. Most want to judge the directors bent and he, theirs.

Not all casting directors are asked, nor do they want, to make deals. Deals can be a royal pain in the neck or sometimes a challenging game. It helps if you have established some kind of estimates with agents when first calling in performers. Today the lawyers do the negotiating for the big names. As we can all see, except those precious few actors who should command multimillion-dollar salaries, the prices have gotten ridiculous.

Salaries now are not the worst part of the deal. If you have a budget, you can probably juggle things a bit, steal a bit from one part to add to another part that is more crucial, but I always tried to be as fair as I could to all, and I never went over budget.

Perks are the *bête noir*. Stars are given first shots at the perks, but it's only practical to try to see that other performers are as comfortable as possible, for then you will get the best out of their talent. It ain't easy.

Often it's hard to find out how many accommodations are available and hard to allot space to the right performers. Many need a private spot to study scripts, rest before a difficult scene, etc. Even for the supporting roles, sometimes agents can really send you round the bend with ridiculous petty points: Who gets the best or biggest trailer or dressing room? Can the car bringing you to the set be just for one, or do you have to share with others? I remember one agent who tried my patience enough that I said, "What color toilet paper would she like in her john?"

Billing order is also a tricky one. Sometimes contractually, the best spots are given, and then you get a wonderful actor in a small but crucial scene—where do you put them? Some studios and producers do not object to a number of actors listed in the opening credits (before the movie begins). Other times they want to limit that desired spot to big names only, and many get left in the end credits. How many names will they allow on one card becomes a problem. Position on that card is important. I'm a believer in trying to make things as equal as possible, as it's easier if you have rules and limits so that, besides the leading actors, the supporting actors can be treated equally.

Most actors are fragile. Many of them have spent years honing their craft and are proud of it. The most important trait for casting directors to me is liking people. Actors are human. Put yourself in their shoes and try to imagine their problems and what they have had to endure for their dreams and aspirations.

The reason Clint Eastwood will not, as a director, read actors is that he hated auditions so much before he broke through that he cannot stand to watch other actors go through that agony. On the other hand, there are actors who love to read, and I must admit that I am a closet ham who likes to read the other parts with the actors.

Rejection is the hardest part of the acting profession. If any good actor is totally wrong for a part and has no chance to be considered for it, I will tell them that rather than let them wait days for an answer. We may discuss why they are wrong and follow up with what other kind of parts we should try him or her in. That at least gives them a bit of hope and saves their ego. I've called back many actors for subsequent readings and later have been able to cast them in parts suited for their particular qualities. I think I read Al Pacino four or five times for different projects before we found him the role in *The Panic in Needle Park*.

When an actor is cast, I telephone their agent with the news; and we begin to discuss salary, perks, and billing. The agent then notifies their client of the offer, and I get a call back with an answer to the offer. If all works out and we negotiate an agreement over the telephone or in my office, I then prepare a deal memo that outlines the main points of our agreement and give that to the production company who is responsible for writing up the actual contract between the company and the actor.

As I mentioned, deal memos and contracts have changed dramatically over the years. *The World of Henry Orient* was my first picture back in 1962. When I came on board, George Roy Hill was directing and had already cast Peter Sellers in the lead role as Henry Orient. It was my job to cast all the other supporting roles. The actress to play the part of Isabel Boyd (Henry Orient's love interest) was finally narrowed down to Lauren Bacall and Angela Lansbury (who was starring on Broadway at the time). The budget for the entire picture was around $1 million, and my casting budget allowed $25,000 for that particular role. Lauren Bacall had made a substantial amount more of a salary on her last picture; however, it was for four weeks' work as opposed to this being only twelve days. I soon got a response from Bacall's agent stating that she would agree to $50,000 plus a percentage of the picture profits. Needless to say, this didn't ride to well with George Roy Hill; and I telephoned Angela Lansbury's agent, and she agreed to our terms. There were very few perks for supporting roles on the film, basically only a few first-class round-trip airline tickets from Los Angeles to New York and a per diem of about eighty-five dollars per day.

My deal memos for the other supporting actors in 1962 were very simple and basically consisted of the following:

> Part: Frank Boyd
>> Actor: Tom Bosley
>> Agent: Kaplan-Veidt
>> $1,250 per week
>> $100 per day rehearsal
>> Feature billing
>> Scheduled for six weeks and four days, which comes to $7,900 (top to $8,000).
>> Rehearsal: Week of July 22–26. Has stock job through August 24 but available for rehearsal.
>> Shooting: September 3–October 18
> Part: Cigar Store Boss
>> Actor: Al Lewis
>> Agent: Kaplan-Veidt
>> $1,000 for four days spread over six working days
>> He must get some sort of billing.
>> No rehearsal
>> Shooting: August 13–August 20

I would send the deal memos in a letter to Mort Leavy who was the attorney for George Roy Hill's production company, Pan Arts; and Mort would do the contracts, and we would have them signed.

In 1967, I cast the film *Midnight Cowboy*, and the deal memos became a little more complicated with a larger cast and budget. When I suggested Dustin Hoffman to play one of the leading roles, he wasn't well-known; however, over the course of preproduction, *The Graduate* was released, and Dustin was able to demand more money for starring in the film. On the other hand, Jon Voight was still a relatively unknown, and I had to go to bat for him to get the part and eventually won out over both the producer and director. Jon was paid $25,000 for the other leading role. There were forty-one other roles to cast in *Midnight Cowboy*, and these deals ranged from one day to two weeks of work. I created the casting budget by hand on two pages of legal paper. In 1967, the Screen Actors Guild (SAG) day player rate for one day's work was $112, for three days was $286, and one week was $392.

My early notes show that Dustin Hoffman was to be paid $150,000 for the starring role, Jon Voight $25,000, and the rest of the cast $37,000, which totaled $212,000. With insurance and overtime, I was looking at just under $230,000 for my entire casting budget. By the end of production, I believe that Dustin's salary had risen to about $250,000 because of his success in *The Graduate*.

My deal memos didn't change too much between 1962 and 1967:

> Brenda Vaccaro: Role of Shirley
>> Agent: William Morris (Ed Bondy)
>> Deal: $2,500 per week, two-week guarantee
>> Dates: Between June 3 and June 28 with a stop date from us end of day June 28
>> Billing: Some kind of star billing first to be billed after Jon Voight unless "Sally Buck" is a bigger name.
>> Note: This was our original agreement; but as of today, Ed Bondy says he will not close the deal unless it is first

of the costars or the last of the costars reading "Brenda Vaccaro as Shirley."

Sylvia Miles: Role of Cass Trehune
  Agent: William Morris (Ed Bondy)
  Deal: $1,500, one week
  Billing: Feature billing in first position of featured players unless the "Sally Buck" role is a more important feature name. (Specifically, we agree that she will be listed before Barnard Hughes.)
  Ms. Miles agrees to put on weight if required and knows she will be shooting "topless."

Barnard Hughes: Role of Towny
  Agent: Ashley Famous Agency (Jane Oliver)
  Deal: $1,000 for three working days in one week, pro rata thereafter (I am trying to change this deal to $1,500 for one week.)
  Billing: Feature billing in no less than third position of featured players
  Note: Mr. Hughes has permission to get out of his performance in *How Now Dow Jones* for the night of May 23. We must work around his matinees.
  Attention: I have changed the deal to $1,500 for one week.

Over the next few years, I cast several pictures, and my deal memos began having to include other issues and clauses for the actor. For instance, I found this deal memo from 1970 when I was casting *Slaughterhouse-Five* for George Roy Hill at Universal:

December 16, 1970

Mr. William Batliner

Universal City Studios

Universal City, California 91608

Dear Bill:

The following deal has been made for the film entitled *Slaughterhouse-Five*:

Paul Lazzaro: Ron Leibman

Agent: Wendor Associates (Phyllis Wendor)

1545 Broadway

LT 1 - 5217

Deal: $5,000 a week, nine-week guarantee

Total: $45,000

One free week. Rehearsals at scale. Free travel days. Three free looping days.

Billing: Second star billing on a line by himself. We have specified no size of type but have agreed to the stipulation that no one else with the exception of Billy Pilgrim may be in larger type that Mr. Leibman. Paid Ads: Mr. Leibman is to receive billing in paid ads only if some actor other than Billy Pilgrim is to be listed, in which case the size of type should conform to the specifications agreed upon for the screen credit. Should it be decided to list Mr. Leibman above the title, that listing does not have to be on a separate line but should be in second position.

Start Date: We have a pay or play agreement, with a shooting date no later than February 25, 1971; however, Mr. Leibman has been alerted to the present rehearsal date of January 18, 1971 (travel: January 16, 1971).

The studio would take the information from this deal memo and combine it with their seven-page Day Player Contract to be agreed upon and signed between them and the actor.

In 1975, Mike Ovitz and a few other guys founded CAA (Creative Artists Agency), which immediately became the powerhouse agency. This changed the art of the deal and the industry for that matter. Some agents developed such an ego that you wondered if they were the actual talent, and many times you couldn't even reach them by telephone. Soon afterward managers came into the process. One day a guy is packing bags at Ralphs Grocery Store, and the next day he's the manager for an actor.

Casting changed. It now became a deal where the agency would sometimes also be representing the director so it would put a "package" deal together with a few of their actors. All the salaries and perks were now negotiated in fifty–plus-page contracts between the studio and agency lawyers—entertainment lawyers. To give you an example, these are some of the negotiating deal points for a not-so-famous actor that were presented to me by her agent:

Compensation

Guaranteed Salary
Deferred Compensation (deferred payments and percentage participation)
Contingent Compensation (tied to overall gross, nominations, and awards)
Overages
Expenses

Billing

Main Titles, separate card, above title
All paid ads (subject to customary exclusions with credit in any excluded
ad in which any other person is mentioned)
Artwork title floor
Likeness parity

Travel and Transportation

All first-class round-trip travel for her, a companion, and her assistant
Exclusive car and driver to and from all airports, sets, and hotels (even
in Los Angeles)
A luxury rental car for personal use at all times while on location with
all amenities

Publicity

75 percent still photograph approval
100 percent nonphotograph likeness approval
Biography submitted for approval
No on-set interviews
Right to approve interviews
No endorsements
No photograph of her using product

Merchandising

No right to merchandise or do commercial tie-ups without prior approval and separate negotiation of royalty
Favored nations on royalty

Miscellaneous Approvals

Script and any material changes
Director and costar
Choice of makeup and hair people
Stunt double
Costumer
Exclusive dresser onset

Assistant

Production will pay assistant $500 per week
Will also provide a reasonable per diem and adjoining hotel room (if needed)
Credit in the end crawl as "Assistant to Ms."
Travel same class, no less than business class if traveling separately

Miscellaneous Items

Dressing facility: star trailer, no one to receive better (with laundry list of amenities)
No invasion of twelve-hour turnaround (forced calls)

Portal-to-portal: thirty-six hours on weekend or fifty-four hours if not on location

Included in Errors and Omissions insurance

Invited with guest, all expenses paid, to any and all premiers on both coasts

A videotape copy of film provided for private use upon final mix and edit

Promotion and Publicity Expenses

With respect to promotion and publicity services rendered by artist hereunder at company's request at a location more than fifty miles from artist's permanent residence, company shall furnish artist with round-trip transportation (first-class, if available and used, and by air, if appropriate). Additionally, artist shall be provided with first-rate one-bedroom hotel suite accommodations, first-rate exclusive ground transportation, and per diem to be negotiated in good faith.

Further Publicity Approval

Artist shall not be required to render any promotional or publicity services absent artist's prior written approval, which shall not be unreasonably withheld or delayed. Company acknowledges that while lender and artist shall act in good faith, artist does not have to do press junkets. Company will make publicity requests through artist's representatives.

And that was nothing compared with what goes on today. Negotiating deal points nowadays can sometimes prevent a movie from being made, as the studios, agents, managers, and lawyers cannot come to an agreement. There are just way too many pots in the fire.

And then there is the Twenty-Million-Dollar (Plus) Club of Hollywood. Past members include Julia Roberts, Tom Cruise, Leonardo DiCaprio, Angelina Jolie, Reese Witherspoon, Tom Hanks, Jim Carrey, Mel Gibson, and recently, Liam Neeson. Brad Pitt, Johnny Depp, and Robert Downey, Jr. are demanding even more.

My Own Casting Process

I was born Marion Caroline Dougherty on February 9, 1923, to Virginia (Mitchell) and Orr Clarence Dougherty in the family home bordering a golf course seven miles outside Hollidaysburg, Pennsylvania. Caroline was my grandmother's maiden name, but she was always called Carrie. My father's Welsh first name was never used, and he was usually just called Doc. I had a five-year-old sister, Doris, waiting for me; and five years later, my younger sister, Virginia, was born to complete our family.

Elda Furry, another Hollidaysburg native, went on to considerably more Hollywood fame than I have known as the gossip columnist Hedda Hopper. Elda's brother was very fond of my mother before she met Daddy and dated her. He gave her a walrus tusk that we kept on the table in the front hall.

About six months out of the year, my mother's aunt, Abigail, lived with our family. Great-aunt Abigail was somewhat like my own Auntie Mame. She was my window to the world—as she traveled a lot—and always had fabulous stories to tell me of the places she'd visited and the people she'd met. Auntie was also a woman with her own mind and principles. She was divorced back in the days when that status for a woman was considered rather scandalous.

When I was still very young, we moved to a house that my father had designed at the Oak Knoll trolley stop, outside Hollidaysburg. Daddy, fascinated by architecture, would have loved to have been an architect. He'd designed us a beautiful home in a woodsy area just prior to the Great Depression. My paternal grandfather, however, made Daddy go into the family hardware business; and then, when the Depression struck, Grandpa moved to Florida, leaving my father with the responsibilities and headaches of running a business in some extremely hard times.

I am not sure it was because it was the house that Daddy designed for us, but my most vivid childhood memories are associated with our Oak Knoll home. Down by a stretch of woods near the house where the lawn ended, there were bars that my sisters and I used to swing on. I was an athletic child, and I'd perform tricks on the bars and spend a lot of time hanging by my legs.

In those days, few private families, only the very rich, had their own swimming pools; but my daddy, with a helper from the neighborhood, built a pool in our backyard. They excavated the hole, built the wood forms, and poured the concrete. They rigged up lights so they could work past sundown when they wanted to. Daddy put a new penny into the cement to mark the year that the pool was built.

There was no filtering material or cleaning equipment in the pool. It was filled by running water from a hose; and, when needed, it was drained by pulling the plug just like an oversized bathtub. We used to get the neighborhood kids to help in "cleaning the pool"; but it ended up being more of a game where we'd swim around with "spears," throwing them at each other while we swam, supposedly cleaning the pool.

Never one to miss an opportunity to have fun, when the pool water got so dirty it needed to be changed, the drain was opened, and the pet ducks we had were allowed to come in and use the pool while it drained. When the pool was being refilled, I remember crawling around on the bottom and playing "alligator."

I do not recall if my first acting role was an alligator, but I would later discover that in those early days, there was little exposure to the world of show business. This was well before television, and my going to the movies was not a regular occurrence. In fact, it was rare. My earliest recollection of seeing a movie was in 1930, a musical with Ruby Keeler called *Show Girl in Hollywood.*

There was some indication in my childhood that I had directorial instincts. I was a typical older sister who resented being placed in charge of my younger sister, Ginny. My mother and Fanny, our family live-in, were doing laundry one day when Ginny was four or five; and Mother decided she was in the way. Mother told me to take Ginny down into the woods and let her play in the fort, a playhouse we had made from a big wooden box that Daddy had helped me build a roof on. Not pleased that I was stuck with my baby sister, I told Ginny to bring her doll and clothes. I suggested she should sit up on the roof of the playhouse, telling her it would be a very nice place to stay. To make my job of babysitting easier, I removed a belt I had on and clinched Ginny to a small tree that the playhouse was built up against. I then went about more important activities, knowing that my little charge, Ginny, was stuck with only one place to play, on the roof of the playhouse, and would not be getting into any sort of trouble for which I might be blamed.

During the building of the pool, Daddy had a huge pile of sand for mixing the concrete. It had been rained on and dried so often that it eventually turned into a hard mound that became a perfect place to build an igloo. Digging out a tunnel and a big round dome inside, I furnished it with a little rug, a candle in its own little niche carved in the wall, and a hand-wound Victoria with some records for entertainment. Of course, I told Ginny all about it but forbade her to enter it for quite a long time. When I finally did relent, I told her to be very careful when entering the tunnel. She made it through the tunnel and promptly sat down on one of my favorite records and crushed it. Little sisters!

I suppose I was considered a tomboy as a child. I certainly was not interested in dolls like my sisters. Daddy built me my own workbench in the basement and furnished it with small-sized tools. In later years, my carpentry came in handy when I had my own places to live. He also bought me a single-shot BB gun, and I became a darn good shot. My targets were chipmunks—a memory that would later cause me terrible angst—and I am now a member of many humane societies, worrying about elephants, gorillas, dolphins, whales, and, of course, dogs and cats.

We lived next door to a snooty neighbor, Mrs. Seeds, who was known for her very elegant, well-publicized gardens, having been featured in *House and Gardens* magazine; and yes, her name was really Mrs. Seeds! She frequently called our mother to ask if she could borrow Ginny. Ginny would go over to help with finding Mrs. Seeds's eyeglasses. More often than not, Ginny would explain, "Mrs. Seeds, they're on top of your head!"

Mrs. Seeds paid no attention to me until she noticed me shooting chipmunks on our property. She inquired about my hunting services as the pesky chipmunks were ruining the flowers in her lovely gardens. At such an early age, I became a hired assassin!

I remember having had my share of other childhood mistakes. One day I took a pair of scissors and cut the fringe off all my mother's Persian rugs. I was merely trying to neaten up their appearances. That was the only time I can remember getting a paddling and thought it very unfair, since I felt I was only trying to help. I also made the mistake of taking a knife and cutting the bark on a number of little trees growing in the woods. At that time, I wasn't aware that by cutting the bark all the way around the trunk of a tree, it would die because the sap could not rise. I was really chastised for that, but nothing could match the guilt I felt for destroying those trees.

As much as I remember everything else, Christmas was made unforgettable by our parents. We had a big sun porch off the living room in the house that had screened doors and windows in the summer and was glassed in for the winters.

Daddy put up newspapers to cover the glass doors so that we three girls wouldn't see the elves coming in to set up the Christmas tree. I remember putting my ear up next to the glass and thrilling to the sounds of the elves working inside. Head Daddy elf worked for weeks on that room after our bedtime. It created a great sense of anticipation and excitement before Christmas Day.

I would leave cookies for the elves on the fireplace mantel at night, and they were always gone in the morning. Daddy even went to the trouble to take a boot and make footprints in the ashes of the fireplace on Christmas Eve, so we knew that Santa had come through the chimney. He then removed all the newspapers from the sun porch doors; and a beautiful Christmas tree, complete with a Lionel train running through a mountain and around a little village, awaited us on Christmas morning. It was such a glorious, thrilling sight on those Christmas mornings as we opened the gifts Santa had left us.

One of the best Christmases we ever had was when everyone got out of the "bug room." I had gotten scarlatina at school but never got the full-blown scarlet fever, which I immediately gave to my two sisters. Both Mother and Aunt Abigail had bronchitis, each in their rooms at the either end of the hall; and Fanny came down with something equally debilitating, so the contagious ones—plus a nurse—were relegated to Fanny's room, the famous "bug room."

We had a big circular staircase from downstairs to the upstairs hall. Daddy set up a cot for sleeping at the head of it and rigged up a communication system, running cords and buzzers to Mother's room, Auntie's room, and one for the bug room. As a result of his efforts, Daddy caught a terrible cold from the draft that came up the staircase because he was sleeping in the hall. All that pain and suffering was the prelude to one of the greatest Christmases we ever had for just in the nick of time, everyone recovered, and we were out of quarantine.

When the Depression hit, my father was unable to keep the hardware business going and was forced into bankruptcy. He moved from being the owner of two successful stores in Altoona to becoming a traveling sales representative for a large hardware corporation. During this time, he was away from home much more than any of us would've wished.

Perhaps the toughest part of those hard financial times was when my parents were forced to sell our Oak Knoll home. I, unfortunately, did not make it any easier on them because I cried so terribly when they told us we had to move. It must've been a horrible time for Mother and Daddy, but this home in the woods was a wondrous place for an eleven-year old.

Our family then moved to Hollidaysburg, at 1005 Allegheny Street, which was an old gloomy Victorian house. Ginny was the only one who didn't seem at all phased by the move, as she was thrilled when she could walk to school. Since I escaped the mini epidemic of scarlet fever, I suppose it was my turn to suffer the next physical calamity, which came through on a very lucky note. I was riding my bicycle when I was hit by a car and thrown up to the hood, with my head hitting the windshield. My physical injuries were relatively minor, but for as long as I can remember, my sisters said that was the reason why "Marion was brain-dead."

All the Dougherty girls received a very good education. My sister, Doris, received a full scholarship to Highland Hall, a prep school in Hollidaysburg. She was such a good student that they offered me a scholarship after attending one year in the public high school. Money was exceedingly tight for everything, but our education never suffered. When it came time for me to go to college, Aunt Abigail sold her AT&T stocks to help. I remember Mother walking up Allegheny Street several houses away to see a government official about getting me a senatorial scholarship for Penn State. The neighbor was a friend of the family, and I knew that this was a serious embarrassment for a very proud and proper lady. I did receive a scholarship for my first two years, and because my grades were so good, it was extended to cover my full college education.

During my first year at Penn State, I studied hard and made the dean's list. Many years later, I told my own great-niece, Sarah Virginia Bent, to do the same—get on that list at first and then you'll always get the benefit of the doubt from then on. Sarah went on to graduate from Penn State University-Phi Beta Kappa.

Throughout my childhood, we occasionally went to visit my mother's brother, Uncle Charlie, and his wife, Reba, down in Swarthmore. My uncle, Charles D. Mitchell, was an artist on several fronts. He directed one play every year, and often he and Reba could be found in the cast. When their theater company outgrew its very modest surroundings and had gained success, Uncle Charlie went to New York and made a very detailed study of the New York theaters. He planned and built his own theater at Swarthmore, which was known to be a direct copy of the New York playhouses, with excellent acoustics, seating, and design.

Uncle Charlie's primary occupation was an illustrator for magazine art. His illustrations appeared in the *Saturday Evening Post*, *Redbook*, *Cosmopolitan*, and other magazines of that day. When Uncle Charlie was a young artist, Charles Dana Gibson met Charlie and took an interest in his art. Gibson was a much older man, a famous illustrator who had published a popular book called, *Our Neighbors*. With an eye for female beauty, Gibson was responsible for those lovely old pictures of females that were referred to as "Gibson Girls."

Charlie invited Gibson to dinner with his family, and when Gibson saw our mother, he wanted to draw her. He asked if she would come and pose in his studio for him. My grandmother and Grandfather Mitchell would not allow that, but he was invited to come to their house and sketch her; and he did, which is how our mother, Virginia Mitchell, became a "Gibson Girl."

My immediate plan after college was to go and work as Uncle Charlie's protégé; however, he died from a cerebral hemorrhage while I was in college, so that dream died with him.

While I was away at college, Daddy became a successful salesman and decided to move our family to Carlisle, Pennsylvania, which was located more in the center of his territory. Unfortunately, none of us really liked the new house he found. It was somewhat small and was done up in a sort of bright orange stucco. I called it the "orange crate." What I do remember most was that the garage was loaded with all the hardware and other items that did not sell during the bankruptcy sale. Daddy would try to sell these things and use that money to repay the men and women who had worked for him in his two Altoona stores. They were paid 50 percent (as you can do in bankruptcy) of whatever their salaries were in those last few weeks before collapse. It took several years, but he finally paid them 100 percent of what they were owed. I was so proud of Daddy, and that taught me a great lesson. Now I have often been called "cheap," especially when dealing in contracts for performers; but this lesson taught me to be honest, although frugal, and to have a better respect for the use of money.

The third and final home that my daddy bought was an old farmhouse on Pine Road in Boiling Springs, between Carlisle and Gettysburg in Pennsylvania. Mother and Daddy would go driving outside of town, dreaming of somehow getting an old colonial home, although they were sure they couldn't afford one. One Christmas Day, Daddy gave Mother a large suit box, and when she opened the box, it revealed a model of an old farmhouse he had made amid beautiful fields. Somehow he had bought a farmhouse for my mother! The deed, which remains in our farmhouse, is signed by Richard and Thomas Penn, governors of the province of Pennsylvania, on October 21, 1766. It designates how the property should be delineated by a man pacing off the boundaries of fifty acres of land, starting at a black oak tree, which was at the Yellow Breeches Creek, mentioned in the writings of the Civil War. The land was deeded to James Weakly, whose family still owns much of the land in Pennsylvania.

This fabulous old farmhouse was built in three stages over the years and is now joined into one. I cannot tell you how many years my parents took to restore it to its natural beauty, including ripping out floors of linoleum and exposing foot-wide planks. The farmers who were living in it had tried to "modernize" the house, taking away all its original characteristics. Underneath the floor in one of the bathrooms was a horse's skull that was placed there to ward off evil spirits. Beneath the bricks in the attic fireplace wall was a very old brown whiskey bottle, apparently hidden after being polished off by one of the workers.

Our Uncle Charlie's daughter, Doreen, who by now was in charge of buying and funding things for Winterthur, which is Delaware's equivalent of Williamsburg, adored my mother and came to stay with her and oversee the transformation.

The property and the farmhouse (now only several acres set in the middle of a prosperous dairy farm) had a small creek along which were lovely old willow trees. I named it Willowick (the wick from Bailiwick). Whenever I went back to visit (I was now in New York), it was like stepping into an old Currier and Ives print.

When my parents passed away, Doris and I did not want the house to pass out of the family, so we told our youngest sister, Virginia, that she could have it for whatever she got from selling her home in Harrisburg. She still lives there, and hopefully it will pass on to one of her four daughters' families, and the memories of our wonderful parents will continue to live on.

While attending Penn State University at the age of sixteen, I was studying liberal arts, and a friend of mine convinced me into participating in the dramatic society, known as the Penn State Players. Soon afterward, I was cast in a production of Shakespeare's *The Taming of the Shrew*, and discovered that I was sort of a ham and loved acting.

Don Taylor was a fellow Penn State Player, much loftier than my position as a bit player, although they'd taken two characters and combined them into one for me to play. Don played Petruchio, and he cut a dashing figure on stage, for he'd let his hair grow out long and then he curled it! Don was a handsome man with the most gorgeous head of curly reddish hair, which caused quite a stir on campus, for this was before men let their hair grow long.

We had a friendship that threatened to turn into something more, but never did. Don moved from his Penn State Players tenure into Moss Hart's 1943 Broadway production of *Winged Victory*, playing the role of Pinky. After Broadway and a stint in the military, he settled into Hollywood where he was probably best remembered as an actor for his roles in *Father of the Bride*, *I'll Cry Tomorrow*, and *Stalag 17*. He eventually moved into directing television and features films that included *The Final Countdown*, *Escape from the Planet of the Apes*, *Damien: Omen II*, *The Island of Dr. Moreau* (1977), and the musical version of *Tom Sawyer*.

My first lead was playing Abby Brewster in Joseph Kesselring's *Arsenic and Old Lace*. This was the story of Mortimer Brewster, a man about to go on his honeymoon, when he discovers his little old lady aunts and a sinister brother have been murdering off visitors at their home. I thought my being cast was very funny, for on Broadway, the role was played by Josephine Hull, who was short and pudgy, whereas I was tall and skinny.

I followed with *The Man Who Came to Dinner*, a broad comedy by Kaufman and Hart about a famous lecturer, Sheridan Whiteside, who, injured outside the home of the Stanleys, proceeds to move in on doctors' orders and wreaks havoc on their lives as he tries to solve all their minor family problems. In this production, I played Nurse Preen, the nurse hired to contend with the demanding, injured egotist.

Then graduation was soon upon me. A. C. Cloetingh, the head of the drama department at Penn State, was very well thought of in dramatic circles within the college world. He had called me in and told me he thought I had talent and should study acting. He said that there were only three really good places to go, San Francisco's ACT, Chicago's Goodman Theatre, or the Cleveland Playhouse. I thought to combine the interest of working as an illustrator with my Uncle Charlie, who passed away, with studying and working with scenic design. I figured I could probably pursue that at the Cleveland Playhouse where I'd decided to go since it was closest to my family home in Pennsylvania.

When I headed to the Cleveland Playhouse to study set design, I thought my chances of having some success were enhanced, not because

I was overflowing with talent, but because it was 1944, and most all of the set designers were men and had gone into the military serving in World War II. What I soon ended up doing was holding book, which meant following along with the script during rehearsals, cuing actors, writing notes, stage movements, etc., for the director. After holding book on several plays, I was finally asked to play a part by an improbable person.

I received a call from someone speaking on behalf of Mr. McConnell, the five-foot-seven-inch-tall head of the Cleveland Playhouse. He did not like women who were taller than he was, so for my first months there, he never spoke to five-foot-nine-inch little me. They were casting *My Sister Eileen*; and they'd not been able to cast the part of Violet, the prostitute. Mr. McConnell directed someone to "Find Dougherty, because she is the only one I haven't bothered yet."

They gave me some pages of the script and had me walk through it for Mr. McConnell. The first time he spoke to me was after my very first "audition" when he said, "I thought you came from a good family?"

I got huffy and replied that I certainly did come from a good family.

"Well then, how did you learn to walk like that?" he asked.

I guess that was a backhanded compliment, and he gave me the part of Violet. I still don't know if I should've been flattered by his comment or worried.

My friend, Lansdale Daley, played the lead; and the show was pretty darn good, so we were invited to make our own little contribution to the war effort and toured with our production to the nearby camps and hospitals where soldiers were recovering from their battle wounds. We had been warned not to take it personally if our audience was sparse, sound asleep, or prone to just get up and leave in the middle of the performance as their injuries and medications demanded. I'm proud to say that we did not lose a single-audience member. As Violet, I wore a spangled dress so tight and slinky, I literally could not sit in it, and I got a downright rapt reception from those rooms full of lovely wounded men.

Perhaps there were omens that I should've noticed as I continued my acting career. The next play that I did was *Thracian Horses*, a tragedy not only in the Greek drama sense but also for my acting. The scene was set in the midst of a funeral procession in the background, with a large cast moving in somber grief behind a row of flats, depicting our ancient village. There were only the tops of lanterns and spears being seen as we citizens passed by. I only had a bit part but was feeling particularly lovely and graceful in a flowing yellow gown with my props—a spear in one hand and a lantern in the other—until the hem of my gown got caught in the peg of a flat. Without an available hand to free myself, I kept advancing my arms as far as I could, which wasn't that far, and then trying, unsuccessfully, to make it look like an integral part of this sad procession. I lowered my props and finally had to lie down between the flat and the back of the wall of the theater, which was a space no more than two feet, and let the rest of the actors behind me stumble as best they could right over me.

My next role was handled with equal decorum. In Thorton Wilder's *The Skin of Our Teeth*, I played one of the three Muses, being led in a terrible rendition of "Jingle Bells" by a very serious actor who, as the song began, developed a bad case of the hiccups. One by one, the other two Muses became too convulsed with laughter to continue singing. I was the last to drop out, which sounds like an admirable accomplishment. The truth is it was such a strain to maintain my composure that while I did manage to keep singing, I also wet my pants. This seemed to be something I did on a regular basis, come to think about it. I was backstage one night in another production, waiting for the opening curtain, when that same urgent biological need hit me. I whispered frantically for the stagehand to hold the curtain, but it was too late; he'd already raised it two or three feet, and there was no turning back. In those days, we wore leg makeup instead of stockings, thanks to the nylon shortage during the war. I can still remember praying as I made my entrance that the unstoppable trickle down my leg through all that makeup would somehow be mistaken for a run in my nonexistent hosiery.

Those acting experiences were invaluable to me in my future casting career. They allowed me to develop firsthand the empathy for actors and the problems they face, not to mention their bladders. During this time, I also got to know Lansdale Daley; she was the leading ingénue of the Cleveland Playhouse. Everyone at the playhouse seemed to be paired up in some way or another. Some were gay and lived together. Some were married to other members of the playhouse; so Lanny and I, who became fast friends, wound up sharing a room at a boarding house for a couple of years.

Actor Ray Walston was at the Cleveland Playhouse at the same time and knew us both well. Many years later, after our time together in Cleveland, I cast Ray in *The Sting*; and a few years after that, Ray drove to Malibu to visit George Roy Hill. Ray pulled up in his car as George and I were walking down a long driveway to his house. Seeing George and I together, Ray was a bit taken aback and mumbled, "Oh, I thought you and Lanny," followed by a long embarrassed pause. I laughed and told him we were dear friends, and she now had four lovely children and lived in Boston.

You might think that my negative onstage experiences in Cleveland would explain my decision not to pursue an acting career, but I abandoned acting for a completely different reason. I'd heard story after story about herds of actors standing on stages in New York and hearing the director sitting back in the audience say, "Okay, you, you, and you can stay. The rest of you are excused." I was never wild about rejection in my personal life, and I couldn't imagine actively welcoming it into my professional life.

Two years after the Cleveland Playhouse, many of the group I had spent so much time with left for New York City to try to break into theater. So I allowed my group momentum to carry me to New York, but Broadway managed to limp along without me while I landed a job designing windows for Delman's at Bergdorf-Goodman in a little studio in the cellar. My starting salary was forty-five dollars per week, and I felt like a queen when Mr. Delman eventually raised it to fifty dollars.

Adding to this embarrassment of riches, a friend from the Cleveland Playhouse called me one day and asked if I'd like to take over a large and lovely six-room Park Avenue apartment that she'd been renting. I'd been living in a fifth-floor walk-up with three other women just beneath the Fifty-ninth Street Bridge, which was not exactly a posh neighborhood. The Park Avenue apartment was a bit of a complicated arrangement; the renters of record weren't allowed to sublet, and they had gone to the West Indies for a long vacation, so there were a few mechanics involved in paying the landlord every month without my name or even my existence being revealed. However, it was a great space and well worth a little inconvenience.

I'm not sure if I was just naive in those days or simply not too bright. I'd been in that apartment for weeks before it began to strike me as odd that an unusual number of strange men were phoning on a very regular basis, asking to speak to several different women that I'd never heard of. After hearing that Elaine or Lindsay or Susan were not at home and were not expected, these men would ask what my name was and if I were available. Finally, duh! I started asking a few questions of my own and discovered that I was living in the hub of a call-girl operation! Fortunately, none of the callers had the address; they only had the phone number, which was listed in an ad for "Massages," and they were calling to make an appointment for someone to come to their apartment or hotel.

Resisting the opportunity to change careers or just supplement my income as, lest we forget, I convincingly walked a prostitute without ever having been one, I admit that I did kind of enjoyed the adventure of simply answering the phone for a while. That changed one night when a friend of mine I worked with at Delman's walked me home after we had changed the windows.

He'd heard the stories about my unique list of callers, and when the phone rang, he insisted on being protective and heroic and grabbed it with a great, "I'll handle this!" I silently cheered him on as I listened to him, his voice dripping with sarcasm, making sure that the man on the other end of the line felt appropriately small and sleazy for having called. He then handed me the phone with eyes rolling and announced, "He claims he's your daddy." It was my daddy, and he greeted me with a puzzled, "What's going on there, kid?" I came up with some lame story that I knew he saw right through; although my mother, God bless her, never did catch on. Soon after that, the NYPD vice squad started a major crackdown on the proliferation of call-girl operations on Park Avenue.

Around that time, I happened to run across some syringes in a bedroom dresser drawer. I was as naive about drugs as I was about everything else, but I wasn't that naive. It was definitely time to move. It was also time to get out of the Bergdorf's basement, where the "studio" for window designers was located. I came across an ad stating that the Rueben H. Donnelley Co. was paying $150 per week for a three-week course in selling ads for the telephone company's yellow pages. Wow! A way to put a little bit of money away! I became very interested in these courses and decided to give it a try; only problem was that we were all assigned to the Brooklyn office, and we were given five sections of the borough to work: Brooklyn Heights, Bedford Stuyvesant, Sheepshead Bay, Red Rock, and Red Hook.

Some of these areas were very decent and civilized, and then some were quite scary. I once had to pole vault over a desk to avoid a potential business owner client. Another time I had to climb up a fire escape and crawl through a window to get to a customer. I also had on one occasion to walk into a dark pool hall where I found out later that the Mafia was having a serious meeting.

Then one day I got an interesting call from Robert Tucker, a classmate and friend from my Penn State days, and I was all ears. Robert Tucker or Tuckie, as he was often called, was a cute young man with a lovely sense of humor and a guy who was liked by all. He was also a wonderful dancer, and I wasn't too bad either. As Penn State was not near any big city, our entertainment was brought in from outside. At least once a month, a well-known name band was hired to play at a dance given in the large gymnasium, which was known as the "Rec Hall." Tuckie was often my escort, and we "cut a mean rug" at these affairs.

After arriving in New York, we wanted to celebrate and see a bit of the glamour of our new city. We decided to find one of the best hotels for dinner so we made a reservation at the Starlight Roof at the Waldorf-Astoria hotel. We were the first diners to arrive (unfashionably early) and were seated on the edge of the dance floor. The band was just setting up at the time. Upon seeing the menu, Tuckie and I looked at each other in a state of panic, as we quickly counted our resources. Tuckie and I had to select the least expensive entree, a plate of spaghetti, and ended up splitting one order, with me politely feigning not being that hungry. I'm sure the waiter recognized right away that we were a couple of kids out of our element, but we were saved! The band started playing, and we got up to dance. The band also realized we were a couple of naive kids, and they were wonderful to us; they played just for us, and we were quite good.

When some early customers arrived, it became a type of floor show with Tuckie and me, the only couple there, dancing up a storm. Even our waiter was amused and never gave us a dirty look when we left a tip composed of all the loose change we had left after paying for our one shared entree.

Now a few years later, here was Tuckie calling me with an intriguing offer that both stunned and delighted me. He'd been hired to do casting for a popular television show called *Kraft Television Theatre* and said that he needed an assistant. Now Robert was well educated but knew absolutely nothing about acting or talent for that matter, and I never did quite understand how he'd managed to get hired. What I did understand was that he was offering to pay me $300 a week to assist him in making appointments for actors to come in and read for parts at *KRAFT*.

Not a difficult decision!

Ah, Those Golden Years!

*K*raft *Television Theatre* was one of the original and most prestigious dramatic anthologies presented in the "Golden Age" of American dramatic television. The telecasts began over NBC-TV on May 7, 1947, and aired on Wednesdays at 7:30 p.m., with only thirty-two thousand television set owners. The following year, programming was moved to 9:00 p.m. It was the only sponsored full-hour television show to use alternating directors. It was also the first dramatic show to use the coaxial cable when it opened in 1949, linking the east to the Midwest. Within five years, the amount of television set owners escalated to over twenty million. Other shows from this "Golden Age" included *Studio One*, *Philco Television Playhouse*, *Robert Montgomery Presents*, *Goodyear Television Playhouse*, *The U.S. Steel Hour*, and *Lux Video Theatre*.

When I showed up for work in the J. Walter Thompson building at 420 Lexington Avenue, I soon learned that J. Walter Thompson, the largest advertising agency in the world at the time, and the agency who hired Tuckie for *KRAFT,* did not have it in their budget for him to have an assistant. I ended up working directly across from Tuckie's desk in this long narrow room on another much smaller show of the time that was also sponsored by *KRAFT*, called appropriately, *Believe It or Not.* We were then told we weren't supposed to talk to each other.

All television productions of those early days of the drama for were done live. The first season of *Believe It or Not*, beginning in March 1949, was a half-hour program that featured Robert L. Ripley seated in a "living room setting" as he recounted tales of strange stories. Not long after I was hired, Robert Ripley passed away and was replaced by Robert St. John.

I recall one of the shows that I cast, a scene called for a knight in full armor. For some Murphy's Law reason, the armor didn't arrive until after the final rehearsal and only minutes before we went on air. The director called for the knight to make his entrance. Nothing happened. He then scanned his huge bank of monitors and realized that there was no knight to be found on any camera.

After several moments of treating the television audience to nothing but a blank empty set, the director wisely cut to a commercial, and a search was launched for the errant knight. It turned out the actor was outside his dressing room, on the floor, where he'd tripped and fallen on his way to the set. Having never worn a full set of armor before, he couldn't figure out for the life of him how to get back up. Finally, some stage hands helped him to his feet and propelled the poor man onto the set just as the unusually lengthy commercial break ended.

We weren't the only ones with "live" problems. Eva Marie Saint was caught rising out of a pool, except for the fact that when she did so, the top of her two-piece bathing suit did not, and she revealed more of her character than she intended. Another actor on *Robert Montgomery Presents*, in a murder mystery story, was to deliver the solution of the murder when he suddenly went blank in the last few minutes of the show. They were off the air by the time he remembered, and the audience never did discover who the murderer was.

Paul Newman told me about the time that he was exchanging serious dialogue with his leading lady kneeling in front of a fireplace; in those days, directors sometimes tried "artsy" shots, including shooting through a fireplace. As the two actors were about to cross to a balcony for the next scene, as it had been blocked, they suddenly found that they couldn't move. Several crew members had wrapped their arms around their legs, out of camera range, so they had to finish the scene in front of the fireplace. Apparently, the camera on the balcony had blown up.

A few months after my arriving at J. Walter Thompson, Robert Tucker left for a new career outside of the casting profession. I took over his job, casting all *Kraft Television Theatre* productions beginning in January 1950 up until June 1958, and cast well over five hundred weekly episodes.

Just after settling into my new position, one of the executives of that prestigious advertising agency had been caught by his wife *en flagrante* with a secretary, not necessarily his own, on the couch in his office. I would guess that it didn't do a single positive thing for his marriage, and I know that it affected many people at the agency. It wasn't long after the agency executive's indiscretion that led to a memo being distributed throughout J. Walter Thompson, stating that all the couches in all the offices throughout the entire building be replaced and mandated to be no longer than a certain number of feet and inches. It was further understood by everyone that this move would prevent their couches from being used for any other purpose than sitting.

Believe it or not, I was never tempted by the stereotypical "casting couch" method of finding actors for a television or film role. On the other hand, several years later, when we added *Lux Playhouse* to J. Walter Thompson's television shows, I had to share an office with Harold Loeb who cast that show. Harold always had his chair turned around so that he could watch the windows of the hotel across from our office where he could occasionally catch a woman undressing. I had my chair turned toward the door. Actresses who came in to see us would invariably always have two photos and two resumes. Harold's would be sexy shots, and mine would be prim.

The casting process for me was about the excitement and satisfaction in finding the best actor for the role. While sex appeal and looks may help, it is more important that the audience believe that the actors are the character conceived by the writers. I know that when I came to my first casting position in 1949, a brand-new career for me, I had no experience in finding actors or judging their qualifications for being talented and suitable for a particular role. Most of us working on the shows were neophytes just beginning to learn our trade.

In the *Golden Age* of television, the hour-long anthologies as well as many of the other first series were all shot in New York City where there were no contract players, and the pool of actors available was very small compared with those that are available today. Our actors' talent pool mostly consisted of talent from the stage or radio. There were only a few agents such as Pat Harris, the sister of Radie Harris (a New York columnist), who were very knowledgeable. Another was Eleanor Kilgallen, sister of Dorothy Kilgallen, the well-known regular panelist on the television game show *What's My Line*. Both Pat and Eleanor knew theater-trained actors, and you could depend on their good taste as to talent.

There were many radio actors, but it was sometimes dangerous to use them. I was quick to find out that radio actors would give spectacular readings and then, during the week's rehearsal period, got worse and worse every day. If radio actors didn't have any stage experience on their resume, they tended not to be good actors.

Occasionally, "stars" would be brought in from Los Angeles, but the budgets generally didn't allow many large salaries. We couldn't use the currently employed Broadway stars, for the television shows were shot live at nine o'clock in the evening, which would directly conflict with their theater jobs.

I believe that reading the script with an actor is the only way to judge if someone is right for a part. We had no demo reels to watch, which I think isn't a good way to really judge an actor anyway. There were no guidelines established for casting in those early days, so I did what everyone else did and had to learn as we went along.

Maury Holland and Stanley Quinn, the first *KRAFT* directors, also functioned as producers. Maury was a jovial, likeable man, an old hoofer who had been in both theater and vaudeville and knew more about theater than television. Stanley was a martinet and much harder to work with. He really scared me at first. Fielder Cook, another early *KRAFT* director, hired George Roy Hill as his assistant; and George wound up becoming a director. William Graham, who also ended up directing, began as a motorcycle messenger.

Eventually, we had three directors who alternated shows each week, so usually I was working on three different shows at any given time. Sometimes it got a bit hectic juggling and thinking about three shows simultaneously. My nightmare was that I'd send the wrong actor to the wrong place for the wrong role! One week, I would read the script, talk to the director, try to think who would be possible casting choices, arrange to meet, and read them; and the next week, I brought them in to meet and read for the director. The third week, I would do their contracts and send them to rehearsals and, then at nine o'clock Wednesday night, sit in front of the television and pray no one would forget their lines. We were truly "live," and there were no retakes, no dubbing; what you saw was what you got on the air for all the audience to see.

For many actors, having an interview with a casting director can be terrifying, onerous, or a just plain boring ordeal that one really doesn't want to have to go through. We represent jobs and doors to open.

Knowing this, I just try to first talk to actors about anything that comes to mind, or I'll ask them if there's anything they want to talk about. Sometimes it's their dramatic prowess, their hometowns, whatever it takes to put them at ease with this frightening woman. The damnedest stories come out; and you often can get to learn a little bit about what makes the actors tick, including whether they have a sense of humor, which is essential to learn if they prefer comedy or tragedy. Often, the actor will leave feeling relieved, saying that it wasn't all that bad. If the actor happens to seem right for a part in something being cast, I may ask them to read a bit of a scene with me. For the larger, more important roles, it's only fair to let the actors read the whole script; however, sometimes that's not possible. Actors can teach you a lot sometimes what not to do. I've learned from some who were wrong for a particular role but sparked some little idea, and I found myself saying, "Oh, now that's interesting. I wonder if that'll work."

I really loved casting *Kraft Television Theatre*. There was so much talent developing at the time, with the beginning and rise of the Actors Studio and all the Broadway, off-Broadway, and off-off Broadway productions. The talent pool continued to grow, and I was in a position of needing almost more good actors than were available with the heavy production schedule *KRAFT* maintained. Yet it never ceased to amaze me at the creative ways actors found to try to get our attention. The *KRAFT* producer, Stanley Quinn, and I were in his office one morning, discussing casting for the next show, when a special delivery box arrived, addressed to me. I opened the box, and out flew a homing pigeon. Unfortunately, poor Stanley was terrified of birds, and he let out a gut-wrenching primal scream and dived to open the window, through which the homing pigeon happily escaped. I eventually learned that if the bird had been with us for more than a few seconds, we would've found a note on its leg band from an actor politely begging for an audition.

There really is no way to describe live television other than to say it required a tremendous amount of effort, concentration, and talent from the actors who had to be letter perfect in the delivery of their lines. They had to maintain a certain pace so that the production would begin and end on time and allow for commercial breaks. When something went wrong, which invariably it did, the actors whose faces were in front of the viewer at home had to make the best of whatever the situation they found themselves in. There were times I really felt for the actors caught in a bind on camera, knowing they were in front of the audience at home.

When *KRAFT* celebrated one of its anniversaries, and the network wanted to boost ratings, I selected a very young, very stunning Paul Newman; and he did one line for us, in the role of a bridegroom. When I made the deal with his agent, he told me off-the-record that Paul would never make it in this business because he looked too much like Marlon Brando. I've been wrong many times during my long career, but never as wrong as that agent.

Those were the obscene days of the McCarthy hearings and the resulting blacklists. While we were never specifically told at *KRAFT* who not to hire and why, we were made subtly aware of what names to avoid and how pointless it was to ignore our instructions. An especially arrogant actor arrived one day to audition for a role in *My Brother's Keeper*, an original teleplay that was written by George Roy Hill. The actor openly carried a pink-colored Communist newspaper tucked under his arm. I held my breath, waiting for some anti-Communist group to rush in and tackle him, but the audition passed without incident. He was so good that despite his arrogance, we offered him the job. I'd previously cast Rod Steiger in a small role in an earlier *KRAFT* production, *The Inn*, and felt that this would be a more significant role for him. He then informed me that he wasn't interested; it wasn't a big enough part. I said, "Then you're a fool, because if you'll notice, this character is alone on camera for a good minute and a half, talking an airplane down with the control tower." That had not occurred to Rod, and he decided to grace us with his presence after all.

The Korean War was the first time radar was used, and this was the setting for the teleplay and an important part of the story. George Roy Hill had some experience with the Korean War, as he'd been recalled as a marine major to pilot planes, which he'd also done in World War II. The war provided him with some wonderful material. *My Brother's Keeper* aired March 4, 1953, and was successful enough to convince *KRAFT* to let George have his first shot at directing. It also helped secure Rod's first Hollywood contract. Soon afterward, he was cast to play Charley Malloy opposite Marlon Brando in *On the Waterfront*.

George Roy Hill wrote a second teleplay for *KRAFT*, titled *Keep Our Honor Bright*, which was centered on a college cheating scandal and aired on October 14, 1953. The main character, Jim, was forced to recount how he obtained an advance copy of an exam and must face an honor committee that offers the possibility of a lighter penalty in exchange for him naming the students with whom he shared the bootleg exam.

Eleanor Kilgallen and Maynard Morris were with the MCA agency and asked me to meet with a young actor named James Dean. I went to see him in an off-Broadway play called *See the Jaguar*, which eventually made it to Broadway. After seeing the play, I agreed to bring him in for a general meeting. When we started to talk, I found him to be shy and sensitive yet fascinating. Throughout our first meeting, he seemed to be off in his own world, sitting in a slouch and staring at the ceiling and all around the office, anywhere but making eye contact with me. He didn't want to talk much about himself or his interests. When I began to talk about the script, he suddenly sat straight up and came to life with tremendous intensity.

Maury Holland was directing the episode, and I asked him to meet with Jimmy; and after they met, Maury agreed to cast him to play the role of Jim. When the episode aired, James Dean played very well in front of the camera and displayed all kinds of mimics and gestures. There were several scenes in which he was able to expose his boyish charm along with a deep-down inner sense of humor. I immediately called him again to talk about another teleplay I was casting called *A Long Time till Dawn*, written by Rod Sterling.

The role that I wanted Jimmy to play was that of Joe Harris, an ex-convict who embodied many contradictions: both a poet and a gangster, smart but having the logic of a child. Freshly out of jail in New York and furious to discover his wife missing, he kills an elderly neighbor who advised the wife to leave him. As the police close in on him, Harris snaps and reverts to his childhood. I had some trouble trying to convince director Dick Dunlap to approve him, but he finally gave in as the rehearsal date grew near.

There was one full week of rehearsals, and after the first day, I started getting calls from Dick and some of the other actors complaining about Jimmy. Dick was shocked when for the first rehearsal, Jimmy showed up late and rumpled and dirty in appearance. I tried to cover for Jimmy and explained to Dick that he probably had to work late or perhaps he overslept. One actor told me that he was just mumbling through his lines, missing cues, and just being rude and difficult.

The following day, I got a second call from Dick who was very irate. "He was late again, and if this happens one more time, forget it and find somebody else!" Dick went on, "Besides that, he's an undisciplined, really deep Actor's Studio type!" I assured Dick that I would immediately find him a standby and asked him to please send Jimmy over to my office after rehearsals.

My office was really tiny in those days, just a desk and chair with another chair beside it. When Jimmy arrived, he shuffled into the chair and sat down. I knew I had a special liking for him, this sweet introspective persona that was just about loveable. I began to give Jimmy one of my polite but firm talking-tos in one of my better Dutch-uncle lectures: "This is no way helps your career . . . It is an important leading role on television, and the part could really play a good step in your career. Reputation is everything. You're much too talented to let this kind of behavior cost you a good job. It is time to shape up or ship out . . . blah . . . blah . . . blah."

At this point, I looked across my desk and could hardly believe my eyes—my "just about loveable" actor had fallen asleep. For a minute, I thought, "Oh well, actors do not make much money when they work at all, and most have to supplement their income as late-night waiters and bartenders." But no one had ever pulled a stunt like that on me, and it was so preposterous that I began to laugh, which roused Jimmy. So having awakened him, I had my secretary bring him a coffee before I finished my harangue and sent him on his way.

He was not fired after all. The next day, he showed up at the rehearsal hall on time and was freshly scrubbed and neatly dressed. I later learned that Dick's father, who was also named James, was visiting and stopped by rehearsals. It turns out he was a farmer, and he and Jimmy began to talk about his farm and the care and feeding of hogs. Jimmy realized that he and director Dick Dunlap had something in common; they were both farm boys.

Many books have been written about him, and I've been interviewed for a few of them, during which my naiveté has been a source of amusement among the authors. I admit it. I did not know the difference then, and I don't always know it now, between an actor who is dozing off from a hard night's work waiting tables and one who's nodding off from being under the influence of drugs.

In the end, Jimmy still had some difficulty with the role. It was very challenging with those different dimensions, and he never became entirely comfortable with it. In fact, there was a clip of his performance that was featured many years later in the documentary, "Hello Actors Studio." In a *New York Times* review of the documentary, the writer explains how Dean's "jittery performance" demonstrates "how annoying the mannerisms of the Method can be."

Jimmy had been cast during this time to play the role of Bachir on Broadway in *The Immortalist*, which opened soon afterward on February 8, 1954, at the Royale Theatre. Elia Kazan went to see Jimmy in the play and arranged for a screen test for him to star as Cal in the film *East of Eden*, which Kazan was directing for Warner Brothers based on the John Steinbeck novel.

It was late in the evening when my telephone rang on September 30, 1955. I picked up the phone, and it was a familiar voice on the other end. My old friend Eleanor Kilgallen said softly, "Did you hear that James Dean was killed in a car accident?"

Many hearts were broken that night.

Before my friend Tuckie had left *KRAFT*, he'd introduced me to Jack Lemmon who he'd cast in a small part for *Whistling in the Dark*, which aired in November 1949. I remembered meeting Jack and later saw him on a television show called *That Wonderful Guy*. When I got wind that the show was being cancelled, I contacted Jack and brought him in for a meeting. Jack had a perfect sense of comic timing and was a good-natured all-American type guy. He had gone to Harvard where he was involved in the Drama Club until the ROTC program placed him in World War II. After the war, Jack got his degree and then came to New York and played piano at the Old Knickerbocker Music Hall, accompanying the silent films of Chaplin and Keaton that were showing. He began to study acting with Uta Hagen at HB Studios and was able to find a few television gigs. After my meeting with Jack, I finally found a role that I thought fit him pretty well in *The Fortune Hunter*, which aired on February 21, 1951. I then cast him in *The Easy Mark* airing on September 5, 1951, and *Duet* airing on January 28, 1953. However, the script that I knew would display his talent was a teleplay called *Snooksie*. The story involved a newspaper's star reporter who became very irritated when his editor assigned him the trivial job of tracking down his spoiled kid's teddy bear. He was so chagrined by such a petty job that he barely noticed a murder he witnessed and the kidnapping of a child star. Immediately after *Snooksie* aired, Jack was cast playing opposite Judy Holliday in *It Should Happen to You*, directed by George Cukor and written by Garson Kanin. He was on his way!

Walter Matthau was a very good talent too; but he was a big, big bettor, and he always seemed to be broke. I first cast Walter in *The Death of Kid Slawson*, which aired June 18, 1952. He was a poker buddy of Harold Loeb and frequently came by my office. One day when it was raining, he took off his shoes, which had holes in them, and propped his feet up on the radiator to dry his socks. Walter played in two other *KRAFT* teleplays, and I used him later when casting *Naked City*. His salary quote was always adjusted so that he was paid part of his actual salary, but another part was paid to his agent to be put into a protected account so he didn't gamble it all away. At one point, we had to deposit his checks in an escrow account to hide them from his gambling creditors. Oh, what a casting director will do!

Anne Italiano was also a regular visitor. She later changed her last name to Marno and still later changed it to Bancroft. It was Anne

Bancroft that she was cast in her first major television role on *KRAFT* in *To Live in Peace*, which aired on December 16, 1953.

Christopher Plummer came down from Canada, and we cast him for one of his first American jobs in the *KRAFT* production of *A Dashing White Sergeant* that aired in July 1954. He married Tammy Grimes a few years later; and they had a daughter, Amanda Plummer, who also became a very talented actor.

Kraft Television Theatre was a highly respected television show that produced anything and everything that defined the word "quality" from Shakespeare, Mark Twain, Lewis Carroll, and Tennessee Williams to taking the chance on many brilliant new writers who were emerging at the time. Rod Serling previously had some success as a writer at *KRAFT*, but not enough to sustain him. One day, when I was in Fielder Cook's office, Rod walked into the office with a script in his hand. He said to Fielder, one of the directors at *KRAFT*, "Either I have to sell this script or admit defeat as a writer and join my father's plumbing business."

The script was titled *Patterns*; and *KRAFT* bought it, Fielder directed it, and I cast Ed Begley and Elizabeth Montgomery in it. The show aired on January 12, 1955, and was so successful that four weeks after its live broadcast, it was repeated live for a second time. Its success didn't stop there; it went on to become a movie starring Van Heflin and Beatrice Straight, again directed by Fielder Cook. Rod Serling, who is probably best remembered for his inventive television series, *The Twilight Zone* and *Night Gallery*, continued to make a living as a highly regarded writer until his untimely death.

There were several critics that didn't understand this new medium of television drama, and it took many Hollywood filmmakers and actors by surprise. In the beginning, veteran actors such as Charlton Heston went public and spoke negatively against live television; however, as years progressed, these same critics and actors saw the value of a large living room audience and had a quick change of attitude. It didn't take long before well-known actors began knocking at our doors. I recently read some comments made by Jack Nicholson and his dislike toward television in those days and how it took away from the movie business.

One major problem that we faced were the young advertising executives at *KRAFT* who had no clue about actors, drama, stage performance, or respect. The "suits" (as I referred to them) were only interested in selling cheese and other products. On more than one occasion, I was asked to bring in a highly regarded actor to read for a director, and one or more of these young suits would be sitting in the room. When the great actress, Helen Hayes, finished her reading for the director, one of the young suits interrupted, "Please, can you tell us what you've done?" Hayes simply smiled and said, "After you."

On May 15, 1956, *KRAFT* produced *Profiles in Courage*, which was adapted from the John F. Kennedy book focusing on the Edmund G. Ross chapter in which Ross, a senator from Kansas, had the crucial vote that saved President Andrew Johnson from being impeached. I cast James Whitmore to play Edmund G. Ross. John F. Kennedy, who was a thirty-eight-year-old senator at the time, provided an on-air introduction to a dramatization of his book. I met him the night he came to the show. This was a man with charisma.

Those were fun and exhilarating times. Actor Baruch Lumet from the Yiddish theater came in one day to introduce himself and ask me to hire his young son, Sidney. Sidney Lumet, who started as an actor, later achieved significant fame as a director in New York.

Pat Remick brought in her beautiful fifteen-year-old daughter, Lee, who I eventually cast when she was seventeen and was able to use her in several *KRAFT* teleplays.

The Curly Headed Kid was another one of our teleplays that aired on June 29, 1957. The story was about a young hitchhiker who is saved from being hanged on a murder charge by a crusading, alcoholic columnist who realizes the kid was falsely identified based only on his curly hair. The suits at *KRAFT* told me to simply find the most darling twenty-two-year-old boy that I could. I gave my agent friend Eleanor Kilgallen a call, and she asked me to see a young man that she'd recently started representing. When I met the young man, his sole acting experience consisted of a fifteen minute religious program. He was studying with Stella Adler, which didn't surprise me as all the kids were into method acting. After spending some time with the young actor, I just had a hunch about him and could feel the hair on the back of my neck stand up. He was so gorgeous and could charm anybody with his good looks and long eyelashes, what a darling. I always tend to go by the reading, but this part also did call for a lovely looking young man, and he was all that and more, so I decided to cast him as our curly-headed kid.

Shortly after casting this kid, he signed with MCA, and word came through the grapevine that he was Shirley MacLaine's little brother. By this time, Shirley was already an up-and-coming movie star, but Warren didn't want her help in the business. He was determined to make it on his own. Nobody had a clue, not even his friends at Stella Adler, that Warren Beatty was Shirley MacLaine's little brother.

Warren showed up for rehearsals and was asked to get a permanent wave and use a curling iron on his hair. When the actors began rehearsing their lines, Raymond Massey, a veteran stage actor who was sixty-one at the time, complained to everyone that he couldn't hear Warren when he delivered his lines. Immediately after the show aired, Eleanor Kilgallen called to ask me what I thought of her client. "I think I understood about every third or fourth sentence that came out of his mouth," was my reply. The Actors Studio was in full swing in those days; and every actress was trying to sound like Geraldine Page, while every actor was trying to sound like Marlon Brando, which newcomers generally accomplished by simply mumbling as much as possible. I went on to tell Eleanor I would consider myself lucky if I didn't get fired after that incomprehensible performance, during which a set also collapsed, but that was beside the point. Warren went on to act in several other television series until his breakout performance as Bud Stamper playing opposite Natalie Wood in Elia Kazan's *Splendor in the Grass.* He learned how to act.

Warren later recalled, "It was my first big job, and I was a kid, and I didn't know what I was doing, and was running around and stumbling, and I thought I was acting."

Television was in its early childhood back then. The pace was frantic, especially since we were all new at the whole phenomenon, and none of us particularly knew what we were doing. During the casting process, when I read a scene with an actor, I would try not to emote too much but to give them an energy they could bounce off. I once had a director who had also been a well-known radio actor. He wanted to read with the actor instead of me and was so in love with his own voice that he hardly paid any attention to the bewildered actor.

When asked to come in for a general casting interview, many actors respond, "What shall I wear?" My reply to that was usually, "Anything that will get you through the streets without being arrested."

Since my early days at *KRAFT*, I began to keep organized notes on performers I would see in my office and at various venues, and it became a practice I continued right up until my retirement. A three-by-five index card file of virtually every performer who caught my eye in plays, television, or movies was maintained and became part of my office. I have kept these files with me right up to this day. There has been some obvious winnowing of my card files over the years, but I've always tried to keep those of the actors with whom I met, many which were early in their careers and have gone on to achieve some deserved fame as actors. *(See Appendix 1)*

Eventually, we were able to develop quite a unique and significant acting pool in New York. In some ways, we sort of created our own repertory company, in that I used several actors in many different types of roles and teleplays throughout my nine years as head of casting for *Kraft Television Theatre*. This is a partial list of some of those superb actors that appeared on live television at *KRAFT*: Grace Kelly, Anne Francis, George Reeves, E. G. Marshall, Eileen Heckart, Joanne Woodward, Carl Reiner, Joel Grey, James Broderick, Maggie Smith, Theodore Bikel, William Shatner, Cliff Robertson, Lorne Greene, Sal Mineo, Geraldine Page, June Lockhart, Maureen Stapleton, George C. Scott, Cloris Leachman, Ben Gazzara, Anne Jackson, Eli Wallach, Shelley Winters, Kim Stanley, Roddy McDowall, Ossie Davis, John Cassavetes, Mary Astor, Lillian Gish, Murray Hamilton, Art Carney, Elaine Stritch, Lois Smith, Anthony Perkins, Richard Kiley, Leslie Nielsen, Peter Cookson, Barnard Hughes, Jayne Meadows, Jackie Cooper, Tony Randall, Jack Klugman, Melvyn Douglas, Anthony Franciosa, Eva LeGallienne, Lee Marvin, Larry Hagman, Hope Lange, Claude Rains, Jo Van Fleet, Eva Gabor, Kay Ballard, Barbara Cook, George Peppard, Orson Bean, Fred Gwynne, Rip Torn, Frank Albertson, Margaret Hamilton, ZaSu Pitts, and Patty Duke at age eleven.

In 1958, David Susskind took over production supervision and managed to bring an illustrious television series to an end in just one season. I was unemployed. Despite nine years of great experience in casting close to five hundred shows, I was an unknown. Casting directors didn't get on-screen credit in those days. In fact, the DGA (Directors Guild of America) wouldn't allow us to call ourselves casting directors, claiming they owned the word "director." Some of this would soon change.

A new ninety-minute anthology show, *The Play of the Week*, was going on the air in 1959; and the head of casting, Marc Merson, asked me to sign on as his assistant. As much as I may have needed a job, I declined because Marc was an actor who had become the show's casting person without ever having previously cast anything. He did, however, agree to my alternate suggestion that he and I share the job and each cast every other show.

My first assignment was a Worthington Minor production of Eugene O'Neill's *The Iceman Cometh*. Sidney Lumet had given up his acting career and was now directing this production.

Robert Redford had been studying at the American Academy of Dramatic Arts in New York after he returned from living in Europe for a few years as a struggling painter. Bob had been seen in a production of *The Seagull* and was able to sign at the MCA agency with the help of Maynard Morris and Stark Hesseltine. Eleanor Kilgallen found him a small part in an *Armstrong Circle Theatre* episode; and just before the show went live on the air, Bob recalled another actor whispering to him, "See the red light on that camera? As soon as it comes on, you will have twenty million people waiting for you to screw up." He barely made it through, but the adrenaline rush was something else, and he knew he had to do it again.

When I brought Bob in to read for Sidney, he'd just finished vacationing out in California with his young family and had been out in the sun, and Sidney told me he looked too much like a surfer. I pleaded with Sidney to take a chance with Bob, and eventually, he agreed. I was very pleased that I managed to convince him to hire actors outside the coterie of actors he'd become close to and always used. The rest of the cast was stunning as well and included several of the actors who'd originated their roles in the same play on Broadway.

Jason Robards played the lead role of Hickey and Bob claims, "We got on right off the bat. Sometimes Jason coached me more than the director Sidney Lumet did and he was extremely generous to me. In the play, when his character meets mine, he says, 'We're members of the same lodge in some way.' Because of our personal connection, he invested in that moment pretty heavily, and I'll never forget that line. It was critical for me to pay attention to him. He wasn't preachy about acting, he was an encyclopedia. I learned more watching his nuances that I did from any stage actor."

The experience Bob had acting in *The Iceman Cometh* meant a lot to him and his career. The insights of the play left a mark on him. He recalls a few of the lines from the play, "The history of the world proves that truth has no bearing on anything," and "Men don't want to be saved from themselves because then they'd have to give up greed . . . and they don't want to pay that price for liberty." Bob says, "It summarized what I felt about American life as I was growing up. We were all looking for the good life, but we didn't want to probe too deeply. It was a life of illusions and non-communication, and that had always felt wrong. O'Neill was about reaching for understanding, and working that text made me comfortable for the first time about this life I found myself in. I wasn't yet an actor, but I was in the state of becoming."

I couldn't have been more proud of my work. It was also the first time that I was going to be given a screen credit as casting director on such a meaningful production. The night it aired, I sat incredulously as the credits ran and found myself staring at a screen that clearly read: Casting Director—Marc Merson.

Eleanor Kilgallen, the agent for several of the actors involved, who knew perfectly well who'd cast the show, urged me to sue Marc. If I'd had a good lawyer in those days or the money to pay one with, I probably would have. As it was, I did nothing about it besides a little detective work, through which I discovered that the "mistake" was not all that mysterious. Marc Merson simply erased my name from the credit sheet and had written in his own instead. Marc, wherever you are now, no, I haven't forgotten, and shame on you. Needless to say, the first production I cast for *The Play of the Week* was also my swan song.

Adrift in the job market again, it wasn't long before Herbert (Bert) Leonard phoned and asked me if I'd like to come on board to cast a new ABC dramatic series called *Naked City*, which was to be filmed entirely in New York City. I leapt at it. This was the second incarnation of the series. A half-hour version that had a different cast I had nothing to do with had aired two years earlier. Bert Leonard's *Naked City*, which was an hour in length, ran for three seasons and turned out to be Hollywood's favorite and most convenient way of "discovering" New York actors; and New York was full of brilliant, available actors who were eager to work. I was like a kid in a candy store.

Bert Leonard was a sensational producer. He worked closely with the writers (including the great Stirling Silliphant) and the directors, and he spent countless hours in the editing room. Bert was a hands-on type that is such a rarity in the business. There was no aspect of *Naked City* that didn't benefit from Bert's talent and expertise. Adding to his brutal schedule was the fact that the show was essentially produced in California but shot in New York.

Bert insisted on flying in from the West Coast for the first two or three shows to oversee my casting. I finally told him, not out of frustration, but out of genuine respect and concern, "You know, Bert, you've already got more than enough to do on this show without flying three thousand miles to attend auditions. If you don't think you can trust me to cast the show the way you want, I'll happily step aside so you can hire someone else you trust." He never flew to auditions again.

Screen Gems, the company behind *Naked City*, had already set Paul Burke (no comment) for the lead as Detective Adam Flint. Two wonderful actors, from the original version of the series, Harry Bellaver and Horace McMahon, returned along with a handful of other talented new regulars that included Nancy Malone.

Each week, I'd try to find a guest star—always a "name"—that Bert and I would discuss over the telephone and agree on. Our budget didn't allow us to "import" movie stars from Hollywood, so our guest stars were usually actors who had starred in or had been featured on the New York stage. Beyond that, I was on my own and had complete autonomy. The director would fly in from California the day before rehearsals started; and I'm sure most, if not all them, wondered at first who this upstart Marion Dougherty was, who'd already assembled a cast without a word of input from them. We all became great friends, though. Again by this time, there was so much amazing acting talent in New York to choose from that they made me look good, so the directors came to trust me as much as Bert did.

I'd been impressed by an actor named Robert Morse after seeing him actually upstage Jackie Gleason—no easy task—in the Broadway musical *Take Me Along*. Robert was not above mugging his way through a part, but he was undeniably talented. We'd hired him to play the "name" as one of the two juvenile delinquents in an upcoming episode of *Naked City*. The trick was who was I going to find that could hold their own opposite such a shameless talented scene-stealer?

One day Robert Duvall, who I used a lot for understandable reasons, asked if I would be willing to meet his roommates; one was a young actor who'd been working in theater for many years but couldn't seem to find a job on television or film and was short on cash. As it turned out, Duvall's roommate was an eager, gifted, prominent-nosed, pompadour-haired kid. After we talked a few minutes, I asked him to go over in the corner with some pages from the script, look them over, and then read with me. He did, and I immediately thought, "Aha! No way is this guy going to let Robert Morse or anybody trample over him!"

He was so amazed when I told him he had the job that his first question was, "Who do I have to see?" It took me a bit to convince him that he'd seen the only person he had to see and that there were no catches—no more hoops to jump through—he was hired. It was Dustin Hoffman's first on-camera job; and he did, indeed, hold his own against Robert Morse in an episode titled *Sweet Prince of Delancy Street* that aired on June 7, 1961. I was able to cast Dustin in one other episode, *Barefoot on a Bed of Coals*, which aired May 29, 1963.

Bobby Duvall's other roommate was an actor named Gene Hackman, and I went to see him perform at the Gateway Playhouse in Bellport, Long Island. He had the qualities of a gentle and nice big guy. He happened to be six-feet-two-inches. Although his performance in the play wasn't all that gripping, I decided to cast him in an episode of *Naked City* and later in *Route 66*. Gene's performance in both shows got good notices, and he was soon offered a role on Broadway in the production of *Any Wednesday*, starring Sandy Dennis. That led to Robert Rossen casting him in his first minor film role *Lilith*, which starred my young curly-headed kid, Warren Beatty.

Another actor struggling during this same time was Martin Sheen. I had cast Martin in the episode *The Night the Saints Lost Their Halos* along with Jo Van Fleet and Peter Fonda, which aired on January 17, 1962. Several months later, Martin came into my office and announced, "I can't pay rent." I told him that I had a few scripts coming up that I thought we could cast him in, so I said, "For now, I'll let you do an extra if you get a cap and keep it down on your face and stay in the background." Martin worked as an extra and then followed as an actor in two other episodes, *And by the Sweat of thy Brow*, with Richard

Jordan and Barbara Barrie, airing October 10, 1962, and *Dust Devil on a Quiet Street*, with Richard Basehard, airing November 28, 1962. I think Martin ended up wearing that cap for years.

Was I a soft touch for an actor who couldn't pay their rent or was short on cash? If they were the acting caliber of Dustin or Martin, you bet!

Bert Leonard had started producing another show for CBS called *Route 66*, and he enthusiastically used many of the *Naked City* actors I had found for him. In one of my many conversations with Bert about *Naked City*, I suggested the talented Jack Warden for a *Route 66* role, after he'd shone in an episode of *Naked City*. Bert immediately said, "Great. I'll set him."

An hour later, I got an outraged call from Millie Gusse, the California casting director on *Route 66*. She was furious that I had invaded her professional territory, particularly since she'd also suggested Jack Warden for the same role, but Bert had already hired him on my recommendation.

I apologized the best I could, considering the fact that as far as I was concerned, I was just doing my job. To avoid any further conflicts, I suggested a compromise to Bert. Since *Route 66* was filmed all over the country, Millie should cast all episodes shot west of the Mississippi, and I would cast all the episodes east of the Mississippi. That ended up working very well for me, as from that day forward, there was never another episode of *Route 66* shot west of the Mississippi.

This development left me casting two one-hour shows every week, with no one helping me but my secretary, Jessica Levy, a very bright lady, but not a casting person. It was an insane schedule, but I loved every minute of it and could never have accomplished it if it weren't for the fact that I had no one to answer to but Bert who had total faith in me. If I had to work my way through the layer after layer of studio and network executives who exist today for the apparent purpose of questioning every decision and withholding permission for as long as possible, it would've been impossible to accomplish what I was able to.

During my years casting both *Naked City* and *Route 66*, we most definitely expanded our New York acting pool. Some of the actors featured were Suzanne Pleshette, Albert Lewis, Brenda Vaccaro, Robert Loggia, Luther Adler, David Janssen, Burt Reynolds, Lois Nettleton, Sylvia Miles, Doris Roberts, Tuesday Weld, James Farentino, Peter Falk, Jean Stapleton, Barbara Baxley, Gladys Cooper, Joseph Campanella, James Coburn, Carroll O'Connor, Alan Alda, Burgess Meredith, Sandy Dennis, Shirley Knight, Diahann Carroll, Christopher Walken, Eddie Albert, George Segal, Jon Voight, Cicely Tyson, Piper Laurie, Gene Roche, Tom Bosley, Tina Louise, Chad Everett, Bruce Glover, Soupy Sales, Bibi Osterwald, Grayson Hall, and Barbara Eden among so many others.

Although I never received a raise in salary when they added a second show to my workload, Bert did give me a casting credit on a single card.

On the Rocks

It would be sweet to be able to paint a lovely portrait of my personal life that matched the satisfaction and fulfillment I was gaining from my career in casting, but there was a time in my life that I was involved in a miserable marriage.

I envy those women who realize they've made a colossal mistake and get out of a bad marriage fast. Ethel Merman, in writing her autobiography, *Merman*, had a chapter heading that read, "My Marriage to Ernest Borgnine." Upon turning the page, you discovered that the next chapter began with no additional mention of her thirty-two-day marriage to Mr. Borgnine. That was my first inclination when I began writing, to leave it a blank page. It would be so lovely to be able to forget about it all that quickly.

I was married from about the time I started casting for *Kraft Television Theatre*. The legal part of the marriage lasted some twenty-nine years, although to be honest, it was over considerably before that time.

In the late 1940s, when I'd arrived in New York, I was pretty much your average working girl, putting in my days at Delman's department store, designing windows, and socializing with friends. On one particular evening, I visited a college friend who happened to be singing on a television show in New York. I went to her hotel, and we headed to the lounge to have a drink before she had to leave to perform. My friend had also invited a rather handsome young man to join us by the name of Robert Blossom, and we were introduced.

He was a pleasant man, a year older than I, and when my friend had to leave about a half hour later, Bobby invited me to have dinner. He told me later that he thought I looked sort of pathetic and felt I could stand a good meal. How romantic!

For some odd reason, during dinner, he told me he'd like to introduce me to his dog and his family. I was already seeing someone at the time, but not wishing to be impolite to a man who'd just bought me dinner, I agreed. We got in his car and began to drive to his family's home. We drove for quite awhile, and I soon realized that his family didn't live in New York City, but in Babylon on Long Island, where I met his dog and his parents, Mr. and Mrs. Sumner Blossom.

Sumner Blossom was the editor of *The American Magazine*, which was published monthly by Crowell-Collier from 1906 until 1956. Sumner was a wonderful, well-respected man, and I immediately realized that Bobby's family was certainly quite well off.

When Bobby asked to see me again, I told him that I was involved and had a date with another young man to go to a dance at the Plaza Hotel. Bobby drove me back to my apartment, and I thought that was the end of that.

I was more than surprised when, at the dance at the Plaza, my date was tapped on the shoulder by Bobby, who asked if he could cut in. After that, Bobby and I dated regularly, and my other beau faded into the background. This was at the same time that I was staying in the Park Avenue apartment that had turned out to be the hub of a call girl operation, so I decided to move in with some friends of Bobby's in Babylon.

In the beginning, Bobby seemed to be a lot of fun. In fact, he was a naval officer at the time I met him, and that wasn't his only occupation; he also had a huge passion for boats and sailing, and this turned out to be a big part of his life. It was actually on his boat that I began to sail and became fairly good at it. We had a nice group of friends that we hung out with in Babylon, and since I'm not basically a city person, it was nice living out there and spending time with other people who enjoyed the outdoors as much as Bobby and I did.

This was the period just after World War II, when all the boys were returning home, and everyone was feeling optimistic about their future. It wasn't surprising when all of the friends around us started to get married. Bobby and I kind of fell into that same rhythm and thought it was the natural thing to do. We really didn't think about it too much.

My parents had a wonderful marriage that lasted over sixty years. While I was not one of those girls who'd had an overwhelming passion to get married or have children, I was not against it for any reason whatsoever. Perhaps it was a sign of things to come that neither Bobby nor I came up with the idea of getting married. It was Bobby's parents and especially his grandfather that really set things in motion. His grandfather actually found the apartment in Babylon that we were to live in once we began our married life.

We were married in the Little Church around the Corner at 1 East Twenty-Ninth Street in New York City. My parents and Aunt Abigail attended the small ceremony along with his parents, but we hadn't told any of our friends in Babylon. Bobby had left the navy by this time and had become a salesman for artwork used in magazines. In the mid-1950s, photographs showed up on the scene and quickly buried original magazine art. I had begun my casting career with *KRAFT* almost a year before our trip down the aisle.

Bobby seemed very proud of my casting position, but his opinion soon changed. I recall very well the party where there was a friend of ours who just loved hearing stories about the entertainment business and all the gossip related to the stars. She wanted to know everything that was going on, and it was great fun to talk about it with someone who was so interested. All of the sudden, Bobby got very angry for no reason at all. He was obviously jealous of the attention that I was getting so I learned not to talk much about what I was doing and began having to lead a double life. In the city, I was Marion Dougherty, professional career woman and casting director for *Kraft Television Theatre*; and in Babylon, I was Mrs. Robert Blossom, housewife and first sailing mate.

In the early days of live television, there were not many industry-held parties or events. Part of my job was to see as many plays and movies in New York as I could, and Bobby sometimes enjoyed sharing those with me. We'd often meet friends at Timothy's Bar on Lexington Avenue, and when I think about those times now, it is quite clear to me that Bobby was an alcoholic. My drinking also fueled the fire.

We eventually moved from our apartment to a rental house in Babylon about a year after we were married. A few years after that, I purchased our first home in Bayshore, Long Island, with the money I was making from *KRAFT*. The new home was located not too far from his family and our friends in Babylon.

While my career continued to flourish, Bobby's magazine artwork sales job fizzled, because of the arrival of photographic art that marked the current rage in print media. From the day we were married, we never had a joint bank account, and I paid for all the household bills from my income. As the marriage went on, I picked up more and more of the financial responsibility until it was all mine.

When Bobby's job vanished, he wanted to go into business with a mechanical friend of his and invest in a Jaguar dealership. Bobby's share of the investment capital came from my *KRAFT* earnings. Since Bobby was notoriously late and seemingly complacent about showing up for work any time before noon, it was surprising that their dealership became somewhat successful. For some odd reason, Bobby was late for everything. It seemed I would find myself always waiting on some street corner for him. He would then show up a half an hour late and think nothing of it. Finally one day I asked him why he was late, and he replied, "I don't like to wait for people."

It was surprising that Bobby and his partner could maintain the Jaguar dealership as long as they did with Bobby's work ethic; but he was a very good salesman—charming, knowledgeable, and passionate about cars and especially Jaguars. There came a time when the Jaguar manufacturing company had some kind of a strike, and with all the trouble back in England, Bobby and his partner had to let the dealership go.

Soon after his business folded, Bobby's jealousy became apparent pretty fast, and his controlling nature crept up on me without fully realizing it. I don't know what the rationale was behind his not wanting to look or find a new job, but he seemed content to putter around the house with his boats and cars and enjoy a life of relative ease. Clearly, had I not had the career I had, with money coming in regularly, it would've been impossible for Bobby to have enjoyed the leisure that he did. I was paid a weekly salary from *KRAFT*, which was in the neighborhood of $500 a week. I also had a decent expense account, so we lived comfortably. Bobby would use whatever money he could get from me to buy old cars and boats and then fix them up and resell them, but I never saw a penny from any of that money. That first meal he bought me when he thought I could stand a good meal was also the last of any meals or gifts that he would give to me. Totally lacking any romantic notions, Bobby was not the giving type—no flowers, no candy, lingerie, perfume—nothing.

It became most important to keep my business life separate from my private life. We had a good social life on the weekends with a great group of friends we'd go sailing with, and at *KRAFT*, I was always very busy and happy with my work. My alone time with Bobby tended to be fairly limited, which made my life a lot easier. I have never been to therapy, so I don't know if Bobby reacted to his feeling powerless in his professional life or what led to the root of the true problems. Maybe he felt some sense of helplessness, but something drove him to attempt to control as much of my life as he could, which eventually turned to physical violence. I seldom invited any of the friends that I'd made in the city to come and visit me out in Bayshore on the weekends, and Bobby made it perfectly clear early on that he was not enamored by my family.

My parents only visited once after we got married. During that one visit, Bobby got into an argument with my daddy that was so heated that I became concerned for my daddy's health; since he'd previously suffered from a heart attack. Not only did my family get the feeling that they shouldn't come and visit me, but my visits with them were also extremely limited. Bobby never wanted to go to Pennsylvania, so I missed out on many family get-togethers, and for that, I feel sorry and guilty about to this day.

Once I had plans to go down to visit my family, and Bobby and I got into an argument just before I left. He slugged me, and I fell down and blackened my eye. I still decided to go on my visit, but I had to put heavy makeup on my eye so they wouldn't see the soreness. Prior to that episode, my marriage had become nasty, and Bobby had taken that first step from which I don't think you can ever come back. He had struck me physically. Again, I don't know why he was a violent person with no self-control. In thinking about it, I believe Bobby's family was much colder to him than mine was to me. Bobby's father was not very supportive of him, and economic circumstances certainly didn't seem to be a factor in their family. It was evident they were financially quite a few steps above the Dougherty family of Pennsylvania.

There was no indication in Bobby's parents' marriage that they had raised him to treat women so abysmally. I knew from my own experience that my father never struck my mother. My parents' marriage had been so wonderful that I was not prepared for what mine turned out to be. My parents didn't even argue! The only time I ever heard my father raise his voice was in frustration. Many times my mother was late in getting ready, and my father would yell, "Come on, Virginia. We're going to be late!" That was the extent of any arguing. I guess I was definitely not ready for the real world in some ways.

I am the type of person who doesn't like conflict or fighting and will do whatever I can to avoid it. However, I do not want to give the impression that there was no joy in the marriage, only that joy was very short lived. Bobby and I had a lovely trip to the West Indies in the early 1950s. Back then, it was not the tourist spot it is today. It had the natural beauty of its reputation but wasn't popular among tourists. We were interested in visiting there after we'd seen an article in *Life Magazine* about the islands.

On a second visit to the West Indies, Bobby became friends with a man who had a sweet little hotel on the beach. A few days before it was time to return to New York, Bobby decided he wanted to extend his stay. When I got back to work in New York, I had been experiencing these peculiar pains for some time and decided to have it checked out by a doctor who was the head of gynecology for St. Vincent's Hospital in New York. The doctor took a few X-rays and discovered a cyst that he felt should promptly get taken care of.

I thought it best to get a second opinion, so I made an appointment and went up to the Presbyterian Hospital. That doctor also took X-rays and confirmed the original diagnosis. I waited for Bobby to return home, and he didn't come as he was having such a good time in the West Indies. Finally, I called Bobby and told him that I had to go to the hospital for an operation. The doctor continued to push me for rescheduling the operation, and just like all those times on the street corner, I waited for Bobby.

When he eventually returned, I scheduled the operation. It turned out to be a much worse scenario, much more complicated than originally suspected. The cyst the doctors had seen on the X-rays was in front of another even larger cyst, so I had to undergo a total hysterectomy. After the operation had been performed, I was told that the cyst was beginning to go into the vital organs and that would've been major trouble. At the age of thirty-two, my chances for having any children of my own came to an end, even if I had been of a mind to have them.

In those days, there were no hormone replacement pills, and the operation they'd performed on me had removed much more than anyone had anticipated. At one point, I can clearly remember being at *KRAFT* and being so depressed that I honestly wanted to jump out the window of the building.

As much as Bobby controlled me in getting me pretty much cut off from my family and city friends, he never was able to conquer my spirit and draw me down the battered wife syndrome. It may seem naive to say that, as embarrassed as I was by having a husband who physically hit me. I was proud that he never conquered my mind and made me think the way he treated me was at all acceptable or that I had done something to deserve it. Not that I didn't think it wouldn't, but the physical abuse escalated, and I was already well on the way of being truly afraid of Bobby when he drew a revolver on me in a fit of rage. I had an almost out-of-body reaction to it, wondering what it would look like when the story hit the newspapers of my being shot by my husband.

New Beginnings

George Roy Hill, director extraordinaire who had become a director for *KRAFT* not long after he'd begun assisting Fielder Cook, called and asked me if I might be interested in casting a film for him that was being shot entirely on location in New York City.

George was set to direct *The World of Henry Orient*, an MGM/United Artists co-production with the then unheard budget of $1 million. The studio had hired a casting director, with George's permission, and this person had submitted what I call a "grocery list"; if you list everyone from A to Z, someone in there is going to be right for the part. If that were all it took to cast a production, I believe most anyone could do it. George immediately fired the guy and asked if I was available. I gave Bert Leonard a call since I was still casting the end of the television season for both *Naked City* and *Route 66*. Bert, the gracious man that he was, gave me his blessing; and I ended up moonlighting.

I hardly ever, unless it's a very peculiar role, suggest more than a few actors. If the director wouldn't spark to those initially suggested, I'd go back to suggest others. I never subscribed to that kind of a huge casting list. I'll start with a small group of actors, which although they might not be totally appropriate for the role; for me, they possess an interesting quality or facet that made me notice or remember them.

I was excited about working on my first film because I'd admired George's work on *KRAFT*, both as a director and as a writer of his own teleplays, and also doctoring many other scripts for *KRAFT*. His work on the *KRAFT* production of *A Night to Remember* was brilliant.

This was George's third film. He'd previously directed *Period of Adjustment* with Jane Fonda, Anthony Franciosa, and Jim Hutton, and *Toys in the Attic* with Dean Martin and Geraldine Page.

The screenplay was written by father-daughter screenwriters Nunnally and Nora Johnson and was based on a book by Nora about her own experiences while attending the Brearly School in New York. Nunnally had previously written the screenplay for *The Grapes of Wrath*, based on the John Steinbeck novel and directed by John Ford. Nunnally was living in London at that time since the tax advantages were considerably better. He could travel back to the United States, but he couldn't work in the States, so George had to travel to London to work with him on the script. Early on, they sent Peter Sellers the script, and he agreed to play the part of Henry Orient, a phony musician. George met with Peter to discuss the script and any changes he wanted; however, Peter liked the script the way it was written.

The World of Henry Orient revolved around two young teenage girls who attended an Upper East Side private school in Manhattan and became fast friends when they found out that they both came from divorced homes. Through their romps into fantasy, they discovered they shared an obsessive fascination for a somewhat less than spectacularly talented pianist, Henry Orient. Through their friendship, they help each other through adolescence.

This was Peter Seller's first American film, and when I joined the production team, I began my first film by casting every other important role. I went through my casting index cards and hired several actors I'd cast in television—Tom Bosely, Bibi Osterwald, Fred Stewart, Phyllis

Thaxter, John Fielder, and Al Lewis. I'd cast Al Lewis in several episodes of *Naked City*, and he became most notably known afterward as Grampa on *The Munsters* television series. We considered Burgess Meredith and Walter Matthau for roles; however, we couldn't come to an agreement with their agents on a deal. We cast Angela Lansbury direct from Broadway (as noted earlier), and George had previously worked with Paula Prentiss. Angela and Paula were each paid $25,000 for about five weeks of work.

The big problem for me was finding the two young girls. I found Merrie Spaeth at a friend's Quaker school in Philadelphia, following trips to Hollywood, Cleveland, Chicago, and Boston, seeing hundreds of girls. We covered every female preparatory school within a hundred-mile radius of New York City.

Merrie was a fifteen-year-old from Philadelphia, and although she had no experience outside her school plays, she was one of those rare talents, an absolutely instinctive actor. She had a wonderful humor and an inborn sense of timing. She happened to fit one of the girls' roles, that of Gilbert, as though it was written for her. We had not set her because we still couldn't find anyone to play the role of her friend, Val.

Three days before we were to go into rehearsals, George and I sat in our offices on East Fifty-Fifth Street in various states of panic, facing the fact that we still hadn't found another girl. We had to postpone rehearsals for one week. We made a last massive effort to find a Val, including an open audition for teenage girls. Peter Sellers, having already arrived from London, most agreeably consented to act as bait, since he was as concerned as we in getting the right tormentors for him. Meanwhile, we pledged ourselves to go back over all our lists and call friends, relatives, acquaintances, enemies—anyone who might have or know a fourteen or fifteen-year-old girl who fit Val's description. The open audition was successful in that it turned up several excellent girls whom we could use in other smaller parts, but still no Val.

Jerome Hellman, who was the producer on the film, phoned his friend, Howard Zieff, who was a photographer at the time, and described this girl we were looking for. Howard explained to Jerry that just the week before, a young girl from Rye, New York, had received permission from her parents to do a little modeling during the summer and had come in to do some work for him. Zieff described her to Jerry as kind of kooky but attractive. Her name was Elizabeth Tipton Walker, known as Tippy, and George promptly gave her parents a call.

The following Tuesday, Tippy came into the production office to meet with George and me. We gave her the script to look over for about an hour and then asked her to read some scenes. I remember Tippy's reading very well as she had long light brown hair and was myopic, so she put her nose about a quarter inch away from the print, and as her hair fell all over the script, she started to read. George recalled it as mumbling. We tried again, this time with Tippy wearing glasses, and a few words became audible.

We discovered that she had absolutely no experience of any kind. She was also extremely shy and probably very frightened. George loved the fact that Tippy was utterly honest in everything she said and did. There was no attempt to put on an act of any kind, no airs; nothing felt manufactured. She read very badly, but once she grasped the idea of the scene and understood the thoughts and feelings of the character, she came alive in bits and flashes. When she did this, both George and I felt she was Val.

Both girls gave absolutely charming performances, although their process of achieving them varied greatly. George described them in an interview: "The girls reacted differently during rehearsals and shooting. Merrie was in seventh heaven. It was though she had stepped into a world for which she had been waiting years. Her curiosity about every phase of moviemaking was insatiable. She was happy, confident, gregarious, and no aspect of the production failed to catch her eye or interest her. She spent hours with Peter and the other actors positively grilling them as to their techniques, and what she learned, she applied. However, it was a strange world for Tippy, one she had never thought of entering, and in the beginning, she was withdrawn and frightened. It took time and much courage for her to give herself a new environment and a new character. But when she finally did, she did it totally and without reservation of self-consciousness. And it is this commitment that comes across on screen."

In one particular scene toward the end of the movie, the two girls are hiding outside Henry Orient's apartment; and Val's mother (played by Angela Lansbury) comes out, obviously having had an affair with Henry. Val is shocked. During the shooting of the scene, Tippy was unable to produce tears and didn't want to use an artificial squirter. Instead, Tippy asked George to slap her; and George did, lightly. She then told him to slap her again, only harder this time, which he did and recounts, "I nearly lost my life as a mutinous crew started to growl. I hit her a third time, and finally, the tears came and none too soon for my own health."

The film was shot on location for the most part around Manhattan with the interiors being filmed in a converted hangar at Roosevelt Field in Long Island. It happened to be the same field that Charles Lindbergh took off from for his most famous flight.

George used a montage in the film with the two young girls running and jumping over trash cans, fire hydrants, whatever they could find. He used a trampoline to give the effect that the girls were flying, an idea he cheerfully admits to having stolen from Leni Riefenstahl's film, *Triumph of the Will*, when she filmed the 1939 Olympic divers jumping from a high board through the air without ever seeing the ground. He also shot that scene in slow motion, which was a technique rarely used up until that time.

I very much admired a red chiffon dress that Angela Lansbury wore in the film, and at the end of the production, she gave it to me as a gift. I thanked her so much and took it home, but it was not really my size. Angela was a bit more endowed than I, I'm sad to say.

George always had great music in his films as he had majored in music at Yale. It was the love of his personal life, and he paid a good deal of attention to the music. I remember he'd hired David Gersten to score the film, and one day when they'd assembled a full orchestra for the film and finished a bit early, Gersten pulled out a piece that he'd written for himself and used the orchestra to hear how it sounded. It had nothing to do with the film whatsoever, and when George caught wind of this, he was so pissed off he replaced Gersten with Elmer Bernstein.

Aside from *The World of Henry Orient* being my first feature film, it was also costume designer Ann Roth's first feature film credit as well. Ann and I have been friends ever since, and we've worked together on several other of George's films.

In the midst of casting *Henry Orient*, actor Jack Weston called me; and he was wondering if I could cast a film that his brother, Sam, was producing called *One Potato, Two Potato*. I had known Jack from *KRAFT* and was intrigued enough by the script to want to help cast it.

Larry Peerce directed, and the two leads involved in this interracial love story were Bernie Hamilton and Barbara Barrie. Others that we cast included Harry Bellaver, one of my marvelous leading character men in *Naked City*; Robert Earl Jones, the father of James Earl Jones; Vinnette Carroll; and Richard Mulligan. The movie, I believe, was the first time an interracial love story had been told on film with an African-American actor starring opposite a Caucasian actor. The film was so low budget that my "paycheck" ended up being a case of Chivas Regal scotch, which made my husband, Bobby, a very happy man.

The World of Henry Orient and *One Potato, Two Potato*, my first two movies, were both chosen for the Cannes Film Festival! In addition, both George Roy Hill and Larry Peerce were nominated for the Palme d'Or, and Barbara Barrie won Best Actress at Cannes for her performance. *The World of Henry Orient* was also nominated for the Golden Globe Best Picture Award.

George Roy Hill had a house in Saltaire on Fire Island, and he had a little catboat that he kept in my backyard since I lived in Bayshore on an outlet. He'd come out on the weekends to get his catboat and sail to Fire Island across the Great South Bay, and he soon began talking to me about his next film project based on the James Michener book, *Hawaii*.

During that summer, George had rented a sailboat and had plans to sail to Block Island with his wife, Louisa, and their four children. When Louisa got sick and couldn't start the trip, George asked me to go along until he could get to Block Island since I was a good sailor. It was a sailing trip of a couple of days, and Louisa would meet George and the kids on Block Island while I returned to New York by plane. George explained that if I'd go on the sailing trip, he'd try to get me the casting job on *Hawaii*. If I got the job, I would have to pay for my return airline ticket from Block Island myself. George already had a reputation of not being very liberal with his money.

I paid for my flight back to New York anyway, and a short time later, George called me and officially asked me if I would like to be the casting director on *Hawaii*. I was terribly excited about seeing the state of Hawaii. My great-aunt Abigail had been there in the early 1900s, in the days when you sailed to the Hawaiian Islands. I remember her description of the Hawaiian Islands had greatly enchanted me as a child. When she told me about them, I knew that one day I must be able to go to this enchantment too.

An Epic Tale of Casting

Perhaps one of the most difficult casting challenges of any of the films that I cast in my career was *Hawaii*. It was my second film with George Roy Hill and only the third film that I cast. I was not aware that the epic nature of the novel and film would translate into an epic tale of casting. Throughout this entire experience, I was able to absorb a tremendous amount of knowledge, and it proved to make every movie I cast following it a comparative breeze!

Hawaii told the history of the Hawaiian Islands from the very moment they were formed back in the prehistoric times right up to the present day—around 1959—when the novel was published. James Michener examined the people and culture of the islands as well as the effects on them as those that came to Hawaii throughout the islands' history brought about dramatic changes.

Part of the daunting task of bringing the novel to the screen, a feat that Michener himself deemed dubious since the book encompassed far too numerous characters and spanned such a great length of time, was to try to figure out what sections of the book to dramatize and what sections to cut. There was no other way to encompass the entire novel in one film by any endurable length for an audience.

The Mirisch Company purchased the film rights for $600,000 only weeks after the novel was published. They first hired Oscar-winning director Fred Zinnemann (*From Here to Eternity*, *A Man for All Seasons*) to direct the film version of *Hawaii*. Zinnemann was overwhelmed by the wealth of material in the novel and fully intended to shoot the entire book. From early on, George Roy Hill had told his agent to inform the Mirisch Company of his interest in making the film should there ever be any changes in arrangements. George's second film, *Toys in the Attic*, was produced by the Mirisch Company.

Zinnemann and Daniel Taradash, who had collaborated with Zinnemann before he won an Oscar for his screenplay *From Here to Eternity*, spent two years working on trying to create a workable screenplay for *Hawaii*. In 1962, after $2 million had already been spent, Zinnemann was finally ready to go before the cameras. The only problem was that they had created a script so immense, that the completed film would have a running time of about eight hours and would require two showings of four hours each on successive nights to see it all. This was Zinnemann's idea, but United Artists and the Mirisch Company refused to go along with it.

The Mirisch Company requested that Zinnemann cut the screenplay to something of manageable length for an audience. Zinnemann then fired Taradash and hired Dalton Trumbo (the blacklisted screenwriter who had finally been allowed to write using his real name again) to handle the job of reducing the screenplay. Nearly two years later, when Trumbo had completed his draft of the screenplay, Zinnemann's interest waned dramatically in the project and he abandoned it.

The project sat for another year or so before the Mirisch Company gave the property to George. Only they know why George was chosen, as his previous film credits did not even faintly resemble the size, scope, and budget of *Hawaii*. They did, however, like George's idea of concentrating the story on the middle of the novel, telling the story of the missionaries and their attempts to establish Christianity in Hawaii, taking the story up to the arrival of the Chinese immigrants and their impact on the Hawaiian culture. As George states, "The only thing that I did realize in taking on this epic film is that Michener's story is not only the birth and life of Hawaii and its people, it is basically the study of what happens when various cultures, backgrounds and religions are amalgamated on the same small island. It is a microcosm of the adjustments to be made in today's world if we are to survive. That is the single most important theme. Hawaii itself is a prime example of learning how to live together."

George's original idea of using a cast of unknowns to create the realism he was interested in was greeted with much less enthusiasm by the Mirisch Company. With box office concerns on their mind, they got George to compromise his original vision and agree to cast star names for the Caucasian leads. The Mirisch Company, with George's approval, had cast Max von Sydow and Julie Andrews as the lead missionary characters, Abner Hale and his bride, Jerusha. Richard Harris was also brought on board to play Jerusha's former love, a dashing sea captain, Rafter Hoxworth.

I don't think it escaped George's eye that of the three "big name" stars that were signed, only Julie Andrews was a major star at the time, having just appeared in the Oscar-winning Best Picture, *The Sound of Music*, and winning the Oscar for Best Actress the year before in Walt Disney's *Mary Poppins*.

Max von Sydow was just starting to do American films at the time. He was already established in films in his native Sweden and would achieve some semblance of fame as Jesus Christ in George Steven's *The Greatest Story Ever Told*; however, that film was not released until the middle of the filming schedule on *Hawaii*, so the Mirisch Company would have no certainty that von Sydow would reach the American audience and perhaps become a star. Max von Sydow was Ingmar

Bergman's leading man for several years. He was very professional, but George worried that his accent might get in the way. When Max gave a very good reading, George agreed to cast him. He also made the choice to cast Max's two sons in the film, Claus, who was good in it, and his younger son Henrik, who was a real terror on the set as he was so curious; and everything he touched, he'd destroy.

Richard Harris had appeared in the 1962 version of *Mutiny on the Bounty*, starring Marlon Brando and Trevor Howard, and received an Oscar nomination for Best Actor in *This Sporting Life*, playing the angry rugby player, Frank Machin; but his fame was still pretty much confined to England.

George and I started seeing a few actors in New York and set John Cullum, Caroll O'Connor, and George Rose for supporting roles before heading to Los Angeles. When we arrived in Hollywood, I made it a point to see John Kelly, the casting director for Zinnemann's attempted film production. He was a nice man who did not offer much encouragement. He said to me, "Forget about trying to find true Polynesians. They don't exist." He tried to explain that there had been so much intermarriage with the Chinese, Portuguese, and Americans, that no one would look like the original Hawaiians. Kelly added that even if you could find true-looking Hawaiians, there were no trained actors in Hawaii and no agents for any actors. Most all of the pictures that had been previously made in Hawaii were cast from the mainland.

That was a bit discouraging to me, but it made me more upset than anything and determined to prove that Kelly was wrong; although I had no idea what I would find there. In my initial discussions with George over casting, he emphasized that just as he intended to show what negative effects the arrival of outsiders had done to the Hawaiian beliefs at the time, societal as well as religious; he wanted to show the beauty of the Hawaiian people and had every intention of using true Polynesian actors and extras to accomplish that.

Even casting the non-Hawaiian roles proved to be more daunting than we'd thought. When we were working on filling the part of Reverend John Whipple, the missionary doctor, I'd become accustomed to studio executives and West Coast agents being shortsighted in the casting process. I actually had one actor come in and read for this role who told me that while he had never played a doctor, he had played an intern in one film! Who on earth did he think would care about that? The role was a significant supporting role, and George and I both agreed that Gene Hackman would be terrific in the part. We both knew Gene's work, and I'd cast him a few years earlier in *Naked City*.

The Mirisch Company had been run by David Mirisch and his younger brother, Walter. David had a massive heart attack, and the production was taken over by the younger Mirisch, who seemed a bit nervous about being in charge. George, thank God, had complete creative control on *Hawaii*; but as a courtesy, he would always tell Walter what actors we were interested in. I remember when we told him about casting Gene Hackman, Walter asked what other films he'd been in. We told him he had a small part in the film *Lilith*, and Walter was aghast. He told us, "Well then forget it. Find someone else!" Gene had appeared in *Lilith*, but it was the film that followed *Hawaii* that would be his breakthrough role as Buck Barrow in *Bonnie and Clyde*. We explained our familiarity with Gene's talent on television and stage, and despite Walter's trepidation and over the studio's objection, George and I set Gene for the part. Luckily, Walter never found out that Gene had also never played a doctor before! I have never understood the "cliché casting" idea and how it took hold so strongly as to rob studio executives of their imaginations. In 1972, when Gene won his first Oscar for Best

Actor in *The French Connection*, I had to exert every bit of my willpower to not call Walter and say, "See, we told you so!"

In Los Angeles, we added Michael Constantine, Lou Antonio, Malcolm Atterbury, and Torin Thatcher to the cast. Our offices were located in less than stunning quarters because of a fire that had forced a relocation of the production offices. I met Dorothy Jeakins, who designed the costumes for the film. Her office was near ours, up a flight of stairs in a somewhat rickety building. At the top the stairs, there were three Oscars, courtesy of Dorothy's movie costumes.

Dorothy was one of the most fascinating looking women I'd ever seen. She had an amazing character face and personality to match. I explained to George that this is the kind of face we need for Max von Sydow's mother, Hepzibah Hale, so we cast her in that small but touching role. Dorothy handled the role with surprising ease, stunning Julie Andrews who was watching the scene where Dorothy bids farewell to her son as he leaves for Hawaii. The makeup man offered to squirt glycerin in her eyes, but she refused. Everyone was impressed when the tears came naturally down Dorothy's face, and Julie asked her now she was able to do that. "It was easy," Dorothy told her, smiling impishly. "I just pretended that George replaced me with Edith Head." Edith Head was the most famous costume designer in Hollywood at the time.

In the MGM version of *Mutiny on the Bounty*, I seemed to recall that it had featured many Polynesians, so I went to visit the casting people there as I thought they might have helpful material. The casting offices at MGM were in a line, and I started with the lowliest casting person and worked my way right up to the head of casting. None of them had any notes. There were no photos, and they hadn't kept any files. They were absolutely no help whatsoever; in fact, they reiterated Jack Kelly's suggestion, "Forget trying to find real Polynesians! There aren't any."

The two-mast brigantine, *Thetis*, which in the film carries the missionaries from New England to Hawaii, was built in Norway and sailed to Hawaii for the filming sequences there. The second unit work actually began in February of 1965, which filmed the ship 150 miles above the Arctic Circle off the coast of Norway—substituting for the passage around Cape Horn at the tip of South America—these were the days prior to the Panama Canal.

Shooting the Walpole, Connecticut, and Yale College scenes were filmed in Old Sturbridge Village in Massachusetts in April of 1965; and the interiors of the New England scenes were shot immediately afterward at the Goldwyn Studios in Los Angeles. By the summer of 1965, filming was well underway. George had decided to film the screenplay as much as he could in chronological and continuous order so that the filming schedule would end with all the other scenes shot in Hawaii.

With George working on the *Thetis* storm sequences on the Goldwyn lot, I was preparing to leave for Hawaii to begin casting the Polynesian-speaking roles as well as the extras there, when a young man entered my office. Robert "Bob" Crawford said that George had told him to come and meet me and that he thought Bob would be right for the part of Cridland, the cabin boy on the ship. George had previously directed Bob in the Playhouse 90 production of *Child of Our Time*. Bob still looked about sixteen at that time when I cast him, and he became a lifelong friend of both George and myself. He continued to work with George behind the camera on several of George's films after *Hawaii*, eventually producing George's later films.

In the 1960s, there was not a big talent pool available of different ethnic actors, so casting associates usually went out to scour neighborhoods, restaurants, schools, laundromats, or wherever they thought they might locate groups of the ethnic backgrounds they were looking for. Now here I was, on my way to Hawaii to find the "nonexistent" true Polynesians.

I arrived in Hawaii late in the evening, after dark, and was met by a few production representatives. There were only a handful of people there who were working on the production, primarily the location and set construction people. They met me and took me out for dinner, and we got a little swacked, and then I went to my hotel, the Ilikai in Honolulu on Waikiki Beach. I was given the bridal suite as I was planning to set up my casting office somewhere there too. Exhausted from the plane trip and dinner, I went directly to bed.

The Hotel Ilikai was a brand-new hotel, and I was the first person to occupy its bridal suite. It was a luxurious suite. In the morning when I awakened to open the draperies, it revealed a breathtakingly beautiful view of Waikiki. It was like waking up to a dream.

Just about everyone in Honolulu was excited about the movie; and William Ewing, the editor of the *Honolulu Star-Bulletin*, as well as radio stations and other media were giving the film lots of preproduction publicity. There was a big buzz about the film production, as it was an important event for them, and they astonished me by making a big fuss over me. I was interviewed on both television and radio as well as in the newspapers.

The studio wanted me to bring over an assistant from Los Angeles, but I said no. I wanted to hire Hawaiians or at least *hapa haoles* (part Hawaiians) and hire locals. It turned out to be an extremely wise decision. I was introduced to Kinau Boyd Kamilii, who in turn introduced me to two other ladies, one a pure Polynesian, Carolyn Wright Glassmeyer, and Tita Ruddie Spielman, a *haole* woman with connections to the Dole pineapple family. Tita had great connections everywhere, although I don't think she was the least bit Hawaiian, except in her heart.

We were shown to our office in room 220 on the ground level of the hotel and again had this breathtaking view of Waikiki Beach with all the surfers. The hotel management brought in a catalog for me to order my office furniture as my huge room with a room behind sliding screens for my two assistants were virtually empty.

I could've ordered anything I wanted for the office; but instead of furnishing it with plush furniture for your usual big-wheel office, upon the advice of my new Hawaiian assistants, I ordered a steel desk, a desk chair, and a chair to go beside the desk. The same furnishings were ordered for the gals and nothing else, leaving the huge room almost empty. We needed to cast hundreds of people for the film, and since we were casting not only the speaking roles but also every one of the extras, we needed the empty space.

At the time, there was some resentment against Hollywood because the movies that had been made there with supposed Polynesians in small parts—most recently *Blue Hawaii, Diamond Head, Gidget Goes Hawaiian*—were cast with people of mixed races. The Polynesian people resented the fact that they used people who were obviously not of the original Polynesian race.

My message to the Hawaiian people was that George Roy Hill has insisted on getting real Polynesians, telling them what we want to do is show the world what beautiful people you are, and if you want this to happen, we must be able to see you. I also talked about George and what his movie would show—the true story of how we *haoles* ruined their lifestyle with our ways—all in the name of Christianity.

For this reason, I welcomed the publicity I was getting from the media. I'd hoped that the executives back in Hollywood would not hear what I was saying, but they were too busy thinking of how to use actors from the States, not believing it possible to find any local talent. I literally beat the bushes to get our message across. On Sundays, I'd go to the churches, way out in the boondocks, to talk with the congregations. Many times there were only a handful of people in attendance.

So bit by bit, the word spread by that marvelous system of communication—the coconut grapevine—that I was not a bad *haole*, and that this *haole* is okay, and maybe we should go and see what this is all about. My success was helped by the combination of the women I'd hired locally and the local publicity we were getting. Since there was not anything earth shattering newsworthy in the world at the time, the film production and casting process benefited tremendously with media coverage.

The sparse decoration of my office at the suggestion of my "girls" proved a terrific idea for eventually entire families would come in—parents, grandparents, children—and plop down in the huge vacant spaces of the room. Sometimes they would sit on the floor and play their ukes and whistles for me. Having entire families come in also made it much easier to get the word out about what we wanted to do. I would tell them about the film, in which they'd be playing Hawaiians in a village many years ago. Then these families would go out and tell their friends and neighbors and relatives, and soon we had lists of hundreds of people who would like to be in the movie, and all true Polynesians!

Once I had passed muster with the Hawaiians, there were one or two problems that I thought I might face that didn't turn out to be problems after all. In the script, there's an important scene where the ship comes into the harbor for the missionaries' first sight of Polynesians. To welcome a ship sailing in, a whole village would take to the water to greet it. Most important are the young boys and girls who row the dugout canoes. These beautiful young girls swim out to the ship, and as was appropriate to the period of Hawaiian history, the young women wore just a wraparound skirt, if that.

This was before nudity was as prevalent as it is today. One of my casting assistants, Carolyn, called up the women who were going to be swimming. Carolyn's patois went something like this: "Hey, Mama, what kind of *waius* you got? Watermelons? Oranges? Or Lemons?" She made a funny game of talking to the mothers of the young girls so they would give permission to let the girls be "swimmers," and they could also be in the scene. I found out that I was the only one that was terribly worried about having the young girls performing topless, as most families were thrilled to have their family member participating in the film whatever the mode of costume.

I relied on my assistants to make sure that our extras in the film were all Hawaiian. With word so widely spread about the movie being made in Hawaii, there were many Portuguese that tried to pass themselves off as Hawaiian. My girls would start talking to them in Hawaiian, and when they didn't have a clue what was being said to them, we sent them on their way. Many African Americans also came in, thinking they could pass themselves off as Polynesians. I would at least see them, but my girls would say *pepolo* (blackberry) to me, and we thanked them for coming in and sent them on their way too. The Hawaiian extras were all very delighted to be part of the film, but within a few weeks, some were coming to me and asking, "Don't we get extra money for beard pay or for growing our hair long?" It didn't take long for them to catch on to the Hollywood way of doing business.

There are a couple of scenes in *Hawaii* that required special attention to the extras that we'd hire. The Ali'i Nui's (Hawaiian queen) mode of transportation was ten or twelve bearers who carried her in a full-sized dory held aloft by poles supported on the bearers' shoulders. Julie Andrews's character, Jerusha, joins the Ali'i Nui the first time this mode of transportation is seen in the film. I knew the cameras would be heavily on the extras' faces, and they'd need to be in great physical shape in order to handle the load, so I wanted to find very strong good-looking men for the bearers. Originally, they were going to make a very light dory of balso, but when they found out the Ali'i Nui we were planning to cast weighed well over three hundred pounds, and with Julie Andrews on board as well, they realized we needed to use a real dory.

I learned from someone that the local police department only hired Polynesians. They let me go through their books with the police identification photos, and I was able to pick out the ones from the books that looked like they had the best physiques with good-looking faces. Once I had selected those that I liked, I got the police department to allow them to grow their hair long, so it would be the appropriate length when the scenes were shot. I next moved to the firemen and got the same cooperation from them. Several of the policemen's hair became very long throughout the production schedule, which caused the hats they wore to ride much higher on their heads than usual. The tourists who visited during this time couldn't understand what the deal was with their long hair as this was before long hair on men was in vogue.

When we were casting locals for some of the minor roles, the most persistent actor was a young Jewish girl, who started coming into my office at least three times a week, angling for any part she could get in the film. I told her repeatedly that I was sorry, that I couldn't possibly use her because she didn't look anything like a Polynesian. After umpteen visits to my office, I was worn down to the point where I told her that I would put her on the missionary ship for the arrival scene. She could play a missionary's wife, but she would have to wear a bonnet that would hide her face, for not only did she not look Polynesian, but she didn't look like a New England missionary either.

There was something about this young woman that intrigued me. She was born in Honolulu and told me her mother named her after Bette Davis. Her two sisters were named Judy, after Judy Garland,

and Susan, after Susan Hayward. Apparently, it hadn't been very easy growing up as a Jewish girl among a mostly Asian community, and she'd developed quite a strong personality. She began working at the Dole Pineapple factory at the age of thirteen and was planning to study drama at the University of Hawaii. Although it was a minor role, and her first, Bette Midler managed it just fine.

There were about a half a dozen important Hawaiian-speaking parts in the script. Queen Ali'i Nui, her husband/brother, their children Keoki and Noelani, and the Hawaiian girl Illiki, who was taken in by Reverend Hale's family, all these roles required considerable acting talent as well as certain physical demands. Local people helped by suggesting those I should look up, and I first selected some who seemed the right age and had the look which we wanted. I then asked them to come in and talk to me and read a little scene. If I felt they might have potential, I tried to coach them a little bit in their reading, so that by the time George arrived, I'd have a group of potential actors for him to at least see.

Having checked with the schools, the East-West Center suggested a twenty-eight-year-old student there who'd graduated with a degree in anthropology and was currently a student at the University of London, where he was studying for his master's degree in political science. Manu Tupou Taunaola was a Tongan by birth but was raised in Fiji.

When I first met this six-foot-five-inch towering Tongan, I was more than a little impressed. He came in to read for the part of Keoki, the son of Queen Ali'i Nui, and read a rather difficult scene for George and me. We could not believe our ears and luck! The hair on the back of my neck stood up again, which is always a good sign for me. Manu's speaking voice was startlingly stunning, a deep rich baritone with a lovely accent, and a very good reading. He made the perfect Keoki.

George had originally planned to have the opening narration in the film done by a trained actor, but upon hearing Manu's voice, he changed the screenplay to have his voice played over the scenes of tropical vistas as the story of the Hawaiian gods unfolded; and this flowed right into Keoiki's speech at Yale college, which was the first speaking scene in the film.

Manu turned out to be not only a fine actor but also a real prince of Tonga. Manu's ancestors had conquered some of the Fijian islands, thus bringing many Tongans to Fiji, whose people weren't Polynesian. Named Manu Topou Taualogo Fata Fehi, Manu became a lifelong friend of mine right up until his death in 2004.

For Kelolo, the husband/brother of Queen Ali'i Nui, I had wanted somebody fairly tall with an imposing figure. Ted Nobriga, a former University of Hawaii football player, who was the head of the Power and Light Company, filled the bill splendidly. *Hawaii* was Ted's only film, but he appeared afterward in various roles in the *Hawaii Five*-O television series.

Prior to George's arrival in Honolulu, I'd planned to go to the islands of Ni'ihau and Lanai, looking for people to use in the film. Ni'ihau was a very small privately owned island with only about 250 Hawaiians living there. They spoke only Hawaiian. There were no cars, electricity, or modern appliances. Tourists weren't allowed on the island as it was kept as it had been in the olden days. It took some time, but I was eventually given permission to go there and see if there were any inhabitants who would be right for our film. I had met one or two in Honolulu and realized after talking to them that these people were totally naive and would be ruined if exposed to modern life, so I turned down my chance to go there. I would've loved to see the island and its people, but I knew it would have been a cruel jolt to expose them to modern times.

I did go to Lanai, which was basically a huge pineapple estate owned by the Dole family. There were about one hundred thousand workers and their families living there. No hotels or tourism, just pineapples and forests of the most beautiful Norfolk pine trees, my favorite tree. I saw quite a few of the men who were painfully shy and not really interested in leaving to be in Oahu for a film. I doubt if any of them had ever seen such a foreign thing.

When George arrived in Hawaii, we began touring the other islands of Kauai, Maui, and the big island, Hawaii, in search of actors for the parts left to cast, which were primarily the three female characters, Malama, Noelani, and Illiki. We were scheduled to leave for Hong Kong the following week to cast the Chinese roles of Nyuk Tsin and Mun Ki, characters who were brought over from China with a boatload of Chinese immigrants to Hawaii.

For the part of Noelani, I found a beautiful young lady name Elizabeth Logue just before my trip to Hong Kong, and she was cast as the daughter of Queen Ali'i Nui.

At the last minute, George decided the script needed his energies more than the Chinese casting, so while George continued to work with Dalton Trumbo, I set off alone on my quest to find Nyuk Tsin and Mun Ki. I arrived in Hong Kong and was met by two men whose command of English was very poor and whose car was a rattletrap. I soon realized that Chinese lower classes don't like to say no in answer to any question. It is far more polite to say yes. It doesn't matter which answer is the correct one. I also had heard of young women being sold into "slavery." Well, it was late at night, and strange thoughts were running through my mind. I have to admit, though, that I was scared silly.

We finally arrived at the renowned Peninsula Hotel, famous for the scenes filmed there in *Love Is a Many-Splendored Thing*. I was not prepared for the state of my room, which was decorated in mold. It was a lovely shade of mold, but still, it was mold. That along with the thought of being driven all over Hong Kong in that ratty car with those two men made me telephone George. He told me, "Speak up. Let the hotel know that the room is unacceptable and call the Run Run Shaw Company, the leading movie production company in China, and get a decent car with a driver who speaks English. You are representing a big American film company."

The next day, I was moved into a very nice room, minus mold, which overlooked the harbor, and was met by Run Run Shaw's own limousine and driver. It taught me a good lesson to assert yourself and pretend you're important. That was sometimes hard when you're used to telling people, "I'm just a naive kid from a farm in Pennsylvania with hay still in my ears."

Hong Kong was a fascinating place to visit and offered me some new experiences like eating pigeon. Peter Chen Ho, an actor I met there, had a boat and offered to take me on a tour of Hong Kong by water. We went to the end of the harbor and saw many junk boats lined up that were decorated and lit with lanterns and populated by the finest prostitutes Hong Kong had to offer. Eventually, I cast two leading Asian film stars, Jeanette Lin Tsui and my boat tour guide, Peter Chen Ho, as Nyuk Tsin and Mun Ki.

Upon my return to Hawaii, I continued to see many ladies for the part of Malama, Queen Ali'i Nui, a very key role in the film. The character was based on the wife of King Kamehameha. In the early days, the mark of Polynesian beauty was a very large lady, which nowadays would be known as obese. The character description from Michener's novel was based on reality, and Malama was described as six-foot tall and weighing over three hundred pounds. The biggest problem was that Malama had to have grace and regality as befit her stature as Queen Ali'i Nui in a body that wouldn't be looked upon today as true beauty. In my search, all the large ladies I met lacked either the height or the dignity and beauty that we needed. Malama was perhaps the most difficult role

I ever had to cast, and I wasn't able to find our Malama on any of the Hawaiian Islands.

George and I set off to do some scouting of locations for the prologue and casting the role of Malama. We headed to Tonga, where I believed we might find our Queen Ali'i Nui. When I was traveling through the West Indies in the late 1950s, there was a calypso song that I'd heard about the queen of Tonga on Coronation Day. At the coronation of Queen Elizabeth, a rainy day when the other royalty and dignitaries present rode in closed coaches, the queen of Tonga insisted on riding in her open carriage. She said that if the people can stand in the rain to see us, then we must ride with the top of our carriages down so that we may be seen by them. That simple act caused the people to regale her through the procession; the people loved her for that decision. I remember seeing a film of her, a very large, imposing lady, pure Polynesian and as regal as they get. I knew we couldn't hope to cast the actual queen of Tonga, but I found out that many women who lived there were very large ladies, and I went with the hope that we could finally find our Malama.

Originally, the Mirisch Company had wanted to cast Juanita Hall as Malama, Queen Ali i' Nui. I don't know if they considered her a "name" as she had achieved considerable success as Bloody Mary on Broadway in *South Pacific* as well as acting in the film version. George was promptly horrified, telling the studio that she was a good performer but was the wrong ethnic background and not anywhere near physically correct for the part. We told the studio we'd lose all our Polynesians playing in the film if we brought a non-Polynesian to play Queen Ali' i Nui.

When our plane landed on Tonga, an island slightly smaller in area than Manhattan, I saw a group of businessmen waiting for their plane, all nicely dressed in jackets, ties, and skirts! I had never seen men in *lava-lavas* before. We were taken to the capital, Nuku'alofa; and as we got to the center of the city, we passed the queen's palace, a charming Victorian house with a lawn that led down to the harbor encircled by a low stone wall. On the lawn was an old sea tortoise that was blind and had initials carved in the top of its shell, purportedly by Captain Cook, which I'd read about before.

There was a lady in Tonga who was physically right for the role of Malama, but she was shy and couldn't really have handled the acting involved with the role. She was a relative of the ruling family, and though expressing some interest, she did fear that she wouldn't be allowed to do it.

One day I was walking down the dirt road by the queen's palace, and I saw a tortoise ambling down the road toward the harbor. I realized that this tortoise out for a stroll probably belonged to the queen. I called out to a policeman, who was absolutely gorgeous in his *lava-lava* with a Sam Browne belt, an Australian hat bent up on one side, and sandals. This was the uniform that all Tongan policemen wore, and what a handsome sight they were! The policeman retrieved the tortoise before it could head down to crawl into the sea and thanked me.

George was very mean to me in Tonga because he wouldn't let me take photographs of the policemen who were standing in the main crosswalks on little stands directing traffic. Traffic in downtown Nuku'alofa didn't include many cars as they were scarce, but there was plenty of bicycle traffic and little carts drawn by donkeys. George didn't want them thinking we were tourists, but frankly, I wouldn't have cared.

The men on Tonga had oak-tree-like thighs, and one night when we were having cocktails with the chief of police, I thought we might hear timber rattling from his massive thighs moving. My dear friend, Manu, who was also Tongan, was also blessed with those thighs and always had to have his slacks tailored.

Both George and I had iffy stomachs but were obliged to attend a feast given by a head chief at his home in Nuku'alofa. The feast began with a ceremonial drink of *kava*, which we were told you have to accept because it was a "no-no" to refuse. We watched them grind roots in a huge wooden bowl, add some liquid, and then pass the finished concoction in a small bowl. It tasted like what I imagine the water in the bottom of an umbrella stand might taste like, only with a mean kick to it! There were toasts made. Soon our stomachs felt much better, our heads a might woozy. I found out later that many people get high off *kava*. It recently showed up in the health stores and pharmacies in the States, but while it is supposed to calm you down, it's not good for your liver.

I had witnessed these darling little piglets running around the yard. Needless to say, I was more than a little shocked to see one of these little darlings in front of me on a huge tray, with an apple stuffed in its mouth, roasted to perfection and surrounded by all types of luscious fruits and vegetables. Not wanting to offend but a bit horrified at the thought of actually eating one of those cute little piglets, I told myself I would taste just a small portion to be polite. The piglets had been roasted in an *imu* (pit in the ground) and were sinfully delicious, so each of the three times I went back for more, I reminded myself that I was just being polite.

We may not have found anyone for our cast there, but Tonga was an island filled with charming, gracious people; and we certainly didn't view our stop there as a wasted effort. Besides, I saved the queen's tortoise.

We then traveled to Fiji and found no one there who was at all suitable to play Malama. We were only there for a day before we moved on to Pago Pago and American Samoa on the island of Tutuila. George and I had come to Pago Pago not to look for actors but to scout locations for prologue scenes that he hoped to shoot there. George wanted to scout islands off the eastern shore called the Manu'a Group, which included the islands of Ta'u, Olosega, and Ofu. We stayed in a Quonset-type hut in Pago Pago. George tried to charter a boat to go out to the Manu'a Group, but there was some big meeting of government officials and chiefs in Fiji, and all the boats we thought we could charter were out of Samoa and on their way to Fiji.

The American Samoa governor, Mr. Lee, was very helpful in coming to our rescue, telling us that a large commercial boat was due in that afternoon and that he would arrange for that boat to take us on the Manu'a Group. We'd have to leave at midnight to catch the right tide. I didn't get much sleep at the thought of sailing under a full moon from Pago Pago into the unknown South Seas.

The ship I had dreamed of turned out to be a mangy, beat-up freighter with a permanent list and crew who'd been at sea for several days and weren't at all happy to have to leave their homes and return to duty after a few hours of rest. They looked more than a little mutinous to me. Not in any position to question our accommodations, the captain showed George and me to our "stateroom," a tiny cubicle with bunk beds and one small porthole. I chose the upper bunk, thinking it might be more out of reach of any rats. We hadn't been in our bunks long when a shoe went whizzing past my head, scaring me to death, but nailing a huge spider on the wall. Thanks, George. I then went to sleep feeling less secure on the upper bunk, because of the appearance of the spider and imagining all the other assorted vermin that I realized wouldn't be confined to the floor.

Our passage to the Manu'a Group was a very rough trip; and George got seasick, although he was now an accomplished sailor. Somehow I survived and at the light of day found my way to the galley. Waiting for me there was a huge vat of vile coffee and greasy lumps that passed for biscuits. I ate them; George did not.

Early that same morning, we anchored off the islands. Two long boats came out to meet us, and we surfed our way into shore. By the time we arrived on the island, George and I were starving to death.

Life on the island was primitive. The houses consisted of huge poles set in a circle with thatched conical roofs and, for privacy, bamboo curtains to close at night. They were all open to the soft ocean breezes; and in several of them, I saw large pieces of Victorian furniture—beds, bureaus, chests—obviously not made on the islands, possibly American or British. We found out that they were received in exchange for fruit or timber from trading ships that passed by.

The children on the island had never seen a white woman before, so I was something of a novelty. As we walked around, we were followed by groups of children, giggling and owl-eyed. They'd walk up behind me and touch my bare arms or legs to see what this white skin felt like.

We were assigned two chiefs, a talking chief who understood our language and would interpret for us and a walking chief who knew all the trails. George took Polaroids of the chiefs surrounded by many children. The people were fascinated by the Polaroid shots, and we began taking pictures of people and handing photos to them. Their reaction was as if we had just performed magic. We went to three or four villages and finally did our best to stave off our hunger with some bananas.

Most of the people had never been to the big island of Samoa and knew little of the world; therefore, it was a bit of a shock to see construction near the landing off the harbor, which would be like their town plaza. A hut was being built for television viewing. I can only imagine what it would seem like to those children who would soon be exposed to its television programs. In a way, it was wonderful; in a way, it was sad, for it would surely take away their innocence.

The footage that George had hoped to get in the Manu'a Group was never shot as the prologue sequence was later dropped from the final screenplay.

Our last stop in the South Seas was Tahiti, noted for its beautiful Polynesian women. We were hoping to find the young girl, Illiki, who becomes a servant girl to the characters played by Julie Andrews and Max von Sydow. Instead of finding her, we were told by an American-born businessman, David Cave, that we should look up the LaGarde family with the possibility of finding our Queen Ali'i Nui, Malama.

David owned a car rental service in the sleepy port town of Papeete, and we drove out to the LaGarde home with David and his French wife, Leonne, to handle any translation for us. Leonne introduced George and me to Jocelyne Bredin LaGarde. Jocelyne was not intimidated by talking to Americans, which intrigued us; but then again, if I stood six-foot-one-inch tall and weighed three hundred and thirty-three pounds, as Jocelyne did, I probably wouldn't be intimidated either. At forty-one years old, she had an absolutely beautiful Polynesian face.

Jocelyne's mother had died when she was a child; so she and her older sister, Helene, were adopted by an aunt, Anna LaGarde, the head of the French-owned telephone company on the island. In Tahiti, adoption by a relative was a common practice. Both Jocelyne and her sister had attended a girl's convent school in Papeete. The mother left her daughters with interests in copra and vanilla producing lands so she'd never worked before.

Jocelyne spoke only French and Tahitian, so we explained as best we could in our broken French and through our interpreter, Leonne, why we were there. After we finished our explanation, George asked Jocelyne if she'd be interested in coming to Honolulu to be in a movie.

"Jamais!" Jocelyne bellowed.

Even if I hadn't known the French word for "never," I knew her response was less than positive.

In an interview Jocelyne later gave to the *Honolulu Advertiser*, she said she felt sorry for us when we told her we would not be able to start filming without casting Malama. Honestly, I think Jocelyne, who had a great heart, was just intrigued with the idea. When we told her she would have only two months to learn English and that Leonne would help her accomplish that, this regal woman couldn't resist the challenge and accepted our offer. Leonne Cave worked alongside Jocelyn daily with a tape recorder and the screenplay, which had nearly twenty pages of dialogue to be memorized for the role of Malama.

When we left Tahiti, I could hardly walk to the airplane because the flower *leis* that were given to us were actually made of seashells, and I was given a ton of these amazing creations. Our South Seas trip concluded with a brief stop at Bora Bora where, still in search of our Illiki, we didn't even find many people living on that island. I eventually found the lovely Lokelani Chicarell when we returned to Hawaii, and she became our Illiki.

George returned to his work, and I returned to my casting office at the Ilikai Hotel. Jocelyne's taped line readings were sent to me when I was back in Hawaii, but since our offices were so scantily supplied, I would go over to the basement in the local Sears store, and the salesman would let me listen to the taped cassettes on one of their machines. With each successive trip that I made to Sears, I could tell by the progress she was making that Jocelyne wouldn't have any difficulty being understood on camera.

Eventually, we brought Jocelyne to Honolulu. We had to purchase two seats on the airplane. She'd never been off the island of Tahiti, except to go to Bora Bora, which is very near Tahiti. There were two things that frightened her when she arrived. The first was that she'd never seen a cigarette machine before, and she was a smoker. Second, at the Iliki Hotel, where she was also staying, they'd installed one of the first outdoor scenic elevators. Jocelyne had never seen an elevator, much less a glass one that rose and descended on the outside of the building. She regarded both of these things as voodoo.

Our primary location site on the island of Oahu was located on the western side of Oahu, next to the Makua Military Reservation. Our company was scheduled to build an entire village that represented Lahaina in 1825, complete with *peli* grass and rice straw. This location had been chosen for its remoteness, since there were no modern buildings within site, and for its similarity to Lahaina, the city on Maui where the actual story was set. Makua Point had the mountains as well as a beach along with a harbor that happened to resemble Lahaina's. There remained only one thing to be done before the construction of the sets could begin.

My three casting associates told me that the area of Makua Point was an area of sacred ground. I'd listened to their stories of the building of the Kaanapali Pass that goes across Oahu from north to south. That area was also a noted sacred area; and they had many accidents, and even a few deaths occurred during the building of the pass until they found a *kahuna* to come in and bless the sacred land. Upon the blessing of the land by Reverend Abraham Akaka, there weren't any more accidents and no more deaths during the building of Kaanapali Pass.

Hearing of the many spirits who inhabited Makua Point and at the urging of my girls, George and I went to see Reverend Akaka, who was renowned on the islands and was also an important *kahuna*, a Hawaiian priest. After we secured the Reverend Akaka's services, I telephoned the Mirisch Company and asked them to make a small contribution to the church. Walter Mirisch then asked me what this contribution was for, and I told him that we needed to get the land blessed by a *kahuna*. Mirisch told me that he thought I was becoming a bit of a *kahuna* myself and managed to cough up all of the fifty-dollar contribution.

George and I, along with Reverend Akaka, went out to the beach at Makua Point late one morning; and the reverend gave a blessing in English first. When he began his blessing in Hawaiian, the big Hawaiian construction workers, whom they called *blalas*, crept out of the surrounding area they were clearing out and stood around us with their hardhats off and listened to the blessing. It was very moving. We had no construction problems in the building of our sets. Reverend Akaka with his prayers had essentially gotten permission from the souls that had died at Makua Point to let us make our film there.

On Jocelyne's first day on the set, she was to be in a canoe and rowed out to greet the missionaries' ship, *Thetis*, in the harbor. After looking at the heavy swells, she said in perfect English, "How can I smile when I'm going to be sick?" We all soon came to realize that Jocelyne had a lovely sense of humor. Jocelyne had packed on an additional 46 pounds by the time filming had begun. While her three hundred seventy-nine pounds worked well for the part of Queen Ali' i Nui, it obviously wasn't good for her health. During the filming, Jocelyne had an infected toe and was sent to the hospital where she was diagnosed with diabetes. Because of the severe condition of her diabetes, she was ordered to immediately go on a strict diet. There was some concern, of course, since we were well into the shooting that we didn't want her weight to fluctuate too dramatically. While she did lose some weight, there wasn't any considerable weight loss that came across on screen.

I made the mistake of hiring a Samoan actor who'd previously worked in Hollywood to oversee the extras, not knowing that the Hawaiians disliked Samoans. That error was later corrected by me when I found Tom Kealiinohomoku to replace the Samoan actor. Tom became a good friend of ours, and after filming, he came to New York for a while. His name in Hawaiian was translated as "he who did not have to bow down." When a procession of Ali' i Nui passed, most would have to bow low; and if Ali' i Nui's shadow passed over their head, they were killed.

The shooting schedule was plagued and beset with problems once the production moved to Hawaii. Makua Point, which was rumored to be the driest spot on the island of Oahu, was beset practically every day with rain, gusty winds, and dark clouds. The *kahuna* had taken care of any accidents on the set but didn't seem to have any control over the weather.

Production had to be stopped completely when the U.S. Army used the military reserve next to our location for firing practice on their artillery range. George also had to work carefully and patiently with his four leading Polynesian actors, who were all novices. I knew that George had a marvelous talent for eliciting terrific performances from actors who'd never acted before. I'd seen him do just that with both Merrie Spaeth and Tippy Walker in *The World of Henry Orient*. I was confident that once we found the people that were physically right, with both intelligence and a solid interest in the film, that George could find the performance within them.

As the production schedule went over and we began to lose days of shooting, our initial six-million-dollar budget had risen to ten million dollars by late July, and the end of the production was nowhere in sight. George had no intention of pushing his fragile Polynesian actors any harder than he'd been doing, so as to appease the studio and to lessen the ballooning budget, he brought in Dalton Trumbo to Hawaii on his own dime. He wanted Dalton to basically "unwrite some of his script." This was only possible because George had decided to shoot the film in chronological order. Trumbo then began to work backward from the last page of the screenplay and eliminated characters that hadn't yet been established. Simultaneously, he also eliminated telescoping events that hadn't taken place.

Dalton loved intrigue as much as he did writing and responded instantly. George thought it best not to advertise Dalton's arrival in Honolulu, so it was planned that when George finished shooting each day's work, he'd then work on the script with Dalton in the evening.

As it turned out, Dalton had arrived with news of his own. The Mirisch Company was planning on firing George if they could find a replacement and were busy scouring the countryside for a new director. This seemed to be okay by George because by this time he had no idea how the production was going to end up without a rewrite of the script. This also marked the third time that the Mirisch Company had threatened to fire George. He'd already been fired once during hassles over the script before production ever got started and then a second time when filming was already underway in the Norwegian fjords while he was filming the prologue to the film.

The production stumbled on as Dalton and George worked through the evenings to try to create a final script. George said Dalton was a champion. They did this for a couple of weeks and were somehow discovered by Mirisch, and there was hell to pay.

By the time George's shooting schedule met Dalton's edited pages, about twenty years of the story was trimmed off the script. My trip to Hong Kong had been for nothing, as Jeannette Lin Tsui and Peter Chen Ho were paid and released from their contracts. Our final story would not reach their characters.

With Dalton's news that George's firing was imminent, George took the time to get some things off his chest in a letter written to Harold Mirisch dated July 28, 1965:

Dear Harold,

As you know, I am aware of your efforts to replace me on this film. I can't think of a more dramatic or catastrophic way to have you discover the facts of life about this production, however, I do not wish an unqualified disaster on anyone.

David Picker came to Hawaii to work on the budget and under present operating conditions, all the good will on the part of the crew, cast, myself or any director could not possibly bring the production in on budget with the way the script is written. What is required is a reconception of many of the sections; a drastic simplification through deletions, changes and cuts. I have requested Dalton's presence over here after learning that cuts and changes he had sent through your office have been prevented from coming to me.

To date, I have sent recommendations and urgent requests for action always through the proper channels. Since you plan to replace me for operating your way, I feel relieved of any responsibility to continue to play your game. If I am to be fired, I am going to be fired for doing my best as I see it and not executing any move of your error.

I asked Dalton to come over at my expense and over the weekend we took eight pages out of the script and saved a minimum of $200,000. I will take this Saturday to schedule the following week's work, get the action sequences planned, and rehearse the actors scenes that we have rewritten.

From now on, whenever time and money can be saved on this picture to bring it closer to budget, I am going to take, on my own initiative, whatever measures necessary to accomplish it. I will finally have the personal satisfaction of seeing this company moving fast, sensibly and economically.

Sincerely,

George Roy Hill

Three days later, George was greeted by Ray Gosnell, our assistant director, who said, "You have a guest on set this morning."

"Who's that?" George asked.

"John Ford," Ray replied.

George's heart sank. The legendary John Ford was a replacement he hadn't counted on. If anyone could whip this production into shape, it would be John Ford, he thought. Well, George figured as long as he's going out, he might as well go out in style. When he arrived on set, he walked over to where Ford was sitting, greeted him as cordially as he could, invited him to have a guest shot, then set up the camera; and before the shot, Ford was presented with a cup of hot coffee and a chorus made up of the crew singing, "Bringing in the Sheaves," reportedly Ford's favorite hymn.

George treated him as an honored guest and gave him plenty of opportunity to drop the ax, but Ford observed the activity in great good humor and was very cordial to George, so he began to suspect that he was *not* his replacement. Ford had lunch with Julie "Poppins" and drove off in high good humor without having mentioned anything about replacing George.

That night, when George got back to his rental house, his wife Louisa was standing on the back porch waving a telegram from the Mirisch Company. He was being replaced by Arthur Hiller. Hiller was being flown to Hawaii from the mainland that very same day.

After George was fired, Lew Rachmill, the associate producer, met with the actors. Max and Julie both listened to Lew and then contacted

George and offered to quit in support of him, but George refused their offer, worried that it might affect their careers.

Lew then went to see Jocelyne and Leonne, her translator, to tell her that George was no longer involved with the picture. Jocelyne was in tears at the news. I had done such a good job in extolling George and his virtues in casting the movie that Jocelyne said that she couldn't work with any other director and that she would quit. Lew spoke French and could understand what Jocelyne was saying to Leonne. She wanted to leave immediately and go home to Tahiti. Being the smart lady that she was, Jocelyne, sensing that Lew spoke French, immediately switched her conversation to Leonne to Tahitian, so Lew couldn't understand a word she said. The only threat that the Mirisch Company had on Jocelyne was that she would never work in Hollywood again, which wasn't a likely prospect for a 379-pound Tahitian woman.

Manu was then brought in, and he also told Lew Rachmill that he was quitting the production. Rachmill threatened Manu with never working on an American film again, and Manu responded by telling them to give him his passport and he would leave. I found out later that both Jocelyne and Manu explained to Rachmill that the main reason that the filming was going so slow was because it took so much time to create actors out of nonprofessionals such as themselves, and Mr. Hill was creating something out of nothing.

It all hit George hard, I know, for that evening I had plans to get together for drinks and drove out to George's house. George wasn't angry; he was glad it was all over and just seemed numb to everything. I told him about Jocelyne and Manu quitting and what happened to them. I told him that I was quitting too, but he told me not to. Refusing to listen, I insisted I had to quit because of how I'd sold George to the Polynesian people. I then set about making my own exit plans.

I immediately went back to the Ilikai Hotel and emptied my office of the files and carried them out to a station wagon I'd rented. My terrific trio of associates quit with me, leaving the production at the same time I did. Without those files, there was no way to contact the people I'd hired for the film, so I knew the studio would have to go through me. I turned the files over to some friends and asked them to find a place to stash them and to not tell me or anyone where they put them. I didn't expect the studio to shove bamboo shoots under my fingernails, but I wanted to be able to honestly say that I didn't know where they were. Even for me, it would be difficult to contact the extras since many of them didn't have phones and had to be contacted at local stores, neighbors, churches, or by the "coconut grapevine."

Liliuokalani Kavananakoa Morris, a local woman who was known to be a descendant of Queen Hilo, would've been queen of the monarchy of Hawaii had it continued. I had met her, despite being told by Walter Mirisch to stay away from her. Liliuokalani called me when she heard about George's firing to express her dismay. I told her that I had rented a station wagon and was planning to take Jocelyne out of the hotel because she was being harassed by the studio and was crying uncontrollably. Liliuokalani told me that her daughter, Kekau, had a compound in the hills outside Honolulu. I phoned Kekau, whom I'd also met, and arranged for her to receive Jocelyne later that night; and, after that, I phoned Leonne to tell her of my plans for Jocelyne. I asked Leonne to have Jocelyne packed and waiting outside of the hotel in an hour and ready to go. I then picked her up, and we drove to Kekau's place where Jocelyne would remain until we found out what would happen.

It was not only the major actors who were appalled by the Mirisch's decision to fire George. The Polynesian extras hired for the film had come to think of Jocelyne as their queen and Manu as their prince, so they met with Manu and offered to burn down the village sets at Makua

Bay if he thought that would help. When Lew Rachmill heard about that, he knew the shit had really hit the fan. He was also aware that Jocelyne had left the hotel, and nobody knew where she was.

As an alternative to the planned arson, a petition was circulated with 175 actors names attached. The petition, in effect, told them that because of George Roy Hill's great concern for the authenticity of the Polynesian culture in the film, he was the only one who should direct the film. It also read: "Those of us who have been on the picture since the first day would like very much to have Mr. Hill return and finish the picture *Hawaii.*"

Walter Mirisch, when contacted by a reporter from a local newspaper at the time, was quoted as saying that he had not heard of the petition. Mirisch then added, "I can't take time out right now to get involved in this. This is an inopportune time. I'm in a very important meeting."

The legendary film director, John Ford, was still in Hawaii, vacationing on his yacht, *Araner*, which was anchored at the Ala Wai Yacht Harbor. When he got wind of George's firing, he invited George and any guests he would care to invite to a farewell party on his yacht to be held on Monday night.

The production had ground to a complete halt. A meeting was arranged at George's house for Sunday morning at ten o'clock, with the purpose being as to whether the Mirisch Company should rehire George, having just fired him from the film for a third time.

As George recalls, Walter Mirisch arrived first. The others that attended included Lew Rachmill, the hired gun for the Mirisch Company; Dick Shepherd, George's then agent; and David Picker, who represented United Artists. They all shook hands and sat in chairs around a low coffee table when the front gate bell rang. This surprised George, since all of the full decision makers were at hand. Nobody else was expected as Louisa and the kids were all at church, except his eleven-year-old son, Mac.

George went out to the front entrance to open the gate. Outside the gate stood a beaten-up Ford station wagon with two men sitting in the front seat, and one of them was John Ford. The other man was dressed in a vaguely nautical outfit and turned out to be the captain of Ford's yacht. George didn't know how Ford knew about the meeting, but there he was, and George approached the car.

"What's going on in there?" Ford asked.

"It's a gathering, Mr. Ford," George answered.

"Jack, call me Jack. I thought so. I came over to see if I could help."

"Sure, Mr. Ford, you could be of great help."

Apparently, Mr. Ford was already stewed at 10:00 a.m., and they had some trouble extricating him from the car. But with his captain on one side and George on the other, they managed to navigate him into the living room.

Walter Mirisch, to say the least, blanched when he saw John Ford, having had a recent unpleasant experience with him on the film *The Horse Soldiers*.

George took his son Mac aside and told him to stand by Mr. Ford and get him anything he wanted. Ford wanted beer.

There followed fifteen minutes of total silence, and every once in a while, Ford would erupt and say, "This is the worst goddamn location I ever saw in my life. How anyone could shoot here is a miracle!" He would then fall into silence except when taking a drink of beer and kept missing the table, which led to some scurrying on Mac's part.

Finally, after another long time lapse, the captain made the suggestion that they leave. Ford nodded, dropped his last bottle of beer on the floor, and stood up, but only for a very short moment. He went flat out on the floor. The captain and George got him back on his feet, each grasping an elbow, and brought him down the driveway to where his car was parked. Then he motioned them to stop. Standing there, he turned to George with a satisfied grin on his face and said, "How'd I do, son?"

"You did just great, Mr. Ford," George replied.

"Jack, call me Jack.

The following morning, George was back to work on *Hawaii*, and John Ford gave a wonderful party on his yacht for George. Intending it as a farewell to George's involvement in the production, the party turned into a rollicking celebration of his return to the film!

I knew darn well that since the Mirisch Company couldn't find their queen, and Manu's passport was nowhere to be found, as well as the fact that they had no way to contact the extras who'd threatened to burn down the sets, there was absolutely no way the studio could continue the production. It would have been lovely of them to have been big enough to admit their mistake.

When George returned to the set on Makua Bay on Tuesday, August 3, 1965, he was greeted with a spontaneous rendition of "Hawaii Ponoi," the state song of Hawaii.

George's impact on the Hawaiian people involved in the production of *Hawaii* was made even more crystal clear to everyone twelve days later when the extras, who had banded together, held a *luau* at the home of Albert and "Aunt Gardie" Perkins. The 350 or more guests were announced as they arrived for the Sunday event and were escorted into a tented garden area. The highlight was Jocelyne's arrival, as she was the last to be announced. All the guests rose to their feet as Jocelyne entered, and they remained standing as she was escorted to an upholstered arm chair next to George. Everyone then sat down. Over the microphone, there was an attempt to get everyone quiet for a prayer, and one of the extras hosting the affair shouted, "*E! Kuli! Kokua*! You guys! We gotta say grace!" As the women began to sing the queen's prayer, the hundreds in attendance rose to their feet again; and when Jocelyne started to rise, she was restrained by one of her Hawaiian cousins, who whispered in her ear that she was the queen and should remain seated.

After the prayer, there was a procession of gift bearers that held an overwhelming evidence of the *aloha* that the Polynesians felt for George. He was presented with a Tahitian *caronne* (a floral crown) made of plumeria and fern. There were *leis* of white ginger, carnation, plumeria, and pikake before he was presented with four strands of *ilima,* a *leis* that had been formerly reserved for royalty and had been rarely given to anyone in modern times. The *Honolulu Advertiser* covered the event and claimed that the last time they had seen *ilima* presented was to Queen Elizabeth on her return trip from Australia.

There were other gifts before George was urged to his feet. He was so moved by the heartfelt gestures that he was unable to speak for a moment, tears welling in his eyes, yet his face full of smiles. George did manage an, "I don't know what to say," and followed that with a simple thank you that was drowned out by cheers.

Aside from being terribly moved myself, I found it absolutely delightful that a photograph accompanying the report of the *luau* in the *Honolulu Advertiser* featured a shot of Walter Mirisch chatting with Kathleen Dickenson Mellon, the author, whom Walter had also warned me to steer clear of, which I, of course, had not. In 1952, Kathleen had a book published titled, *The Magnificent Matriarch: Kaahmanu, Queen of Hawaii—1772–1832*, which examined the history of Hawaii at the time when the missionaries arrived. I'd always thought it interesting that in Kathleen's book, which I'd previously read, there were paragraphs from her book that were in our screenplay. I'd also heard stories before that some of Michener's work may not have always been his own. I loved the fact that Walter was not able to resist Kathleen any more than

I was. Kathleen was quoted as saying the production of the film *Hawaii* as well as the response of the Polynesian people to George Roy Hill and the film was "a resurgence of the Polynesian nationalism."

At the end of September, Manu and I hosted a Fijian *luau* at the house I'd rented on Kahala Beach. Jacqueline Kennedy would be the next occupant of the house after we moved out. Manu's friends at the Polynesian Cultural Center helped to prepare and cook the food, native to Fiji, and also entertain the guests. A big pig was roasted in an *imu* dug on the beach in front of the house. The food and entertainment were wonderful with *hula* dancers and a bamboo playing organ.

As the production came to an end, Jocelyne continued to delight and impress us all. There is a very moving scene in the film where Queen Ali' i Nui dies, and Jocelyne was in a gleeful mood when they were filming the scene, probably eager in anticipation for her return home to Tahiti. Jocelyne looked around at the assembled cast and extras, and everyone broke into laughter. Julie Andrews, whose character had to react somberly to Malama's death, said to her, "Please, Jocelyne, can't you be serious for one minute? You're dying." Jocelyne, beaming that great big smile she had, looked incredulous and replied in her halting English, "Me, I not dying. Malama die. Not Jocelyne. I, happy. I want everybody happy. Not sad." Once her death scene was finished, Jocelyne rolled off her deathbed and prepared to leave the set for one last time. Everyone on the set gave her a marvelous send off, showering her with *leis* and hugging her warmly. It was only later in the privacy of her room that Jocelyne could truly acknowledge how moved she was by crying most of the night.

The filming of *Hawaii* finally came to an end in early November 1965. I had to stay on in Hawaii to have an operation to remove two slipped discs in my spine as a result from carrying all my casting files away from the office on the night George was fired. I rented a different beach house for my recovery; and it was a great house with many rooms so some friends—Gene Hackman, Manu, and Tom (my extras overseer)—stayed on too.

As I was not able to move from my bed for about one month following my surgery, my West Indian housekeeper, Muriel, came over to cook for us. As I was prone, I was lifted out to the porch and dumped on a lounge chair each night, and our group played a game of Risk, which usually lasted well past midnight as we were all very competitive. It was a peaceful way to relax, listening to the surf under a tropical moon.

Another amazing thing that happened during my recuperation, something that still brings tears of gratitude to my eyes, was that on one of the first few days at the beach house, two of the *blalas* (construction men who were also extras in the film) arrived, saying they wanted to take me swimming! Muriel got me into my suit, and the *blalas* carried me down to the beach to a deep pool of water surrounded by rocks. The rock formations were home to several moray eels. The *blalas* swam with me to protect me from the eels. I couldn't put any weight on my feet so as not to injure my back any further, so swimming was a safe and therapeutic exercise. The *blalas* would show up every day; and I was never able to get them to accept any payment, any food or drink, but they have my heartfelt gratitude for their magnanimous gesture of friendship.

On October 10, 1966, I was filled with excitement to finally attend the premiere of *Hawaii* in New York City. As we were making our way up the red carpet, I felt a tug on my blouse from behind. The last person I'd expected to see standing there was Bette Midler, who'd snuck under the rope. The film production had brought Bette to Los Angeles for some additional work on the studio soundstage and put her up at the Roosevelt Hotel. She then made her way to New York on the recommendation of her newly found friends Gene Hackman and John Cullum, who'd suggested she come to New York and study acting. Bette enrolled in musical comedy at HB Studios and also attended a class Lee Strasburg was teaching at Carnegie Hall. She was able to land a small part in Jerome Robbins's Broadway production of *Fiddler on the Roof*, which eventually led her to take over the role of Tzeitel. One of her teachers at HB Studios introduced her to a manager at the Continental Baths, a gay bathhouse in the basement of the famous Ansonia Hotel on the Upper West Side. The bathhouse had a disco and cabaret lounge; and with a push from her hairdresser on *Fiddler*, she performed at the club and was introduced as the Divine Miss M, accompanied on the piano by a young Barry Manilow.

Bette became a gifted actress and a marvelous songstress with a great voice and thoroughly delighted and surprised me when she played Radio City Music Hall many years later. I went and requested permission to see her after the concert. When the elevator door opened, the management led about ten or twelve of us into this room, and Bette was standing there looking at the whole group. As soon as she spotted me, she said, "Come here." She put her arm around me and told the others in the room, "This is the reason I am in New York right now!"

Hawaii became the highest grossing film in 1966. It was critically praised and received seven Academy Award nominations. Jocelyne LaGarde did a beautiful job of acting the part of Malama in *Hawaii*. Her performance won her the Golden Globe for Best Supporting Actress in 1966, in competition with the likes of Shelley Winters, Geraldine Page, Vivien Merchant, and Sandy Dennis. Jocelyne was nominated for an Academy Award, and it would be my first trip to the awards ceremony to accompany her. Something told me that she wouldn't win the Oscar, and I wanted to be there for support. Sandy Dennis won for her performance in *Who's Afraid of Virginia Woolf?*

Several years later, Jocelyne would return to Honolulu to have her leg amputated because of complications from her diabetes. She was fitted with a prosthetic leg and had a wonderful reunion with her Hawaiian "subjects."

In recounting the story of the filming of *Hawaii* and my participation in the production, I must say that the making of *Hawaii* was an incredible experience that I've treasured forever, and I had one helluva time doing it! It's a true story of the little guys besting the big guys and the "there are none left" Polynesians winning over the Hollywood moguls.

Brownstone Central

Following my back surgery in Hawaii, I was receiving insurance disability checks from the production company for as long as I qualified. I then went on to receive Social Security disability benefits for the remainder of my recovery, which was for several months upon returning to my home on Long Island. It was during this time, when Bobby did not even try to find a job, that I knew my marriage was coming to an end. We had to support ourselves solely on these disability payments. Being married to a man who was not willing to step up to the plate when I really needed him and to earn a living that would help support us made me a lot more concerned about my future. I came to the realization when I was forty-three years old that I had been paying for everything throughout our entire marriage.

During this time, I tried to get a job teaching school as a substitute teacher. Although I'd been offered an assistant professorship at Penn State in Art History when I graduated, I didn't have the credentials to teach at public schools. What seemed crystal clear was that while I was trying everything in my power to bring additional money into the household, Bobby was not.

I purchased the house in Bayshore, although he did quite a bit of work with plumbing, electrical, and painting. It was a small house that was actually the boating house of a much larger estate. Bobby built an extra wing onto the house, as he was quite gifted at that kind of carpentry work.

The problem was that Bobby was always spending money that was coming in from me. We owned boats and cars, and there would always be a breakdown on one of them, and that would be expensive. He continually wanted to buy another new toy.

When he wanted to build yet another wing on the house, I told him, "Bobby, we don't need it." I had just finished paying off the mortgage, and I had gotten things settled moneywise. Bobby insisted on taking out a $20,000 second mortgage.

"We can't do that," I told him.

"Well then, we'll sell the house," was his patented reply.

Bobby knew that I loved that house and that it was upsetting me, particularly when he told me he could sell it if he wanted to without my permission. Whenever he wanted to buy a boat or wanted to buy a car, he would always just announce that he would sell the house, certain that he'd always get the same reaction. We had purchased the house in both of our names, but he seemed to have forgotten about what had happened when he entered the Jaguar business. To protect the house from it being seized in a possible lawsuit, we'd put the house solely in my name.

My time in Hawaii had brought us as close as we'd ever come to having a child. Once my hysterectomy prevented me from having my own, Bobby and I briefly discussed adopting a little Hawaiian boy. Thank God, we didn't. I had some intuition that told me that if Bobby couldn't control himself as a husband, he wouldn't be any better at controlling himself as the father of a child.

When I finally recovered from my back operation, I made the decision to set up my own casting company since I now had the security of having cast several important television series and three successful films under my belt. With the encouragement and some help from Bert Leonard, I formed Marion Dougherty Associates (MDA).

The first film that I began to work on was a Warner Bros. production, *The Heart Is a Lonely Hunter*, which was based on Carson McCuller's novel. The film was being directed by Joseph Strick; and my most difficult role to cast was the role of Mick, an adolescent girl who strikes up a friendship with John Singer, a deaf-mute who rented a room in her mother's house. Mick would be playing across Alan Arkin, who'd already been set to play the role of Singer.

The director and producers wanted an unknown to play this unspoiled fourteen-year-old tomboy, who was not beautiful, but appealing, and not grown up, but not a child. They asked me to set up a "cattle call" type audition, which I really disliked. I telephoned all the talent agents in town, and we held auditions at the Celebrity Arts Studio at 29 West Fifty-Seventh Street. I recall one exuberant teenager who bounced into the studio and yelled, "I'm here!" I looked at her and said, "Where from?" "The Bronx!" she answered. She then announced herself as "Merle Exit," the stage name of Merle Meyerowitz. I asked her why she'd chosen that name, and she told me because, "It will look good in lights."

Having seen almost two hundred young actresses in New York and not coming anywhere close to finding our "Mick," I then began a search down south. Joseph Strick was in New Orleans and sent me by small plane to Birmingham, Alabama, and Coral Gables, Florida, where other young girls were lining up so I could see them. When I arrived in Coral Gables, I went up and down the line of girls that really caught my attention, and I brought them in to read. One of them seemed a little too young for the part; however, she gave such a fascinating audition, and I also sensed that she had a very special talent, so I decided to invite her to come to New York and meet the director. Although she didn't get the part, little did I know that this fascinating young girl, Margaret Whitton, would eventually enter my life many years later in a huge way.

When I arrived in Birmingham at a theater called the Town and Gown, a friend of mine, James Thatcher, had invited many young girls to come and meet me for callbacks after he'd previously met with them. He informed me that there was a group of not very good choices, a group of good choices, and also someone who'd driven there from another state and had shown up uninvited. I told him that I would see all the girls who'd shown up, including the one from out-of-state since she had gone to all the trouble of coming there.

Sondra Locke was a heavily freckled slender young blonde girl with no chest who drove all the way from Tennessee for the audition. As she read with me, the hair on the back of my neck rose, and I knew that she was an exceptional choice for the role. I was sad that she had a pimple on her nose, was sunburned to boot, and nervously peeled some flaking skin off her nose during her reading, eventually removing the pimple too.

Following her audition, I asked her if she was available to travel to New Orleans, which wasn't far away, so she could meet with the director. She arrived in New Orleans, and Joseph Strick was also impressed by her reading; and about a week later, I called and invited her to come to New York and read for us again. Her mother got on the phone and gave permission for Sondra to come to New York and asked me if Sondra's cousin, Gordon, could accompany her as her escort. I agreed.

Once in New York, Sondra read for everyone else involved with the production and was offered to play the part of Mick. Not long afterward, Joseph Strick had a disagreement with the company over the storyline and was replaced by another director, Robert Ellis Miller.

When production finally began down in Selma, Alabama, I received a call from an irate and disturbed Thomas Ryan, who was the screenwriter as well as one of the producers on the film. Thomas explained that Gordon was not Sondra's cousin, but her husband! The woman who pretended to be Sondra's mother was actually Gordon's mother. This young girl with no chest, who had told me that she was seventeen, had, with the help of her husband, Gordon, bound her breasts, applied the freckles using makeup, and used collodion, a gelatinous makeup that can create bumps and scar tissue, to create her pimpled, sunburned, and peeling skin! It turned out that Sondra was actually twenty-three years old. Thomas went on to say that when this information came out to the press, it would be a nightmare and perhaps ruin the picture. He claimed that the audience would be expecting an adolescent girl, not a married woman. We eventually were able to settle Thomas down, and Sondra was able to remain in the film; however, they demanded that her husband be banned from the set, and she was asked not to drive her car during the production.

The film was released through Warner Bros. and enjoyed critical acclaim for its actors, with both Sondra and Alan garnering Academy Award and Golden Globe nominations. Other cast members included Stacy Keach, Cicely Tyson, Percy Rodriquez, and Chuck McCann.

It didn't take long for Sondra to go to Hollywood either. At a publicity gathering for the film in New York City, Sondra showed up looking every bit of her twenty-three years of age and the polar opposite of the gawky adolescent "girl" I had first met. Sondra was cast in several of Clint Eastwood's films and has actually written a book about her experiences with him.

Soon afterward, Norman Lear asked me to cast his production of *The Night They Raided Minsky's*, which was being directed by a young William Friedkin. We cast the film out of the offices that Norman had in an old bar mitzvah hall down on Second Avenue. One day, while casting a huge street scene, I had filled the lobby with a prestigious group of highly respected actors from the Yiddish theater, many of whom I'd hired before and knew how talented they were.

When they were all assembled, I stepped across the hallway from my little cubicle to Billy Friedkin's office to let him know that the actors were there and ready for him to start greeting them. Unfortunately, Billy happened to be playing music to some gorgeous blonde woman at that moment, so he responded to my announcement with a dismissive, "Tell them to come back some other time. I'm busy."

I was livid and stormed down to Norman's office and announced, "I quit!" Norman asked me why; and I told him exactly what group was waiting to audition, exactly what Billy had said, and exactly what Billy was doing.

Norman, God bless him, was as livid as I was, for he also knew the Yiddish theater folk and said, "Fine. If he's too busy, we'll see these people." So instead of bringing everyone to meet Billy, I brought them to meet Norman, and we cast the roles ourselves. Billy hated me from that moment forward. And from that moment, the feelings were mutual.

The Night They Raided Minsky's was the story of a young Amish woman, played by Britt Ekland, who came to New York City and was hired as a seamstress in a seedy vaudeville theater, which featured the typical vaudeville fare: comics, slapstick comedy, and bawdy sketches with scantily clad women. In the story, there is a romance between a shy and gentlemanly comic, played by English music hall performer, Norman Wisdom, and Elkland's character. She is also being hotly pursued by the lecherous leading comic of the vaudeville theater, played by Jason Robards.

The cast also featured Bert Lahr, the wonderful Cowardly Lion from *The Wizard of Oz*, who died during the filming. Fortunately, the film editor was able to cut the film so that his part was not totally eliminated.

In featured supporting roles were Forrest Tucker, Joseph Wiseman, Denholm Elliott, Elliott Gould, and Gloria LeRoy. Harry Andrews, the British character actor, who happened to be my favorite bit of casting in the film, played Ekland's father, a stern bearded Amish man.

It was during my casting of *The Night They Raided Minsky's* that we came across a brownstone to rent at 153 East Thirtieth Street between Lexington and Third Avenue. This address soon became the new offices of Marion Dougherty Associates (MDA). My telephone number, when it was connected, was 679-0153 (actually OR-9-0153 in those days of telephone exchanges in Manhattan). I called the phone company to thank them for the million-to-one-shot of getting a phone number, which ended with the same street number as the house. They told me that it had nothing to do with them, that sort of thing could not be arranged. I thought it was a rather good omen. When I told someone in the business about my new offices, they said I'd made a huge mistake and would never get any directors or producers to come there because it was too far away from the theater district.

The brownstone had been one of the smaller buildings of a church on the corner, a part of a manse. It was an old home with linoleum floors that we ripped up to expose lovely hardwood floors. In the living room, there was a fireplace that had been completely painted over. I thought it was an old pine mantel until I dropped a tool on it. We then stripped the paint off to find it to be marble. The railing going upstairs was painted black, and we stripped all of it. The walls were cracked plaster that was so old you could see the horse hairs that they'd used to plaster in some spots. To keep the wall plaster stable, we hung wallpaper made with a heavy type canvas.

I wanted to decorate and furnish the brownstone in a Victorian-type fashion with a lot of charm. It was important to me that my offices felt comfortable for everyone who came in, and since I'd been involved in window dressing at one time and had thought about being a set designer, I did a pretty good job of "designing the set" for my new casting offices. The idea was to create a theatrical kind of atmosphere, as that is what casting is, people playing other people. Besides the tremendous amount of remodeling, I bought several throw rugs and chairs for the sitting room and found a perfect roll-top desk for my office.

I'd met an actor named Tom Sprately who was out of work at the time and needed a place to stay. I offered Tom a little room in the basement behind the boiler, where he could live, as I was always worried that someone would break in and steal all my casting files, especially my precious three-by-five index cards. We needed someone to be there for security reasons, and this seemed like a good arrangement. I also rented one room upstairs to an up-and-coming writer named Steve Tesich, who rode his bike everywhere and would eventually win an Academy Award for his original screenplay, *Breaking Away*. There was one other room upstairs, which I rented to my dear friend, Manu, who had played the young prince in *Hawaii*.

My first client in the brownstone was Jackie Babbin. I remember the only room that was cleared of rubble was on the second floor, and we had to climb over this pile of plaster to get upstairs. Jacqueline Babbin was one of the first successful women producers. She worked for David Susskind and later moved on to producing New York–based soap operas, most notably, *All My Children*. Susskind hired women, and there were four or five very powerful women who worked for him. Jackie was producing a television pilot and asked me to help cast it.

Just after my initial meeting with Jackie, I happened to get a call from Dustin Hoffman, asking if I had anything for him. By this time, he'd already completed filming his part as Benjamin Braddock in *The Graduate*, but it wouldn't be released for quite some time. It was a slow summer, and I told him, "There's a small part you could do in a television pilot, but I hear you'll be a big star when *The Graduate* comes out."

"Yeah, so they say, but I have to pay this month's rent," he told me.

I explained that the part was okay; however, the pilot would probably not air until after *The Graduate* was released.

"It can't hurt me, do you think?" he asked.

I said, "No, I don't think so."

So he did it because he needed the money. If an actor feels that a role might hurt his or her career, and I feel they are wrong, I try to convince them otherwise; however, if I think the actor is right, I'll say, "Yeah, it could hurt your career."

The pilot did flop for the most part but certainly didn't hurt Dustin's career. It seemed that every summer for years, when the network programmed old stuff for filler, this pilot was aired, for it had some memorable names in it like Dustin and Gunilla Knutson, a former Miss Sweden who was famous for the line, "Take it off. Take it all off," to the accompaniment of David Rose's song "The Stripper" from the Noxema Medicated Instant Shaving Cream commercial that ran in the mid-1960s.

If my office telephone number was a good omen, it did not take long to prove to be true. The first film MDA handled ensconced in our new offices was *Midnight Cowboy*. I was sent a copy of James Leo Herlihy's book right around the time that it was published in 1965. The movie rights to it were quickly obtained, but it took three years to secure any monies for preproduction. Jerome Hellman was the producer, and John Schlesinger soon became attached to direct the film.

On a hunch, I sent the book to Dustin Hoffman, who read it and loved it. Jerry Hellman was taking off from Los Angeles and heading to Europe, and I asked him if he could stop in New York on his way.

He said, "Yes, but why?"

I told him, "If you go downtown and see a play called *EH!* you'll find your Ratso Rizzo."

Jerry followed my hunch and saw Dustin in the Circle in the Square production of *EH!* The rest, as they say, would have been history, except for the fact that Jerry Hellman, in the liner notes for the recent DVD release of the movie, is quoted as claiming that he found Dustin and had his heart set on him for the role of Ratso Rizzo, a huge lie!

Meanwhile, Mike Nichols's *The Graduate* was released to great acclaim for the film as well as many of the leading actors and none more so than its star, Dustin Hoffman. Dustin's agents immediately declared their opposition to his doing *Midnight Cowboy.* In their opinion, he was a star now and should not have to share the male lead in a movie with anyone. As Dustin states, "After *The Graduate*, everyone said, 'Well, Mike Nichols has this guy who's just playing himself.' I got so upset when I read that, I couldn't wait to prove them wrong, and when I chose to do *Midnight Cowboy*, Nichols called up at one point and said, 'Are you sure you want to play Razzo Rizzo? It's such an unattractive role and you could kill your career.' But I was out to show that I was a character actor. I was very affected by Lee Strasberg when I studied with him; he would say over and over, 'There's no such thing as a juvenile or an ingénue or a villain or a hero or a leading man. We're all characters.' I was maybe twenty-one years old, I'd just come to New York to study and it hit me very strong, because I was a victim of casting. Even today, casting people can kill you. Because you sit down, and before you say a word they're going to look at you and without knowing anything about you tell you, 'Well, you're not a leading man. You're not a juvenile. We'll cast you as a doctor, or a scientist maybe.' What's much more fun is to get to know someone, and then to see a way of casting that most people wouldn't cast me as. You start to see something coming out that is what they are underneath. That is what Marion Dougherty can do."

Dustin was smart. He was committed to playing the Ratzo Rizzo character. He'd already done research to find out what kind of diseases, vitamin deficiencies, or other aliments would cause a slum kid to limp like that and be so sickly. With or without his agents' approval, he had no intention of missing out on *Midnight Cowboy*. It was one of the smartest moves he ever made because he went from a wonderful comic, but clearly a leading man role, to a stark, dramatic character role. To his credit, Dustin has continued to capitalize on both those early career choices and has convincingly played wonderful character roles as well as those of leading men.

Since we now had our Ratzo Rizzo, we needed the costar, Joe Buck. Jerry Hellman suggested, in a typical cliché casting idea, that we cast it on the West Coast, where we'd be more likely to find a "cowboy type." *Duh!* We needed a great actor! Five actors were flown in from Los Angeles to test for the role, but I knew that the real inside track belonged to Michael Sarrazin.

I asked if they would also test an interesting New York actor I liked named Jon Voight. I pointed out that testing him would not cost them any extra money. They liked Jon, but they had their hearts set on Michael Sarrazin.

I then made one of my more unfortunate gaffes. I pulled John Schlesinger aside and, with absolute sincerity, told him that I wasn't comfortable about casting Michael in this particular part because he was too pretty. Since the relationship between Joe Buck and Ratzo Rizzo was such a close and loving one, I was afraid the audience might mistakenly infer that they were gay.

A quick, subtle reaction crossed John's face, just enough to tip me off that this man, who I'd known for maybe two or three days, was himself gay and just emerging from the *closet* at the time. He was graceful enough to pretend not to notice that my foot was lodged in my mouth, and he never held it against me.

Jerry Hellman, John Schlesinger, his coterie, and I were all gathered in a screening room to watch the screen tests for Joe Buck. Everyone knew that John's choice was Michael; so it didn't surprise me, it infuriated me, when the tests ended, and the Michael Sarrazin frenzy swept the group like a tidal wave. I had already expressed myself to John, so rather than be redundant or cause a scene, I simply stood up, announced that I was late for a meeting, and headed for the door. Jerry Hellman heard the anger in my voice and asked what was wrong.

"Nothing. You guys are just making a terrible mistake, that's all," I answered and walked away.

Fortunately, studio stupidity intervened when I could not. The studio that had Michael Sarrazin under contract was willing to let him out to shoot *Midnight Cowboy*, but they refused to make him available for the two-week rehearsal period before principal photography began. Not that they planned to use him for those two weeks, mind you, they just decided to take a position of power that did them no good and hurt their actor. I think, with all respect to Michael, who is a talented actor, it was a lucky break for us.

When John Schlesinger got wind of the studio's position, he said, "My God, how am I going to make this movie without rehearsals?" By this time, the broken record that I was answered, "You're not. You're going to use Jon Voight."

He agreed to sit down again in the screening room with no one but me and Jerry Hellman and review just two of the screen tests—Michael Sarrazin and Jon Voight. After we'd seen the two tests, John turned to me and said, "Well, what do you think?"

And I said, "You know what I think."

Whereupon a little smile came over his face, as he may have thought I would back down, and we've been good friends ever since. It took me weeks to "bully" them, but I knew I was right, and Jon Voight got the part of his life. I honestly think it saved the real meaning of the film.

When the movie came out and was such a big hit, John Schlesinger was on a late-night talk show and was asked by the host how he'd discovered Jon Voight? He then told the television audience, "I didn't. Marion Dougherty found him and insisted that I use him. Frankly, I didn't even want Jon Voight." That was particularly brave and honest of him, since Jon happened to be sitting beside him.

The brilliant Barnard Hughes, father of the well-known theater director, Doug Hughes, did not want to do *Midnight Cowboy*. His part was that of a gay man who tried to hire Joe Buck as a prostitute. Barnard was concerned about the effect on his children if and when they saw the film. I told him the same thing that I've told other actors since then, "It's not you . . . it's a character you are playing. You're an actor and that is your job." When Barney discussed accepting the role with his wife, actress Helen Stenborg, she urged him, insisting, "You'd be crazy not to do it!" Barney recalled over the years that many an actor has sought out his advice on playing a gay character and the effect it could have on one's career. For Barney, the role in *Midnight Cowboy* had a great impact on his future career, and playing a gay character in those days certainly was a much rarer occurrence than it is these days.

There is a large party scene in the film that required a mixture of wild partygoers that was easy enough to cast, considering it was in the late 1960s. One of the great things about the brownstone was that we could look out the window and watch when people would arrive, especially if they were late for an appointment. You'd see people get all primped up before they rang the bell. I remember the day Viva, who'd achieved fame from her connection with Andy Warhol and her appearances in some of his films, came to read for *Midnight Cowboy*. Before she got out of the cab, instead of smoothing her hair, she pulled on it wildly every which way, slashed her brightly colored lipstick from her lips, and came in for her audition.

The most spectacular of the arrivals was without competition, the group of Hell's Angels who came to audition for the party scene. They brought many of their real heavyweights along, and I decided to hire several of them. I was touched before they left when they gave me their hotline number and told me that if anyone gave me or anyone else on the film any trouble, all I had to do was speak up, and they'd take care of it and pass the word around the neighborhood.

I always seemed to get along with all types of people. I think it's just the fact that people like me because I like them. I've succeeded in communicating and getting along well with the Hell's Angels, the Polynesians, the Sioux Indians, and all other types of people. Some people are difficult to get through to, but I somehow do. The weird thing was that Sandy Alexander, the head of the Hell's Angels in New York, had acted a little bit and was quite an intelligent guy. I'll never forget the day he came in with his sergeant-at-arms who should have been cast in *The Munsters*! His head was a brick wall all the way through; he was a mean mother!

Midnight Cowboy achieved a great deal of success and remains to this day a compelling film entertainment. Its' excellent supporting cast featured Sylvia Miles (Oscar nominated), John McGiver, Brenda Vaccaro, Ruth White, Barnard Hughes, Jennifer Salt (screenwriter Waldo Salt's daughter), Bob Balaban, and party scene participants that included Viva, Gastone Rosselli, Ultra Violet, Paul Jabara, International Velvet, and Paul Morrissey—all Andy Warhol buddies. The film received seven Academy Award nominations and was the first (and only) Academy

Award winning, X-rated, Best Picture. John Schlesinger and Waldo Salt also won Oscars for their direction and screenplay, respectively.

An equal number of Golden Globe nominations were received with Jon Voight winning as Most Promising Male Newcomer; and it swept the British Academy of Film and Television Arts Awards (BAFTA), winning in all six nominated categories. Perhaps most noteworthy, regarding the timelessness and the regard in which *Midnight Cowboy* is still held is the fact that in 1994, it was placed on the National Film Registry.

It was a great disappointment to me that my name is nowhere to be seen on the credits of *Midnight Cowboy*. There is no casting credit on *Midnight Cowboy*. It was a result of listening to my husband that I ended the experience on a sour note. My deal with Jerry Hellman called for me to get casting credit in the end credits in first position on a card with no more than two names on it. The number of names on any one card when the credits roll by is invariably part of a contract negotiation, and obviously the fewer names on the card, the more attention your name receives. When I attended the first screening of the completed film, I wasn't thrilled to see my casting credit on a card with three other names on it.

It was even more upsetting to me that my name was not first on the list and that one of the names hadn't done anything on *Midnight Cowboy* except take Polaroid pictures. I felt that I'd more than earned enough respect to have that agreement point honored, especially when Jerry Hellman, who was a "friend," came up with the lame excuse that it was "too expensive" to change it. My husband came up with the bright idea that I should issue an ultimatum. Put my credit on a two name card as promised or take my name off the film completely. I was dumb enough and angry enough to listen to him.

Jerry Hellman chose the second option; he took my name off of the movie. When it was too late, I realized that he had to change the card anyway to remove my name and that it wouldn't have been any more expensive to position my credit for casting as per specified in my deal.

TOO EXPENSIVE! Jerry Hellman is still living off the profits he made from *Midnight Cowboy*. This hurt me more than anything else in my fifty-year career of casting. But then no one ever accused this business of being logical or fair. Up to that point, I had never signed a contract for any of my films. It was a matter of a verbal deal of honesty and good faith.

John Schlesinger was quite angry about Jerry's lousy move; however, he could do nothing about it but apologize to me. I am honored to say that John became a good friend of mine. I loved his honesty, his wonderful eye for the actor's talent, and his humor about himself and others. His talent added much to the art of filmmaking, and he will be loved and missed by all who were lucky enough to have known him or seen his films.

Juliet Taylor, one of today's preeminent casting directors, was the first associate to work with me at MDA in the brownstone. Juliet was working for David Merrick, who at the time was a well-known producer from the Broadway theater. Juliet was interested in the film business and came in to see me. I hired Juliet and she began to answer the phones and take care of the office when I was away. I'll never forget that she'd just broken up with her boyfriend, and every once in a while, I could hear her crying in the bathroom. As time went by, it was very good for me because Juliet was obviously more than a few years younger, and there were certain areas where we could bounce ideas back and forth.

I then met with Bill Treusch, who was with Dudley Field Malone in an office next door to where Juliet had been working with David Merrick. I'd known Bill from an agency called TMI, which was financed

by Bernie Cornfeld until he went out of business. When Bill was at
TMI, he had several up and coming actors he worked with, including
Sissy Spacek and Diane Keaton. I invited Bill to come and work out
of the brownstone and let him take over the basement, which had a
separate entrance. I didn't charge him any rent; instead, I asked him to
negotiate the contracts for MDA, following the disaster that had recently
happened to me on *Midnight Cowboy*. I negotiated all the contracts
with the agents for the actors that were hired, and Bill negotiated the
contract between MDA and the producers for our casting fees. I wasn't
good at negotiating my casting fee; however, I was very good at saving
the producers and directors a lot of money in the casting budget on
their films. Bill also loved to go to the theater and would clue me in if
he came across any good performances.

The one thing that Bill had to put up with was Tom Sprately, who
was living in the basement. It seemed Tom never had a job or any money
and would occasionally feel compelled to walk through Bill's office space
in his underwear to empty the garbage. Tom was also a kind of junk
collector and had a cat named Tikky that seemed to always be in the
way. Juliet told me the cat would sit there and stare at her all day long.

Bill introduced me to his other young clients, which included Lois
Smith, Carol Kane, Christopher Walken, Eric Roberts, Antonia Rey,
Tom Berenger, Peter Weller, and John Hurt. At any given time, people
would just stop by the brownstone to say hello and see what was going
on. Sometimes they'd bring food or something to drink, and we'd hang
around the kitchen and eat. The brownstone felt more like a home
where people could enjoy spending time.

For all of the people I have had working for me, I always avoided
labeling their job descriptions. I also encouraged them to become
involved in the process of casting so that they had a better understanding

of what I was doing. Juliet was the first, but there were others who came along and established themselves as very talented casting directors.

When Nessa Hyams came to work for us at MDA, we were all a little intimidated. Nessa's grandfather, Sol Hurok, was the first to bring the Russian Bolshoi Ballet to the United States for an eight-week tour. He also managed the careers of Arthur Rubinstein, Isaac Stern, and Marian Anderson among many others. Nessa would come to work in her mink coat and fashionable outfits and would always go to meet her grandfather for lunch at the Russian Tea Room, while Juliet and I would grab a sandwich at the corner deli and eat in the brownstone. Nessa went on to become a very important casting director on her own. A few of the films she later cast were *Blazing Saddles*, *What's Up Doc*, *Night Moves*, *With Honors*, and *The Exorcist*.

It wasn't long before Nessa and Juliet began commenting on my sense of fashion. I recall having been invited to attend some type of event, and they both insisted on going out and buying me a new outfit. That happened on more than one occasion.

Wally Nicita also came to work for us at MDA. Wally was a creative writing teacher who was married to Rick Nicita, a young agent at William Morris, which was the largest and oldest global talent agency. When she was laid off from her teaching job, she came to see me, and my first thought was that if she was a writing teacher, she would probably be good at reading and understanding scripts. On her first day, I'd bought a jacket for my husband that didn't fit, and I didn't keep the sales receipt. I gave it to Wally and asked her if she'd return it for me and get the cash. I have to admit that it was an odd thing to ask her to do on her first day. She later told me that they weren't going to give her the money back, and she burst into tears. The customer service woman felt so awful that she gave her the money.

I was always a little careful about what I would say around Wally, especially about the abusive relationship with Bobby, since her husband was an agent at William Morris and I didn't want that to get around. One late afternoon, I returned to the office from a meeting and found Bobby sitting at my desk, going through all my files, and looking at photos of the women. I got upset and said something, and Bobby went into a rage. He was just about to clobber me when Bill and Tom started banging on the door, asking what was going on. That put an end to that one particular episode. In later years, Wally worked with me at both Paramount and Warner Brothers before she began casting films on her own. *The Big Chill, The Fabulous Baker Boys,* and *The Witches of Eastwick* are only a few of her many credits; and Wally produced the film *Mermaids* with Cher and Winona Ryder.

Gretchen Rennell also came to work with us at MDA. She'd been working as a receptionist for Broadway producer Harold Prince and was an agent in training. Juliet introduced me to Gretchen as they both had been raised in Greenwich, Connecticut. Gretchen also worked with me in later years before branching out. A few of the films Grethen cast on her own are *Runaway Brides, The Color of Money, The Cotton Club,* and *The Horse Whisperer.*

At any time, you could walk into the brownstone and feel like you were in a Eugene Ionesco play or encounter any number of inspiring actors and directors. At various times, I had eccentric people living in the basement, upstairs, people that would just come wafting through the room unexpectedly. It really was a wonderful time in my life. Life in the brownstone offices of MDA was basically filled with much good hard work by my various associates and a tremendous amount of good humor that was peopled by a plethora of interesting and talented filmmakers.

MDA began to work with several movies that were primarily filmed in New York City and were definitely flavored with the abundance of acting talent to be found there. During this time, Mayor John Lindsay hosted a large campaign to try and bring film production to New York.

In 1969, we cast a lovely film called *POPI,* which was directed by Arthur Hiller and produced by my good friend, Bert Leonard. Alan Arkin played the father of two absolutely darling Hispanic children. I found one of the children, Miguel Alejandro, who played Junior, at a little theater in the village. We found Reuben Figueroa, who played the younger brother, Luis, at a school near 125ᵗʰ Street after watching him play with a group of kids on the playground. The supporting cast featured Rita Moreno, Anthony Holland, Louis Zorich, John Harkins, Antonia Rey, and Joan Tompkins.

On one of my visits to the uptown East Side neighborhood where the film was being shot, I commented to someone how charming I thought it was that all the tenement fire escapes were decorated with flower pots in which everyone seemed to be growing identical plants. Whoever I mentioned this to got one of the plants for me to take home. I planted it on my sun porch in Bayshore where it grew healthy and very tall until one day some of its leaves fell off. My two cats ate the leaves and immediately started acting like a couple of drunks! I've often wondered if I'm the only person that ever nurtured a marijuana plant into full adulthood without smoking some or having a clue as to what it was.

Cotton Comes to Harlem, another 1969 release, was actor Ossie Davis's first directorial effort. The film's cast included Raymond St. Jacques, Calvin Lockhart, Judy Pace, Emily Yancy, Lou Jacobi, Eugene Roche, J. D. Cannon, Helen Martin (who couldn't remember her lines, but was so good that I later used her several times), and Cleavon Little, whom I adored. There was also a guy who did some cabaret work that I'd heard about named Redd Foxx. I called him in and ended up casting him as Uncle Bud. *Cotton Comes to Harlem* was the first time Redd became widely known beyond the cabaret circuit.

Godfrey Cambridge, with whom I had an awkward history, headed the cast list. I had earlier cast Godfrey in a couple of *Naked City* episodes. I also had gone to see him in an Equity showcase so I knew him quite well. One day, during the period when I was casting *Naked City*, he called and started asking the oddest questions about actors I had hired and actors I had not. Finally, the conversation got odd enough that I asked, "Godfrey, are you taping this conversation?" He said that he was, and I became so furious that I told him I was hanging up. The next thing I knew, a lawyer from Screen Gems, the company that produced *Naked City*, came to see me and was rather upset. It seemed that Godfrey Cambridge was suing Screen Gems for discrimination or something and was using out of context quotes from our taped conversation to support his accusations. The discrimination charge really offended me, especially since it was coming from an actor I had given jobs to more than once. I told the lawyer that I would be happy to take the stand and repeat every word that I said on that tape, in context, and add enough other facts under oath that a suit against Screen Gems, for discrimination of all things, would be laughed right out of court. I never heard another word about it.

By the time Godfrey was cast in *Cotton Comes to Harlem*, his stand-up comedy career had taken off, and I heard he was sensational. He was appearing at the Blue Angel, a prestigious New York nightclub, and I planned to go visit him on the set to congratulate him. When word somehow reached him on the set that I was coming, he said, "Yeah, tell Marion Dougherty to show up so I can bite her white ass!" Always one to believe the "when in Rome" adage, I laughed upon hearing that and announced, "Then you tell him my white ass is on its way!" The producers on the movie were so nervous about the potential confrontation that they begged me not to come. I ended up staying away, not for my sake, but for theirs.

Godfrey had gone completely around the bend by the time *Cotton Comes to Harlem* finished shooting. He was thrown out of the Blue Angel as he was saying very racist things in his act. On the film set, he poured plaster of Paris down the toilets of the honey wagons (mobile dressing rooms), trashed the craft service food trucks, and generally made a nuisance of himself behind the scenes. Despite the trouble between us, I am truly sorry about whatever made him so desperately unhappy. Although we know actors have it "hard" and African American actors have had it doubly hard, particularly in those earlier days, it is a shame to see any talented actor self-destruct.

The Owl and the Pussycat and *Where's Poppa?* were two back-to-back features in which we cast George Segal. The Herbert Ross production of *The Owl and the Pussycat* teamed up George with Barbra Streisand in a wild comedy about a prostitute and a john. The cast included Robert Klein, Alan Garfield, Buck Henry, and Roz Kelly.

Directed by the funny and oh-so-talented Carl Reiner, *Where's Poppa?* has probably gained in stature from the hit is was, when released to something of a cult picture, with the now infamous tush scene. Ruth Gordon played the senile mother of two sons, George Segal, a hapless lawyer downtrodden by life while taking care of his mother, and Ron Leibman, a milquetoast husband who is constantly harassed by muggers in Central Park. The muggers take his clothes in one scene, only to mug him on his return home through the park dressed in a gorilla suit that he borrowed from his brother.

Segal's character was desperate to escape his mother and longing for romance, so when he meets an inept visiting nurse, played by Trish Van Devere, who will take care of his mother, he overlooks her ineptness because of her attractiveness. At a dinner date, which his mother attends,

Segal's character is mortified when his mother yanks down the back of his trousers and begins a wild commentary on his great tush, climaxing with her kissing the exposed cheeks as if it were an irresistible baby. Ruth Gordon held nothing back in the playing of that scene.

Carl ended up using Trish Van Devere as Segal's love interest in her first film role. The other two women I sent him to see, Diane Keaton and Bernadette Peters, managed quite well without this film on their resume. In supporting roles, I had favorites like Barnard Hughes, Vincent Gardenia, Billy LeMassena, Helen Martin, Jane Hoffman, and Alice Drummond. Garrett Morris, of *Saturday Night Live* fame, made his screen debut. Carl gave his very talented son, Rob, a role that bore a remarkable likeness to the role Rob would next play on the television series *All in the Family*. Penny Marshall, who was Rob's wife at the time, can be seen as an extra in the courtroom scene.

The wild and dark comedy was written by Robert Klane, who based the screenplay on his novel, and featured a much darker ending than in the released version of the film. The most recent DVD of the movie offers both endings.

I then headed west in order to cast a film for Elliott Silverstein that was produced by Sandy Howard and titled *A Man Called Horse*. Several years before, I'd worked on a television pilot for Elliott and found him a bit odd and quite funny. He was a little shorter than I was, and on the second day we met, he entered my office by jumping up and swinging on the transom over the door yelling, "I will be taller than you!" He then jumped up on my desk, looking down at me, and said, "See?" I thought that was quite silly, so I took him out to lunch with my arm slung around his shoulder.

A Man Called Horse was to star Richard Harris as John Morgan, a white man who is assimilated into the lives and culture of a Sioux Indian tribe, whose chief was portrayed by my dear friend and MDA brownstone tenant, Manu Tupou. Both Richard and Manu had appeared in the film *Hawaii*. The supporting cast included Jean Gascon, Dup Taylor, and Corinna Tsopei. My moment of real chutzpa came in the casting of a character named Buffalo Head, an old Indian woman. The part was unusual in that the character appears through almost the entire film and speaks not a word of English dialogue. I thought of Dame Judith Anderson for that role. Why, I cannot tell you; it was just one of those crazy ideas that came out of nowhere. But did I dare? I think it had been a while since she worked, but who cared? I managed to track down a phone number for her in Santa Barbara and called her myself. To my great surprise, not only did she say yes, but she even came down to Los Angeles a few days later and met with us. Of course, she was as exquisite as we all knew she would be.

Thanks in a large part to the involvement of the Rosebud Sioux Indians, it was a marvelous and fascinating experience. We wanted to cast as many native Sioux as possible for the smaller parts, so off I went to the Rosebud Reservation in South Dakota. One of the first priorities for my notes and files was to take Polaroids of as many of the tribe members as I could that were willing and interested in working on the film.

The idea didn't exactly sweep through the reservation like wildfire, thanks to a belief held by some Sioux that being photographed takes away part of your spirit. Also, I was alien to these people. I was so grateful on the first day to the few who did come straggling into my little makeshift office, which was a shack set up in a large field that was being prepared for a big "pow wow" for the Rosebud and Wounded Knee tribes. I took two Polaroids of those few that did come in, one for me and one for them to keep.

In no time, word got around that maybe this woman who'd plopped herself into their midst out of nowhere might not be so bad. All you had to do was spend a few minutes with her, and she'd give you a free photo of yourself. My Polaroid and I were busy and popular from then on, taking pictures of all those beautiful faces.

I had the privilege of being at Rosebud for one of their major rituals. The field was filled with thatch-roofed tents in a big oval circle, and the women prepared stew in giant cauldrons. The Sioux had prepared the "stage." There were large poles set up in another large circle with a thatched roof attached, so the audience could stand in the shade. I will never forget standing among the tribal audience one night as the dancers and drummers performed. The chanting, music, and drums went all the way through my body, piercing and thrilling, as they were dances meant to inspire them for upcoming combat. This memory still deeply affects me.

One of the many Sioux who fascinated me was a young man who had left the reservation to take a job as a mathematician in the Silicon Valley but finally had his fill of "civilization" and returned home. I visited his trailer one evening, and on the end table, there was a grainy photograph of a very old man wearing a beautiful fringed jacket. I commented on it, and he explained that it was his grandfather.

We needed to hire an interpreter because most of the older Indians spoke very little English. I particularly loved the introductions. Many of the Indians' names were so captivating and confirmed the belief that the name reflected the mother's first sight or impression after her baby was born. It was enchanting to meet Spotted Elk and Bear Crossing the River after hearing those names in the native Sioux tongue. From my casting notebook on *A Man Called Horse*, just a few of the delightful Sioux names who came to see me were Pete Charging Thunder, Cecil White Hat, Buzzy Thunder Hawk, Agnes Left Hand Bull, Elizabeth Little Elk, Carla May Running Horse, Dawson Shot With Two Arrows, Thomas Bone Shirt, Christine Red Feather, Milton Walking Eagle,

Delbert Thunder Hawk, Odell Standing Cloud, Ross Kills Enemy, and James Never Misses A Shot.

We ended up casting about fifteen Sioux from the Rosebud Reservation and brought them on location to Durango, Mexico, where we were filming. The night they arrived, they celebrated with much enthusiasm. It was quite a night, but the Sioux members of the cast were well worth it.

I had a comparatively minor brush with alcohol on that film myself, come to think of it. A delightful young Caucasian man named Clyde Dollar had been hired as a technical advisor and historian on the film. Thanks to his expertise in Sioux artifacts, traditions, history, and language, Clyde was hired to make sure that every detail of the movie was authentic. While on location one night, he insisted on mixing me a drink called Red-Eye. I'm not sure if I found out before or after I drank it that one of the ingredients was actual gunpowder.

While I was working on the movie in Mexico City, I met Colonel Frank Kurtz and his author wife, Margo, in a little gift shop in the hotel. He was in Mexico on the Olympic Committee; and it turned out that they had a daughter, Swoosie Kurtz, who wanted to become an actor. They were very cordial to me probably because they thought I could perhaps help Swoosie.

Colonel Kurtz was the pilot of the first plane to fly across the Andes in World War II and was the most decorated pilot in that war. He had named his plane the Swoose, for it seemed half swan, half goose. I can remember hearing a Kay Kyser song about the Swoose in the 1940s. Swoosie got her name from that song. "It's half swan, half goose. Alexander is a swoose."

The hottest ticket to the Olympic Games was the female gymnastics competition. The Olympics were being held right after Russia had gone into Czechoslovakia, and Colonel Kurtz gave me two tickets as my husband was visiting me. I ended up in the peanut gallery while my husband sat right behind the Russian generals and judges in the first row. Whenever a Czech girl did a brilliant routine, the Russians remained silent; and whenever the Russian did likewise, they whopped and hollered. Colonel Kurtz told me afterward that Bobby, my not-too-bright husband, would tap the generals on the shoulder so they would cheer for the Czech girl also.

A Man Called Horse was shot and released at a time when the problems of Indians and their relationship to the United States government were often headline news, culminating a few years later with a clash at Wounded Knee that resulted in casualties and was the impetus for Marlon Brando's refusal of his Academy Award as Best Actor. It was a particularly satisfying movie to work on in those times, since it was one of the earlier movies to realistically show the spirituality and way of life of the Native Americans.

The year of 1971 saw the release of more than ten movies that MDA cast or had a hand in casting. There were some firsts among them. Although some of the movies have faded from the memories of all but most ardent moviegoers, a few have achieved near-classic status.

My first experience working with a female director was *A New Leaf*, which was written and directed by the masterful Elaine May. She directed herself in a comedy about a bumbling heiress who is hotly pursued by a money-hungry suitor played by Walter Matthau. It is a funny movie, and Elaine gave me an interesting twist on my casting responsibilities since she wanted practically everyone she knew to be hired for some small part or another, from her maid to her cousins to her hairdresser. Among Elaine's list of friends, I managed to squeeze in some other talented actors such as Jack Weston, George Rose, James Coco, Doris Roberts, William Redfield, and Renee Taylor.

Renee and her husband, Joseph Bologna, wrote another one of our projects that year, a semiautobiographical story of their romance and marriage titled *Made for Each Other*, in which they also starred. The movie was Robert B. Bean's only feature directing credit. While I have grown to dislike having screenwriters sit in on auditions, or downright refusing, in the case of Renee and Joe, when it came to casting the parents of their characters, I really could not keep them away. It provided an interesting glimpse at human nature. I had to find actors to play both of their characters' parents while they sat in.

There was one couple in particular for the role of Renee's parents, which really impressed Joe; and the minute they left the room, he said, "That's it! That's them exactly! They're perfect!"

"What are you talking about? Those people were nothing like my parents. They couldn't be more wrong for this!" Renee shot back, aghast at the thought.

The same thing happened during the auditions for Joe's parents. Renee would find some uncanny similarity between a couple of actors and Joe's parents, while Joe would gape at her as if she'd completely lost her mind.

The casting of the two sets of parents became even more interesting when I read real-life married actors, Olympia Dukakis and Louis Zorich, which was about fifteen years before Olympia's Oscar win as Best Supporting Actress for *Moonstruck*. Louis and Olympia seem to have perfect chemistry in real life, so it was odd that I should end up casting Olympia as Joe's mother and Louis as Renee's father in the film.

Olympia wrote her autobiography, *Ask Me Again Tomorrow*, and Louis has written a book for actors about auditioning titled *What Have You Done?* When I heard about the subject of the book, I reminded him of my favorite story of his readings for me. Louis is one of the great gigglers of all time, and he was apt to start in the middle of a line reading.

When Louis read for *Made for Each Other*, I'd already cast him in an earlier film, *They Might Be Giants*, and I warned him, "Now, Louis, don't start giggling!" That alone set him off, but he got the part anyway; and Louis and Olympia are sweet enough to this day to keep in touch with me.

Our next project was the film *Bananas* for Woody Allen. Woody is brilliant, obviously, and unique to work with. I typically schedule actors' first meetings with a director for fifteen minutes. On the first day of work, I soon realized that Woody was so shy that he did not want those meetings to last more than a minute or two. It was a disaster. He wanted no conversation, no small talk, no handshakes, and certainly no compliments about how great he was. He always had one of his producers in the room to answer any questions the actors might have about the script.

The next day, I began scheduling the meetings for Woody every five minutes in order to make him feel more comfortable, and we finally got down to every two minutes. I always cautioned agents when I made the appointments that the actors were not to take offense at the brevity of their auditions or Woody's unwillingness to chat; it was definitely nothing to take personally.

Woody had a great eye and an amazing memory, so much so that a year later he said to me one day, "Remember that actor in the red beret that we met for *Bananas*?" I thought, after a two-minute meeting, a year earlier? I didn't have the foggiest idea who he was talking about, but we found out later that it was Tom Sprately, one of the basement denizens in the brownstone, and Woody used him in *Everything You Always Wanted to Know about Sex*.

Bananas was the story of Fielding Melish (Woody) and his involvement with a Central American country's revolution. The cast included Louise Lasser (Woody's ex-wife), Carlos Montalban (brother of Ricardo), Charlotte Rae, Stanley Ackerman, and Renee Enriquez. Howard Cosell played himself; and Sylvester Stallone made his debut, of sorts, as a subway thug menacing Woody's character.

I had bought a Lincoln rocking chair for the parlor of the brownstone where we held the interviews. Woody would sit in the chair during these meetings, rocking like crazy out of sheer nervousness. The more he rocked, the more the chair would "walk" subtly backward toward the window.

One day he was in midrock when the chair suddenly raked against the wooden slats of the window's shutters and he leapt out of that chair like a shot, scared silly. From then on, I took it upon myself to gently remind him, every ten minutes or so, to pull his chair forward again.

His "designated talker," one of his producers, called in sick one morning before a day of auditions. Woody panicked and said, "This is terrible! Who's going to talk to these people then?"

"I'll be happy to talk to them," I told him.

"You can do that?" he asked incredulously.

I laughed and assured him that I had been doing it every day for years and years. Bless his heart; he could not imagine having to do such a thing.

We cast *Everything You Always Wanted to Know about Sex* and *Sleeper* out of the brownstone. When Woody called to ask me to cast *Love and Death*, I told him that I was working on another movie.

"But how am I going to cast this movie without you?" he asked.

"Easy. You'll use Juliet," I explained.

Juliet Taylor had been, to drastically understate it, my secretary, assistant, colleague, and much more for years. Woody was still reluctant, so I promised him that if he hired Juliet, I would work with her to take care of him. He followed my advice and hired Juliet; and she's been casting for him ever since, quite brilliantly, I might add, and without any help from me. Besides casting all of Woody's films, Juliet went on to cast *Schindler's List*, *Birdcage*, *Arthur*, *Big*, *Sleepless in Seattle*, *Terms of Endearment*, *Taxi Driver*, and *Close Encounters of the Third Kind* to name only a handful.

My old friend, Norman Lear, hired us to cast a movie for him called *Cold Turkey*. The screenplay concerned the population of a small town in Iowa whose citizens accept the challenge of a major tobacco company to all quit smoking in order to win millions of dollars in a contest sponsored by the company who uses it as a publicity stunt believing that no town in America could possibly win the money.

The town is led in their quest by a local minister portrayed by Dick Van Dyke and is chock full of comedy gems in one of the most talented comedic ensembles ever assembled: Bob Newhart, Tom Poston, Bob and Ray, Barnard Hughes, Pippa Scott, Jean Stapleton, Barbara Cason, Vincent Gardenia, Sudie Bond, Helen Page Camp, M. Emmet Walsh, Graham Jarvis, Judith Lowry, and Peggy Rea.

The incredible character actor, Edward Everett Horton, played a nearly vegetable-like head of the tobacco company and was superb in his last film role. He didn't have a word of dialogue but was terribly funny.

Bob Elliott and Ray Goulding, who'd gained fame with their popular radio show, came in to see me for the movie. The way that they sat huddled together like two scared teenagers, you would have thought I was going to murder them rather than showcase their comedic talents in multiple roles spoofing famous television newscasters of the day in *Cold Turkey*, which was their first movie.

Many years later, I ran into Norman Lear out in California and jokingly threatened to bill him for additional fees after he'd used so many of the cast from *Cold Turkey*, with such brilliant success, in many of his subsequent television series.

I did actually have a hand in some of that, though, when I cast the original television pilot for *All in the Family* and brought Jean Stapleton and Carroll O'Connor to Norman's attention. We cast Jean in *Cold Turkey*, and he was already a fan of Carroll's performance from the film *What Did You Do in the War Daddy?* and I had cast Carroll in *Hawaii*. The pilot was later reshot, and Norman brought in Sally Struthers and Rob Reiner to play the roles of Gloria and Mike.

Along with *Cold Turkey*, which I think remains a classic film comedy, there were two other movies that MDA cast in 1971 that have become classics. *The Hospital*, a black comedy of the highest order, was written by the brilliant Paddy Chayefsky. Paddy won practically every screenwriting award that year including the Oscar, Golden Globe, Writer's Guild, and the BAFTA. The film, directed by Arthur Hiller, starred George C. Scott as a doctor in a New York City hospital besieged on practically all fronts by crisis after crisis that might normally be associated with a hospital; however, there was also a serial killer that was running amok and murdering hospital personnel. All these stressful situations and an unhappy home life were rapidly driving Scott's character closer and closer to a severe nervous breakdown.

Although I had never met her, I had been a fan of Diana Rigg's since seeing her as Emma Peel in *The Avengers*, so I suggested her for the female lead and the film marked one of her first nonclassic film roles, besides playing the Bond girl, Tracy, in *On Her Majesty's Secret Service*. The supporting cast was full of New York actors like Nancy Marchand, Barnard Hughes, Stephen Elliott, Richard Dysart, Katherine Helmond, Tresa Hughes, and Kate Harrington. Stockard Channing and Christopher Guest both made their film debuts in *The Hospital*, with parts that were unfortunately, not credited.

Let it never be said that once I make up my mind about someone's talent, that I never change it. Frances Sternhagen, who played the harried hospital business office employee, constantly trying to get forms filled out properly in *The Hospital*, recently reminded me that back when I was doing television, her agent tried to get her an appointment with me; and I told him, "I'm just not a Frances Sternhagen fan." Frances believes my refusal may have been because of a play she was doing at the time in which she herself thought she was miscast. I did cast Frances, who is a very talented actor, in a *KRAFT* production of *The Lost Weekend*, and went on to cast her not only in *The Hospital*, but in two other films as well.

A favorite children's film that has been around long enough for the children who first fell in love with it to pass that love on to the next generation also came our way that same year. *Willie Wonka and the Chocolate Factory*, based on Roald Dahl's classic story, *Charlie and the Chocolate Factory*, was directed by Mel Stuart, with Dahl writing the screenplay.

I had a fairly easy time casting Gene Wilder and dear Jack Albertson, God bless him; but I looked and looked for a boy to play the lead, Charlie, in the movie. We finally sent Juliet to Chicago and Cleveland to interview potential children. It was at the Cleveland Playhouse, which had a children's theater group named the Curtain Pullers, whose most noted alumnus was Joel Grey, where, sure enough, Juliet found a darling little guy named Peter Ostrum who was absolutely wonderful in the film. He is now a veterinarian.

We had invaluable help from Mary Selway who cast the Europeans, especially the Salts, the deliciously nasty and spoiled Veruca, played by Julie Dawn Cole, and her overly indulgent father, Henry, played by the marvelous character actor, Roy Kinnear. Mary also cast the zoftig Mrs.

Gloop, Ursula Reit, and her boy Augustus, with the hearty appetite, Michael Bollner.

I found Denise Nickerson, who'd been acting for a couple of years on ABC's daytime vampire drama, *Dark Shadows*, to play Violet Beaurgarde and then cast Leonard Stone, as Violet's used-car salesman dad. Paris Themmen played the television-addicted Mike Teevee and Nora Denney his doting mother.

Before we started shooting the film at the studios in Munich, Germany, Gene Wilder came up with the brilliant idea of doing the somersault in the scene when he first meets the children. He wanted to set a tone for the character and portray him as someone whose actions were completely unpredictable.

Willy Wonka and the Chocolate Factory didn't do too well at the box office when it was first released; however, with its release on home video, the movie became one of the more popular rentals of the 1980s.

We cast the film *Across 110th Street*, with a predominantly African American cast, which was directed by Barry Shear and starred Anthony Quinn, Yaphet Kotto, and Anthony Franciosa.

Anthony Quinn, who was an executive producer, sat in on the readings with Barry Shear in the brownstone. I remember Anthony very well because his pants were terribly tight across his privates, which was rather distracting.

Paul Benjamin, who is a very large man, was sitting on one of my antique sofas to read for me; and suddenly, he had some type of a seizure. He got up from the couch and fell immediately down to the floor. The girls in the office say I picked him up; and, if that is true, I don't know how I did, because he was a very big man.

Anthony Quinn helped him upstairs to one of the bedrooms and laid him down and told him to rest. Paul did return and read and got the part playing Jim Harris.

There was some very tough material in *Across 110th Street*. They went for the blood and violence but had the screenplay been edited for integrity it would've really been an eye-opening film about problems in the African American culture.

The screenplay seemed to really touch the actors that came in to read for it. We were reading many men and women, and I'd never seen so many break down in their auditions. The material really got to them. Many of them were reluctant to do the project because it had a Caucasian director. It was after the assassinations of Martin Luther King Jr. and Bobby Kennedy, and there were riots and fires in St. Louis and Chicago.

I had spoken to the Negro Ensemble Company, a New York–based theater company and one of the foremost repertory companies, and told them here is a forum for the problems of African American people to be aired in a dramatic context; and suddenly, the floodgates opened. Everybody in Harlem was banging on the doors and windows trying to get an audition. Anthony Quinn had played so many minority groups in his career that I used it as a hook in my conversation with the actors.

On one of my many forays to off-Broadway, I attended a two play evening down in Greenwich Village at the Astor Place Theater to see an actor that I had cast several times and liked him very much, Matthew Cowles. The first play, *It's Called a Sugar Plum*, with Jill Clayburgh, was so dreadful that my two gentlemen escorts insisted on leaving to go have dinner; but my being so Scotch (a.k.a. frugal) and Matthew being in the second play, I insisted that we wait for Israel Horovitz's *The Indian Wants the Bronx*. Matthew was one of my favorite "delinquents" when I cast *Naked City*, but he came from a spiffy family. His aunt, Fleur Cowles, was the creator and editor for a beautiful magazine called *American*.

The moment that Al Pacino appeared on stage, playing the street punk Murph, the hair on the back of my neck stood up. He was possessed with his character and had so much violence within him that it made me hold on tight to my chair in an almost uncomfortable position. His performance was terrifyingly explosive to say the least. Even Al later admitted, "I discovered something I hadn't known was there." I had come to see Matthew, who was as good as always, as was John Cazale, the other member of the three person cast; but I was absolutely staggered by Al Pacino.

Al had auditioned for Lee Strasberg's Actors Studio when he was a teenager and was eventually accepted four years later. We first started to get wind of Al when he appeared in an off-off Broadway production of *Why Is a Crooked Letter*. However, it was in this off-Broadway production, *The Indian Wants the Bronx*, where he won an Obie for Best Actor. John Cazale won Best Supporting Actor, and Israel Horovitz won Best New Play.

Marty Bregman had also gone to see Al in the play and began to represent the actor. When I arranged to have Al come to meet with me, I was eager to find him some work; but at the time, the only thing that I could offer him was a one line role in the quiet little comedy/drama, *Me Natalie*, directed by Fred Coe. Not an auspicious debut for Al Pacino playing a guy named Tony with his one and only line being, "May I have the next dance?" Juliet recalls Al in the brownstone repeating the line in different ways over and over. The film starred Patty Duke along with a rich supporting cast that included James Farentino, Martin Balsam, Elso Lanchester, Nancy Marchand, Salome Jens, Bob Balaban, Matthew Cowles, and Catherine Burns. The film seemed to disappear not long after it was released; but it had a lovely performance by Patty in a role that won her the Golden Globe for Best Actress in a Musical or Comedy that year, and the movie itself captured the universal theme of the youthful angst of wanting to be accepted, liked, and found attractive.

Al went on to make his Broadway debut, playing Bickham in Don Peterson's *Does a Tiger Wear a Necktie?* at the Belasco Theater. His performance received rave reviews, and Al won the Tony Award for Best Actor.

Al and the production of *The Indian Wants the Bronx* had earlier traveled to Italy for a performance in the Festival dei Due Mondi in Spoleto, and I remember how Al said he loved performing for an Italian audience. When *The Gang that Couldn't Shoot Straight* came my way, I noted the Italian bicycle racer and immediately called him to come in and look at the script. He showed up at the brownstone and walked in with a noticeably dramatic limp and explained that it was a slipped cartilage in his knee.

It was woefully apparent that he was in no condition to play a bicycle racer in the near future, but I wasn't about to let him go. I remember saying to him that because of his injury, I wasn't going to be able to cast him, but I had a script coming up called *The Panic in Needle Park*, for a role in which I thought he'd be good. Considering the part in *The Gang that Couldn't Shoot Straight* was actually a supporting role, and the role in *The Panic in Needle Park* was a leading role, it turned out to be a better deal for Al and also for his introduction to Hollywood. Al had turned down several film projects prior to *The Panic in Needle Park*, and we all worked with Marty Bregman to put it together.

The Panic in Needle Park was directed by Jerry Schatzberg based on a screenplay by Joan Didion and John Gregory Dunne. We needed an actress to play opposite Al who played a heroin addict named Bobby. I soon found Kitty Winn in a New York ANTA production of *The Three Sisters* presented by the American Conservatory Theater from San Francisco.

Neither Al nor Kitty were particularly known at the time. That was one of the great thrills of casting in those days, which happens much too infrequently now. It is rare for many filmmakers these days to take a chance on unknowns, I think, and give them a fair shot in roles that showcase what they can really do.

"Needle Park" is a tiny sliver of land just above Columbus Circle in Manhattan that was known in the seventies as a virtual paradise for anyone wanting to buy or sell drugs. A terrific African American actor named Arnold Williams was playing one of the dealers and looked the part so perfectly in his cape and floppy hat that the police hauled him in one night. I had to telephone the police station to verify that no, honestly, Arnold was not in the "pharmaceutical" business; he was a member of *The Panic in Needle Park* cast and was being paid to dress like that. I had used Arnold in several other films that I cast, including *Cotton Comes to Harlem*, *Across 110th Street*, and *The King of Marvin Gardens*; but to many moviegoers, Arnold may be best remembered in a film that I did not cast, as the smiling, menacing cab driver that gives Roger Moore's James Bond a couple of wild cab rides in *Live and Let Die*.

Alan Vint, Richard Bright, and Maria Jean Kurtz joined Al and Kitty in the film as well as the gorgeous and gifted actor, Raul Julia, whose talent was cut off much too soon. He is missed and always will be. Raul reached his widest audience on stage and in the original production of the Broadway musical *Nine* and several *Shakespeare in the Park* productions. He may be best well-known as the outrageously funny Gomez Adams in the two comedy films based on *The Adams Family* television series.

The Panic in Needle Park was not a terribly successful film, but Al's performance garnered him many rave reviews. Jacob Brickman wrote in Esquire, "Especially Al Pacino and Kitty Winn in the leads, create intensely real people. Their brand of realness feels close to documentary." Al has gone on record saying that he thought Kitty was great in the film, and she wasn't on anybody's breath come Oscar time because the picture didn't do so well. There were also those not so nice reviews. Al remembers Kitty Winn once telling her grandmother how affected she was by the criticism of *The Panic in Needle Park*, and her grandmother said, "Well, that's awful. You should quit."

Hollywood and Francis Ford Coppola soon discovered what I knew the minute I saw Al on that little off-Broadway stage. In his next film, Al was cast as Michael Corleone in *The Godfather* films; however, in the beginning, the producers were against casting Al until they screened eight minutes of *The Panic in Needle Park*, and then he was set.

When Al was suddenly unavailable for our Italian bicycle racer, I thought of Robert De Niro, who had seen some success in independent films like *Greetings* and *Hi, Mom*, both directed by Brian De Palma. *The Gang That Couldn't Shoot Straight* was directed by James Goldstone, with a script written by Waldo Salt and produced by Irwin Winkler and Robert Chartoff who later went on to *Rocky* fame.

Robert De Niro was as much into researching any new role as Dustin Hoffman had been when he played Ratzo Rizzo. I decided to cast Bob as the Italian bicycle racer; and on his own dime, he set off for Italy to learn what the appropriate Sicilian dialect would be to use for the role of Mario Trantino, a phony priest, thieving immigrant from southern Italy, and a bicyclist. As Bob recalls, "Everything I do is different. I could see someone in the street who has some quirk or eccentricity, and that one little thing would be interesting. It could be just that simple—say it's just right for the character—or get a picture in my mind of people I know or have seen. Then I start working on it and picking up things here and there. Of course you always bring something of yourself to a part, but to me acting means playing different parts, trying to get as close to the reality of a character as possible, learning his life-style, how he holds his fork, how he carries himself, how he talks, how he relates to other people. It's hard to do, because it means you always have to keep looking. Some days you find nothing, other days you're inspired and you see a lot that's exciting. That's why I like to travel before I do a part . . . so I can feel I've prepared as well as I can and I've earned the right to play the person."

At that time, Robert De Niro was not what could be considered a "hot property," but he was certainly being noticed. "I wasn't what you call an attractive person," he points out. "I wasn't being snatched up for certain roles in movies. Therefore, I had to work harder. The more you become a star the less preparation and hard work seem necessary. There is more temptation not to do right by what you do. But a star really has more responsibility. You know, I had somebody tell me once—he had done some films, but he didn't have that much experience—'You just cut away. You don't have to worry about the actors.' But if you don't have anything that's interesting to watch, that's real or that grabs you, whether it be actors or real people, then no matter how beautiful the photography is or how great the editing, it's not going to make any difference."

Besides Robert De Niro, I cast Jerry Orbach, Leigh Taylor Young, Lionel Stander (who had just returned to the United States from Europe after being blacklisted), and Jo Van Fleet, who was a terrific actress and worked for several more years but was beginning to show the first signs of what I and others believe was Alzheimer's disease.

The script called for a dwarf, and I happened to be in a delicatessen around the corner from the brownstone one day, getting a sandwich for lunch, when I saw this little person behind the counter. I am not very bold and didn't want to go up and ask, "Have you ever acted?" So I waited until he left and approached another clerk in the store. It turned out the guy had been in a few plays downtown, and we invited him into the office for an interview. Upon entering the office, wearing a derby and a checked vest, he promptly jumped up on top of the desk and sat puffing away on a huge cigar. Herve Villechaize was quite a character, and we all liked him at once. His most notable other film appearance was in the James Bond film, *The Man with the Golden Gun*, but Herve achieved his greatest recognition for playing Tatoo on the television series *Fantasy Island*.

Burt Young also appeared in *The Gang That Couldn't Shoot Straight*. When I first gave a "general" (a meeting with someone for no particular part to cast, just someone whose resume and photo interested me) to Burt, he told me that he was a button man in the Mafia, a sort of gofer. During our meeting, he explained that one night he was getting coffee in a diner, and sitting beside him was a pretty young woman who asked him what he did for a living. "Oh, I'm an actor," Burt offered as the first thing that came to his mind. She was so impressed that he figured, "Why not try that?" He said that he found the name of Lee Strasberg and the address of the Actors Studio and wrote a three-page letter extolling himself from the Mafia. He went on to say that at the end of the first page he wrote, "If you want to discover different and exciting types, then you should keep on reading this." Someone obviously did and arranged a meeting for Burt to join the Actors Studio!

I cannot recall the details or the reason behind it, but Burt suffered a terrible family tragedy. It had something to do with his wife at the time and his late son, Richard. Having just heard the news, he came to the brownstone in tears. I canceled whatever appointments I had and kept him in my office and helped to talk him through it. I guess he just didn't have anyone else to turn to. He has remained very paternal toward me, being the second person to offer to take care of my-less-than-loving husband, Bobby Bloosom, just as the Hells Angels had.

One day I received a call that an acquaintance of mine, who was an agent, had died suddenly. He was married to a woman that was also an agent, and he had lived a double life as a homosexual. I knew that he kept his private life hidden from his wife, and in a small safe behind his desk, he kept male pornography. I asked Burt to accompany me to his office, and Burt "opened" the safe, and we were able to remove the contents before his wife was able to discover it. They had a child, and I felt it was something neither of them needed to find out. When Burt was able to "crack" that safe, I was more than convinced that he, indeed, had lived an interesting life prior to becoming an actor. Several years later, Burt was nominated as Best Supporting Actor for his role as the brother-in-law, Paulie, in *Rocky*.

The Gang That Couldn't Shoot Straight opened in December 1971, and the critics were of one voice in their praise for Robert De Niro. He practically stole the film. This was the start of his cornering the market on character alienation. His preparation was serious, his roles were brilliantly conceived, and his stardom was earned. I will always be proud of that casting too.

Peter Bogdanovich presented me with an uncomfortable problem when he asked me a favor while casting *The Last Picture Show*. Peter asked me to track down a gorgeous young model named Cybill Shepherd, whom he'd seen on several magazine covers.

I found her and scheduled a meeting, before which Peter reminded me that I would have to see her naked. She would be doing a very brief nude scene in the film, and he wanted to make sure she had no stretch marks, on a twenty-year-old no less! I could see my reputation headed straight for the toilet if I asked or even allowed a young woman to completely disrobe at an audition.

So instead I called Cybill's agent to discuss the problem, and we arrived at the compromise that I would see Cybill in a very small bikini instead. I still remember how mortified and awkward I felt escorting this young girl into the ladies' room for her to change from her street clothes into a tiny bathing suit.

I cast Cloris Leachman in *The Last Picture Show* as well as Eileen Brennan and Ellen Burstyn, none of whom, thank God, I had to ask to appear naked. Ellen was nominated for an Academy Award for Best Supporting Actress, along with Cloris who won. Her character, Ruth Popper, the coach's wife, in her loneliness, reaches out to one of her husband's young athletes in an ill-fated affair.

While I have enjoyed a good relationship with nearly all the directors with whom I've been fortunate enough to work, I must say that I probably most enjoyed my film experiences with George Roy Hill. George was a fantastic director who, while he received accolades along his career path, probably will not be regarded in history as one of Hollywood's foremost directors because of one facet of his person.

Most widely admired movie directors are inclined to be recognized for a particular genre or type of film: John Ford for westerns, Preston Sturges for screwball comedies, George Cukor for "women's" pictures, David Lean for historical epics, Cecil B. DeMille for epic epics, and the like.

George, simply put, refused to confine himself to one type of filmmaking. That is not to say other directors haven't ventured off the path of their greatest claim to fame occasionally, but I think George made a conscious decision to only pursue film projects that were terribly interesting to him, not giving any thought to trying to duplicate his previous successes by restricting himself to other film projects of a similar genre.

George was a much-loved man who had wit and humor and was also quite handsome, I thought, with a complete understanding of what made a good story that helped him sail over the rough spots that invariably arose in the making of a film. He loved actors, and it was reciprocal.

None of George's films were alike; he handled epics, musicals, westerns, dramas, comedies, and romance all with equal aplomb. But in all of George's films, as there was in the man himself, there was humanity and humor. I had the pleasure of working on most of George Roy Hill's films. Whenever George would call and ask me if I could help cast his next picture, I would do whatever I had to do to rearrange my schedule.

On a few separate occasions, I was asked to sit down with George and do a series of taped interviews, once with Loring Mandel for a tribute being organized for George at the Metropolitan Museum of Art and later with George's memoirist. I was hesitant at first, as I explained to them that someday I planned to write my own memoirs and wasn't sure that I wanted to share my own personal stories. We made a compromise that whatever was discussed during these sessions could be used by either of us, and George provided me with a transcribed copy of all our taped sessions. Throughout the following in regard to the films that we worked on together, I've done my best to separate George's comments in italics and intersperse them with my own so as to better understand his filmmaking process and our working relationship.

Slaughterhouse-Five was based on the popular novel written by Kurt Vonnegut. The screenplay was written by Stephen Geller and was a riveting story about Billy Pilgrim, a seemingly ordinary man who found himself bouncing around all the stages in his life, never knowing from one moment to the next whether he'd be the family man at home with his wife and children, stuck in the middle of World War II where he is captured by the Germans, or off on the distant planet of Tralfamadore with the movie blonde bombshell, Montana Wildhack. He continually lived his life in either the past, present, or future.

We almost didn't do the film, as we could not seem to find the right actor to play Billy Pilgrim. We searched in both New York and California and even went to England looking for the right actor. Having considered just about everybody that one could think of for this part, including big name actors, we realized it just did not work. At one point, George said to me, "Well, you gotta find somebody. I don't care if you go out on the street and pick someone."

Once back in my brownstone, I looked through a big pile of photographs and resumes that were stacked on my roll top desk. These were all people that I had not yet had a chance to meet. There was one photo that I had kept because I thought it looked so funny. It was this Caucasian kid with a type of afro hairdo with great big pink ears that stuck out and such a silly face with the roses in his cheeks that were very prominent. I don't know why I called him, but I did.

His name was Michael Sacks, and just out of Harvard, he had done nothing except one week of stock theater up in New England. I asked him to read for me, and every so often, the hair on the nape of my neck rose up as he read scenes with me. I suddenly realized what it was that made him so right. He was a totally naive kid, and so was Billy Pilgrim. Although the novel and film took Billy from age fifteen all the way into his eighties, he retained this type of naiveté throughout.

> GRH: Billy is not an ordinary hero. In fact, there is very little about him that is heroic at all. He is a young chap who should not have been in the Army. He was shaped like a Coca-Cola bottle and was the son of a Unitarian minister. The character was one of a reactor; he didn't drive any scenes, and it was a tough part because he wasn't ever the hero of the scene or the victim of the scene. He just wandered through as kind of an everyman without anything particular to recommend him

or to build on in terms of character. Billy just floated from stage to stage. He had a kind of sweet, goofy, sad-sack quality. Unlike most of the modern film heroes that are gangsters or outlaws, Billy Pilgrim had a very gentle soul.

The trouble with reading well-known actors was their personalities were so strong they automatically ruined the part. They weren't right for it. There is a line in the movie that refers to Billy, "You could carve a better man out of a banana." That was Billy, and it's pretty hard to play a banana!

I then called George and told him that I may have found our Billy. He asked me what he'd done.

"Nothing," I said.

"Are you out of your mind?" George replied.

"No, I'm just doing what you told me to do. Remember, you said to just go out and get you someone. Well, I did, and I think you should meet and read him."

Incidentally, I would not have dared suggest someone with little or no experience if I didn't know George's skill in directing. I had seen him work with nonactors before and knew what magic he could use on them. I felt Michael had both the right look and good instincts as an actor. He was surprisingly raw, and it was hard to keep him from acting.

Paul Monash had bought the rights to the novel and was the producer. So as a courtesy to him, we let him see some of the actors that we read for Billy. Paul had told us before that Billy Pilgrim must not be played by a Jewish actor, insisting that he had to be a Christian kid. George and I said we understood. When Michael came in, it was a rainy night in the middle of winter. I obviously had to tell Michael my predicament of him being Jewish, so I told him to bring a sailor's cap, and when he arrived, I sent him upstairs to wet down his frizzy hair in the bathroom and put the sailor's cap on.

I always had a typed list of people reading for those who would be listening so they could jot down comments as each person read. On this list, where I arranged to have Michael read last (another trick I've used before), I gave Michael a new Nordic last name, Anderson. We had the readings, and Michael read well and left the office.

George then turned to Paul and asked, "Well, what do you think?"

"Oh my god, he's Billy Pilgrim," Paul replied enthusiastically.

"You don't think he looks Jewish, do you?" George pressed.

Paul, who happens to be Jewish, said, "No, I can smell a Jew a mile away."

George and I finally did tell Paul that Michael was Jewish; and Paul, to his credit, was a good sport about it, and so we had found our perfect Billy Pilgrim. By the time George finished with rehearsals, Michael began to acquire a considerable acting technique.

Slaughterhouse-Five was Henry (Bummy) Bumstead's first film as an art director with George. There were several art directors to choose from on the Universal lot, and George decided to meet with Bummy. Bummy had won the Academy Award for his art direction on the film *To Kill a Mockingbird*. He'd also worked with Billy Wilder, Michael Curtiz, and Robert Mulligan and had made several films with Alfred Hitchcock. When George first met Bummy, he thought he was too amenable and too agreeable; however, he had outstanding credits and was available, so George hired him as the production designer on *Slaughterhouse-Five*. Bummy was a darling, great big man with a big, round, sweet face.

George and Bummy started to scout locations for a site to recreate the bombing of Dresden in both Yugoslavia and Hungary and finally made it to Czechoslovakia and discovered the small village of Most, a place that the government planned to tear down because of the richness of the coal that was underneath. Bummy produced many preliminary drawings, and they decided that Most and Prague would be ideal as the primary locations. Now what they had to do was to convince the Communist government. They met with officials for two solid days and discussed what sets would have to be built as well as the amount of extras needed to shoot the scenes. Several days later, the officials gave an estimate of what it would cost to shoot there. It was amazingly inexpensive. The money saved in that area enabled the film to produce those beautiful shots of Most and Prague. Bummy claimed we could not have possibly built the sets in the United States as it would have been much too expensive.

All the wartime sequences were shot in Czechoslovakia, and they spent nearly three months carefully working out details before principal photography began. Since the country was dominated by Russians, all phases had to be negotiated; and surprisingly enough, there was no attempt to censor the script. Shooting began in Prague, Czechoslovakia, on January 31, 1971.

The supporting cast for *Slaughterhouse-Five* included many actors who I'd worked with in the past as well as a few that made their film debut: Eugene Roche, Ron Leibman, Sharon Gans, Valerie Perrine, Holly Near, Perry King, Kevin Conway, Sorrell Booke, and John Dehner. I can't take credit for Valerie Perrine for an agent in Hollywood suggested that George see a Las Vegas showgirl he represented. She was just right for Montana Wildhack, and I later cast her as Honey Bruce in *Lenny*, opposite Dustin Hoffman. Besides the principal actors, the rest of the cast and crew were local, including all the boys who played the American POWs.

There is a character in *Slaughterhouse-Five* that appeared in some of Kurt Vonnegut's other books named Eliot Rosewater. Vonnegut's fifth novel was titled *God Bless You, Mr. Rosewater*. George wanted

Kurt himself to play the part, and Kurt agreed; however, when George saw the dailies, there was an obvious makeup problem. And when they needed to reshoot, Kurt wasn't available. There was only one guy I knew at the moment that would be right for the part, and I told George that the only person I knew who is this great big bumbling guy who is so dear and could play this part was Bummy.

With George's blessing, I told Bummy I had a part for him in the film.

"Oh no, I couldn't do that," he responded in typical Bummy fashion.

Eliot Rosewater's scene in *Slaughterhouse-Five* was in a hospital bed beside Billy Pilgrim during a visit from Billy's mother. He had a few lines, and it was his first and only acting part. From then on, every Christmas, I received a card from Bummy that was signed, "Eliot Rosewater."

Several scenes were set in Dresden, Germany. During World War II, there were only old men and boys left in the city; the rest were all army. There was this marvelous man who came in to read by the name of Friedrich Ledebur. He was a count who had played Queequeg in John Huston's film version of *Moby Dick*. I also found a beautiful sixteen-year-old boy in Munich named Ekkehardt (Nicky) Belle, who played the physically demanding role of a young German soldier. Nicky had to run at top speed through the burning rubble, taking several falls at full speed; and he really banged himself up, but he kept charging on. He also was required to run into a burning building for several takes and got himself pretty scorched in the process. George really admired Nicky a lot for his efforts and thought he had a lot of guts.

Sharon Gans played Billy Pilgrim's wife, Valencia. In one scene, she was given a new white Cadillac for her birthday. It was a flashy car; and later in the film, she takes it out for a wild ride rushing to the hospital in a panic, thinking that Billy is dying. It was the funniest scene in the film, despite the fact that her character ends up being killed upon crashing into the hospital and dying of carbon monoxide asphyxiation. George used the white Cadillac as the ultimate symbol of American middle class and accentuated its destruction by having it rammed by a German Mercedes Benz in the high-speed ride to the hospital. Terry Loften, one of Hollywood's best stunt drivers, did all the driving for this scene, appropriately dressed up as Valencia Pilgrim, of course.

There was a terribly sad scene in the film where this sweet guy, an American soldier, Edgar Derby, played by Eugene Roche, picked up a piece of Dresden statuary in the ruins of Dresden after the American bombing, an exact replica of one his wife had owned that had been broken by their son back home in the States. He was then shot by German soldiers for looting.

Ron Leibman played Billy Pilgrim's nemesis throughout the film, a disgruntled, nasty soldier with a huge chip on his shoulder. At the very end of the film, he shoots Billy Pilgrim.

> GRH: One of the reasons I selected Czechoslovakia was that Prague is a beautiful Baroque city very much like Dresden was before the bombing. I designed one entire sequence, the arrival of the guards and POW's as they marched through Dresden, to a Bach keyboard concerto. Glenn Gould scored the film and I wanted the music to personalize the city so that we'd have an emotional response to it and the bombing wouldn't be just another statistic.
>
> The major production sequence in the movie was the re-creation of the day Dresden was bombed. Dresden's normal population of 500,000 had swollen to over one million by an enormous influx of refugees, and we had to find a location where we could show the hungry and displaced people pouring

into town on that particular day. I needed to shoot the entire sequence in one day and most everyone thought I was nuts. I wanted to set-up the shots in the morning, break for lunch, and then shoot in the afternoon. We broke up the assignments and Bummy went in one direction, his Czech assistant went another, and Ray Gosnell, the assistant director, went yet another. They went over everything and we got all the shots that afternoon. Everybody pitched in.

The tactics of firebombing are pretty frightening. The first wave would drop cluster bombs to tear the roofs off the houses and then they would drop incendiaries to set the interiors on fire. Once these fires got started they would suddenly link into one tremendous inferno that would build up winds of hurricane velocity sucking anything moveable from miles around into the center where the temperature would range from 600 to 1000 degrees Celsius. The only possible safe refuge was deep shelters and even in many of these, the occupants suffocated.

We used some footage from the actual bombing of Dresden on the night of February 13, 1945. The footage was shot by the British when Lancaster bombers dropped a preliminary linking of bombs to produce multiple fires that eventually became an entire city in flames.

Another major production sequence was to construct the ruins of Dresden after the firebombing. Our idea was that since they were to tear down the town of Most to get at the coal on which it was built, they would first tear it down to our specifications for shooting before they leveled it off completely. Bummy had sketched it out well, but unfortunately in their enthusiasm they tore down more than we wanted them to so we had to reconstruct some of it. It was so cold outside when they were rebuilding the sets that the paint would freeze on the brushes and I'll never forget Bummy running back and forth giving the guys booze as they worked to get it done. He made many new friends that day.

Slaughterhouse-Five was George's second film to go to the Cannes Film Festival, nominated for the Golden Palm and winning the Jury Prize. Perhaps the most remarkable thing about *Slaughterhouse-Five* for me, personally, was that George gave me a single card credit in the main titles directly below the actors. This was a total surprise for me. That was the beginning of my credit being in such a good position, and not only for me but also for practically every other casting director, who, once word got out, demanded the same. George did this without my asking for it, which is only one of the many reasons he was a man so easy to love.

Producer Robert Weitman hired me to cast a very limited number of roles for the film *Shamus*, directed by Buzz Kulik and starring Burt Reynolds and Dyan Cannon. Producers are always looking out for ways to save a buck, and there are good ways to accomplish this, and then there are bad ways.

When I joined the production, they had a lot of actors on hold for cameo parts. None of them were particularly impressive; and in total, there was a lot of money tied up. I informed Buzz and Robert Weitman that I could cast better actors than those on hold and also save the production much money, which I did—a whole lot of money, in fact.

Burt Reynolds played a detective named Shamus McCoy who lived in a second-floor loft apartment somewhere in the Bronx. The set furniture consisted of this huge pool table in the middle of the living room that was also his bed. A somewhat ratty kitchen was off to one side.

Usually, I never had time to go to the sets, but for some reason, I went out to this Bronx location one day. Buzz was introducing me to people whom I'd never met before like Dyan Cannon. She was rather cool to me, I thought. After meeting several other people on the set, Buzz said, "Do you know Burt Reynolds?"

I had cast Burt when I was doing *Naked City*. Burt came over and said, "Do I know Marion Dougherty?"

He grabbed me and bent me over backward in a Valentino-like swooping kiss. Just before he kissed me, with my head turned back because I was almost upside-down, I looked at the part of the set that I was facing, which was the kitchen; and through a window jumped a big orange cat.

"Oh my god, it's Morris!" I said, upon which Burt promptly dropped me to the floor.

Disgruntled, he said, "I've never been upstaged by a cat."

But this was not just any cat! This was Morris the cat, the real Morris, and he was incredible. I watched that take of him coming through the window four different times. He would jump through the window and move to exactly the right spot on the counter during each take. No offense, Burt, but he was quite an animal.

The *Shamus* cast included John P. Ryan, Joe Santos, Beeson Carroll, Kevin Conway, and John Glover. The well-known opera singer, Giorgio Tozzi, was also in the cast. I still have a lovely painting of a Hudson River scene that he gave to me.

After filming was over, on the advice of Buzz Kulik, who was aware of the significant financial contribution of my recasting those cameos with New York actors had saved the production, I wrote a letter to Weitman with my figures of how much the production had saved. I suggested in the letter that since the savings was such a substantial amount, and since I ended up casting many more parts that I was originally contracted to, that perhaps Marion Dougherty Associates should be paid a little bit more than the $3,000 fee my company had been paid.

I'm still waiting for a response to that letter. Fucked again! I guess Weitman's foible was being unfair.

Years later, I was flying on the same plane as Dyan Cannon and found out that my initial judgment of her may not have been accurate. I was slightly disabled with a knee damaged badly in a Sixth Avenue pothole and was forced to use crutches to get around. When we landed in Los Angeles, I was preparing to make my way to the exit door with many other passengers attempting to get around me in a hurry to get out. Bless her heart, Dyan would have none of it, and she literally halted the pedestrian traffic around me and made everyone wait until I had exited the plane before she allowed the rest of the passengers to disembark.

John Houseman had been around a long while before he made a breakthrough debut as a movie actor at the age of seventy-one in *The Paper Chase* as Professor Charles Kingsfield. Houseman founded the Mercury Theater along with Orson Welles. He also taught acting at Julliard School of Fine Arts, and while it was not the first time he had appeared on the movie screen (an uncredited bit part in *Seven Days of May* was his first on-screen appearance), *The Paper Chase* changed his life drastically.

Director James Bridges had been a student of Houseman's many years earlier and was really responsible for remembering him. With a cast that included Timothy Bottoms, Lindsay Wagner, Graham Beckel, James Naughton, and Blair Brown, Houseman pretty much ran away with the film garnering glowing notices from film critics that pushed him toward his winning the Academy Award for Best Supporting Actor.

The first time a screening for the public was held, John came up to me afterward, and I told him how wonderful he was in the part.

"Oh, do you think you could use me in something else again? That was so much fun." He responded.

After *The Paper Chase*, John Houseman acted in several movies, proving himself as adept at comedy as he was in dramatic roles. He worked right up until the time of his death in 1988 and became a wealthy man acting in other films and also the television series based on *The Paper Chase*, for which he is so well remembered.

Another highly enjoyable George Roy Hill film, *The Sting*, came my way not long after *Slaughterhouse-Five*. George called me one morning at the brownstone and told me he was sending over a script that he wanted me to read right away. He said it was a very intriguing script and needed my opinion on something.

Paul Newman had been set to play the part of Henry Gondorff and was leaving that afternoon on a cruise ship to Europe. Paul wanted to know who George had in mind to play opposite him. George told me that he wanted Robert Redford, since they obviously knew each other, and had worked together on *Butch Cassidy and the Sundance Kid*. The problem was that Newman's character was written somewhat older than he'd previously been playing, and the other role of Johnny Hooker was a character of similar age. George wanted my opinion as soon as possible.

Dutifully, I set aside everything and sat down to read the script. I can remember being fascinated by it; I just raced through it. The screenplay was so well written, and when I got to about three of four pages from the end and was sitting on the couch in my office, I threw the script on the floor and yelped, "Oh shit!" I had reached the point in the story where both of the lead characters were shot. I thought to myself, "It's such a great script. Why did they have to ruin it by killing these two likeable characters?" Halfheartedly, I picked up the script and read through to the end and realized that like everyone else, I'd been had by Davis S. Ward's clever script. George got around the age discrepancy in the original script by agreeing with my suggestion of leaving Newman's character slightly older and functioning as a mentor or an older brother type to Redford's character. He then called Paul and told him that both he and I thought readjusting the two characters' age and relationship would work out fine and that was that. Paul agreed. George then called and asked David to rewrite the character of Johnny Hooker to be slightly younger than in his original script.

I am quite certain that George had been hoping to come up with a script for Newman and Redford since their wildly successful collaboration on *Butch Cassidy and the Sundance Kid* a few years earlier. So we had our two male leads and high hopes that their magical chemistry would still be intact.

When we got to Los Angeles and started seeing people for the supporting roles, word had already spread around that there was a woman's part, Billie, available in a film with Newman and Redford. Every agent in town besieged me with these Playboy playmate types.

Finally, one agent asked me if I remembered Eileen Brennan. Of course, I did. I had seen her in a play in New York quite a few years back, *Little Mary Sunshine*, for which she'd won the Theatre World Award that year, so I asked the agent to send her in.

George was with Universal at the time, and we were casting out of these bungalows they had for the different directors on the studio lot. George had a very lovely one with a big living room and smaller offices to the side. In his big office, he had a grand piano that he played beautifully, music being another one of his passions.

On the day that Eileen came in to see me in my little back office, she appeared in a long sequined black dress with a red piano shawl around her shoulders, and I just burst out laughing. As it turned out, she was eight and three quarter months pregnant at the time. She looked at me in that terrific deadpan expression that only Eileen has and told me she had dressed especially for me and hoped that I still had the sense of humor that she remembered me having.

We read about two pages of the script, and that was enough for me—she was great. I told her that George was seeing people the following day, and she was excited about meeting him. I told her, however, that there was only one stipulation for her reading with George, "You must come dressed in the same outfit you have on now."

"Marion, I couldn't do that. I knew that you were funny, but I can't come to see George Roy Hill dressed like this!" she protested.

"Then you don't get the appointment," I told her.

Eileen acquiesced and showed up the next day in the same dress. I did not say boo to George ahead of time. He was in his office playing his piano when I told him I thought I had found the actress for the part of Billie. He was playing away when in walked Eileen. George took one look at her and fell off the piano stool he was laughing so hard. The part was hers.

The Sting was a remarkable movie. I don't think that I called in more than one person for each part. It had to be one of the easiest films that I ever had to cast. It just fell together like magic, and the ESP between George and me worked beautifully.

When we were in New York casting the second most important woman's role, I called in an actress to play Loretta. Loretta was the waitress in the diner that Redford's Johnny Hooker frequented. He makes a pass at her, and they wind up in bed together at some sleazy joint. The character takes a surprise turn when it is revealed that Loretta was actually a hit woman for the villain who tries to kill Johnny Hooker after their one-night stand.

Now Dimitra Arliss is not a very sexy woman. She has a hawk face and can be mean-as-hell looking. When the studio people out in Hollywood saw her picture and knew that we were going to cast her, they told us we could not do that. "This is Robert Redford. Why would he go to bed with a hatchet-faced woman?" I countered their protests, explaining that this is not Robert Redford, this is a small-time con man named Johnny Hooker, and he's not going to find Sophia Loren behind the counter of a lousy blue plate diner.

I told George about the studio's concerns with casting Dimitra; and it didn't seem to bother him, although he would face concerns from another front as he explains:

> *GRH: When Eileen Brennan and Dimitra Arliss showed up for our first rehearsal, both Newman and Redford blanched. They were obviously expecting them to be more conventionally attractive. They came up to me and said, "Those aren't the women you're going to use for the parts are they?" I pulled them aside and answered, "Look, give me a week and if you're not enthusiastic about them at the end of the week, I'll change them." Of course, this was a shoo-in because the minute they started to act together, both Paul and Bob came up to me and said how wrong they had been and how great the women would be in their parts.*

Then there was the part of Doyle Lonnegan, who was the head mobster of an American crime organization and was the mark for the big con in the film. We had originally wanted Richard Boone (*Have Gun, Will Travel*) for the part because he had the right look. I got hold of him down in Florida on the telephone, and he was just so drunk there was no talking to him. I found out that he was really a mean son of a gun and drank an awful lot so we weren't sure what to do. Peter Boyle was also strongly considered for the part.

It was George's wife, Louisa Horton, who suggested Robert Shaw. The studio again told us the script calls for an Italian American in the Mafia; and once again, I had to give them a call. So Robert Shaw is English; we'll make him Irish. I had to say to George, "You know, just because you and I are Irish doesn't mean that an Irishman couldn't be the head of a crime syndicate in America. He doesn't have to be an Italian, and we know Shaw can do an Irish accent."

A few days before filming began, Robert Shaw was in a squash game and injured his knee. He called George and said he was sorry that he would not be able to do the picture. George found this unacceptable. If you've seen *The Sting*, the character of Doyle Lonnegan walks with a limp and a cane. It was very effective for the character and one of those things that could be seen as a wonderful choice by an actor; but in reality, because of the squash injury, the limp and cane only added to his masterly performance.

I had terrific fun assembling the supporting male cast. This was the first movie that Harold Gould made, and he became our Kid Twist. I remember George said to me, "I want Adolphe Menjou for the part of Kid Twist." And I sharply replied, "Oh, thanks a lot. He's been dead for fifteen years." But I knew exactly the quality he wanted and had seen Harold Gould in John Guare's play *House of Blue Leaves* in New York. He perfectly captured the Adolphe Menjou quality that George was looking for. It was Charles Durning's first big film as well. He became the determined police lieutenant, William Snyder.

There was another kid in the cast named Jack Kehoe whom I adored. I had cast Jack in *The Gang That Couldn't Shoot Straight* and *The Friends of Eddie Coyle*. Jack had a big scar on his nose, and I once asked him about it. He told me that he was drunk one night and was with a friend when he fell down and got his nose caught in a grating on the street and tore off the end of his nose. His friend got the piece of nose from the grating and took him to the emergency room where it was sewn back on. Jack played Joe Erie, and it was purely circumstantial that Jack's role required him to have his nose broken by Durning's ruthless policeman character.

Ray Walston was famous from his hit 1960s series, *My Favorite Martian*, during this time. I knew Ray from when we were young actors at the Cleveland Playhouse, so when I asked his agent to have Ray come in and read for George, they said he was too famous as Uncle Martin; and he would not read, but he would meet. I explained to them that the voice was invaluable because his character called the races in the horse racing con that Newman's and Redford's characters were attempting to achieve. I told them if they wouldn't let him read, I would personally call him since we were old friends. They held fast. I then called Ray, knowing that he would come in, and he gave a terrific performance as J. J. Singleton.

Dana Elcar, Jack Heffernan, Robert Earl Jones, Charlie Dierkop, Sally Kirkland, Arch Johnson, Brad Sullivan, Pauline Myers, Billy Benedict, and Tom Spratley (my tenant and security in the brownstone's basement) rounded out a first-rate supporting cast.

The Sting opened strongly on Christmas Day in 1973 and became a much talked about film and certainly delivered on that buzz by garnering ten Academy Award nominations. During the publicity junket, George gave an interview where he discussed my casting:

> GRH: *Marion Dougherty helped cast the rest of the picture once we got Newman and Redford set. When Marion reads a script, she takes notes and has an idea for two or three actors for each important role after a first reading. The director's job is to*

get a good shooting script in place and then cast it properly. After you've done that, the success or lack of success of the film is more or less decided. If somebody is miscast, it doesn't make any difference how clever you are with the camera or how spellbinding the actor or actress is, it's just not going to work. There are many aspects to casting and the search for an actor to play a character is always a frustrating one. That is where Marion is so gifted. When Eileen Brennan walked in the door, before she sat down, I cast her. You know when a person is really right. In this case, it was her gestures, the way she sat down, and the way she spoke. I didn't audition her; I didn't need to audition her. She was just right for the part. When I'm working with Marion, I'm constantly asking her to get me dead actors. I'll say, "Bring me Claude Rains, or bring me Walter Huston, or Bert Lahr." You can describe what kind of person you want by using other actors as role models. I've worked with Marion for a long time and we both had the same ideas in casting THE STING. Marion knows what I'm looking for and always finds someone to fill the bill.

I never thought I was egotistical, but I guess I am a tiny bit, for I really loved this interview when he gave me a copy of it to read.

The Sting became the Academy's Best Picture of 1973. George followed up his Director's Guild of America Award by winning his only Oscar as Best Director. *The Exorcist* was also nominated for Best Picture, and I was worried that it might win. Juliet Taylor and Nessa Hyams cast that film for our office, and it was a hard choice to know who to root for. Not really!

Bummy took home an Oscar for Art Direction along with Set Direction by James Payne. Edith Head won for Costume Design, William Reynolds for Editing, and David Ward for Original Screenplay.

Marvin Hamlish received an Oscar for Best Original Score, and to be honest, I'm not exactly sure how that worked out since the music from *The Sting* was pretty much all Scott Joplin rags. Marvin adapted all the tunes as per George's arrangement, but Joplin was the original composer.

George's oldest son had purchased a Scott Joplin album and was playing it at home when George had another brilliant idea for the film. He felt that these songs perfectly captured and enhanced the action and flavor of *The Sting*. Having previously worked with a young Marvin Hamlish on Broadway, he hired Marvin to come in and play the piano. George knew that the time element was a little off, with Joplin having composed at an earlier date than the film's action took place. One of the many side benefits of the success of the film was that there was an almost immediate and prolonged interest in Scott Joplin's nearly forgotten ragtime music.

I was back home in Bayshore, giving an Academy Awards party, when George won his Oscar. We were all sitting in the living room when George's name was announced. He had just started making his acceptance speech when the first mouse I'd ever seen in my home ran under a table. There were two friends sitting at the table who jumped up and screamed, and with all the commotion, I never heard what George said. I found out afterward that George said that he could not have lost because he had three ringers: Newman and Redford and Marion Dougherty.

My Parents - Virginia and Orr Clarence Dougherty.

My Sisters - Doris on my left and Virginia on my right.

"Willowick" our family home in Pennsylvania.

Me at Penn State University.

My early days of casting for KRAFT TELEVISION THEATRE.

Manu Tupou and Jocelyne LaGarde during the filming of HAWAII.

My MDA associates at Brownstone Central (L to R)
Wally Nicita, Juliet Taylor and Gretchen Rennell.

(L to R) - Paul Newman, George Roy Hill and
Robert Redford on the set of THE STING.

My Casting Associates - Gretchen Rennell, Wally Nicita
(center), and me at George's ranch in Malibu.

Clowning around with Paul Newman during the filming of
A LITTLE ROMANCE (L to R) Sally Kellerman, Joanne
Woodward, Jack DeMave, Thelonius Bernard, George
Roy Hill, me, Camille DeMave and Paul Newman.

(L to R) - Chris Crawford, Tanja Crawford, Robert Roussel, Robert Crawford, myself and George Roy Hill (lower right hand corner) having dinner and relaxing on the Fisher's Island location while filming THE WORLD ACCORDING TO GARP.

George Roy Hill as he's finishing the daily New York Times crossword puzzle on Fisher's Island.

George Roy Hill, Robert Roussel and Robin Williams on location while filming THE WORLD ACCORDING TO GARP. The "Magic Gloves" scene which they're shooting was shot directly in front of the coop apartment I purchased years later.

George Roy Hill's film production company PAN ARTS in Los Angeles (L to R) - Jack DeMave, Kaela Crawford, Camille DeMave, Matthew Crawford, Tanja Crawford, Bob Crawford, Robert Roussel, Judy Kelley, Chris Crawford, George and Pat Kelley.

One of the Studio's publicity photos.

My bedroom overlooking Central Park at
George's 920 Fifth Avenue apartment.

Having dinner with George, Paul Newman and
Joanne Woodward at the apartment.

Robert Roussel, me and Colin Irving (John Irving's
son) on the set of FUNNY FARM.

Opening night for A SALUTE TO GEORGE ROY HILL at the Metropolitan Museum of Art in New York with Glenn Close, Robert Redford and George (I'm seated in the lower right hand corner).

George and me on vacation in Puerto Vallarta, Mexico.

Celebrating George's 73rd birthday at the apartment (L to R)
Robert Roussel, Paul Newman, Valerie Perrine, George, Mary
Tyler Moore, me, William Goldman and Robert Levine.

My Great Escape

One of my old roommates from college, who was now living in New Jersey, came to visit me at the house one day in Bayshore and brought her darling little daughter with her. My husband, Bobby, also met her that day; and while I do not know any specifics of their relationship, nor do I want to, they did pursue one beyond that day in Bayshore.

I remember on Christmas Eve, Bobby was not home until very late, and I suspected where he had gone. I was there trimming the tree and doing everything in preparation for Christmas, which always used to be such a joyful time. I found out later that he had gone to visit my ex-roommate and delivered a lot of toys he'd bought for her little girl. I got more than a little suspicious after that and extremely pissed off. Years later, my ex-roommate did finally apologize to me.

Things worsened when Bobby and I were in the brownstone one night, having drinks, and he went upstairs to talk on the phone. I overheard something that made me know he was talking to "her." When we were driving home along the parkway, I said to him, "I know who you were talking to and that's on *my* telephone bill."

"I was not!" he said.

"Oh yes, you were," I insisted.

"No, no, you're absolutely wrong," he lied.

"Wait until my phone bill comes in, and then I'll know for sure," I baited him, which was not smart.

Bobby backhanded me until I saw stars and yelled, "I'm going to throw you out of this fucking car!"

My first thought was that I couldn't jump out of the car because he was driving too fast. When we came off the ramp, I had decided I was going to jump out of the car. He then threatened to hit me again, and I told him, "Bobby, don't be crazy. You'll go to jail for this!" That incident produced more than a few bruises. I was so ashamed having to show up at the brownstone in my sunglasses in the middle of winter and wear them all day long. I was too embarrassed to say anything to Juliet or Wally, but they knew what was going on.

I'd been secretly looking for a way to get out of my marriage since 1965, and not solely for reasons of physical abuse. It sounds amazingly trivial to me to say that the reason I knew I couldn't go on with the marriage was Bobby was not there for me in a very basic way I needed him to be. I knew that he would never be able to change. Now nearly ten years later, I seized my chance to leave my marriage. To be more accurate, it was my escape.

David Picker called me one day out of the blue and offered me a job. He was starting his own production company, Two Roads, and asked me to join him. I hadn't really known David that well, despite having met him briefly during the filming of *Hawaii* when he was an executive for United Artists. When I learned that I was to be the only other person in his production company besides office staff, I asked him, "Why did you select me?" He responded, "Because every movie I've seen that I really liked, I would look at the casting credits, and it was always your name."

In a recent interview, David commented, "Marion understood movies, and everybody wanted her. We had a good relationship, and she was a delight to work with and very smart. It was also a pleasant career move for me to enable her to go beyond. I trusted and could rely upon Marion. From day one, she was much more than making lists, she was a natural at what she did, and I loved and respected her for it. In fact, I felt privileged to be able to work alongside Marion." Bless his heart.

I accepted David's offer and eventually left Juliet Taylor solely in charge of MDA in New York. Gretchen Rennell was working with us during this time, and we were in the midst of casting *The Day of the Locust* for John Schlesinger.

Based on the novel by Nathanael West, Waldo Salt's screenplay was a penetrating look at Hollywood in the 1930s that examined both the movie business (those in it and those that wanted to be) as well as the times. There was an Aimee Semple McPherson type character called Big Sister, and I thought Geraldine Page would be right for the part so I invited her to come in and see John at the brownstone.

Geraldine Page was a brilliant actress and a delightful person who always seemed too occupied with her family or career to ever spend all that much time worrying about what kind of impression she made. She showed up at the brownstone with two of her children in tow, both of whom were eating and spilling ice cream all over the place. Geraldine's hair looked like a fountain at Versailles. Whatever one may have thought of her as a person or the image she projected, she was a consummate actor who vividly brought Big Sister to life and so richly deserved the Oscar she finally received for *The Trip to Bountiful.*

I was interested in Jack Warden, a terrific actor that I had used before, and by that time he was a big enough name so his agents refused to let him read for the part. They did, however, inform him that there was interest in him for the part; and Jack, professional and secure man that he is, agreed to come in and read. Jack understood why I needed him to read; and although he gave a great reading, he had a presence that was too strong for the character, and I reluctantly couldn't use him.

We cast Billy Barty in a featured supporting role as one of the little people. Gretchen Rennell helped us bring in some little people as her father was involved with Pan Am, and they used to hire them for certain repair work on the wings and engines. Jackie Earle Haley played Adore, a child star with his overbearing stage mother played by Gloria LeRoy. Jackie did the part extremely well, and it was not until *The Bad News Bears* and *Breaking Away* when true movie fans realized that Jackie was very much a young man.

The supporting cast included Donald Sutherland, Karen Black and Burgess Meredith along with William Atherton, Richard Dysart, Bo Hopkins, Lelia Goldoni, Jane Hoffman, Madge Kennedy, and Natalie Schafer. Dick Powell Jr. did a cameo for us playing his famous father. Burgess Meredith was nominated for an Oscar for Best Supporting Actor.

The first production that I became involved in at Two Roads with David Picker was *Juggernaut*, a thriller set aboard a cruise ship that starred Richard Harris and Omar Sharif. Mary Selway handled the casting of the movie in England, and I assisted David, who was the executive producer.

David had hired his own secretary as well as Virginia Raymond, a friend of mine since we'd worked together during the *KRAFT* television days. Virginia became my assistant, and we also had an office boy who David hired because he knew the young man's family. David was convinced the young man was either going to become a major executive or land in jail. Jeffrey Katzenberg, presently one of the studio heads at DreamWorks, was that office boy who would bring us coffee in the morning.

Jeffrey was already an up-and-comer looking toward his future. One day, when I was not there, he asked Virginia for copies of my files of actors and my resource materials. He knew I had some up-and-coming young actors and also wanted to know from Virginia who my favorites were. It was not "please" or "ask Marion if this would be all right?" I did not hear about the favor asked of Virginia until a long time afterward, and that is another reason Virginia and I are still friends to this day. I must say Mr. Katzenberg is doing very well without my list of actors, having not long since sued Disney for $500 million and won.

Lenny, directed by Bob Fosse, was the first production I cast while working with David's company. The film was a biographical look at the troubled life and career of the outrageously talented comedian, Lenny Bruce. The role of Lenny was first offered to Neil Diamond, and he turned it down. Al Pacino was then considered; however, the part eventually went to Dustin Hoffman. It had been a successful play before it made its transition to screen, and Cliff Gorman had won the Tony for his portrayal of Lenny Bruce on Broadway; however, the producers felt he wasn't as bankable of an actor as Dustin. David Picker was the executive producer, while I handled casting most of the principal and supporting roles. Beverly McDermott was in charge of casting some Florida locals for the smaller parts.

My first introduction to Bob Fosse was in California at the Beverly Hills Hotel. We had a meeting in his room, and he ordered us sandwiches for lunch. During lunch, he told me that he wanted Joey Heatherton to play Honey, the woman Lenny Bruce marries.

I said, "Joey Heatherton, with that squeaky little voice? She can't act!"

Fosse did not pursue the matter, and we talked about some of the other parts. I then went back to report to David.

"Well, how'd it go?" asked David.

"Do you know who he wanted for the part of Honey? Joey Heatherton!" I replied indignantly.

"Marion, he's living with her and having an affair with her right now," David quietly informed me.

Oops, that's me and my big Irish mouth.

At one point, they offered the part to Raquel Welch, but she turned it down because she thought she couldn't play it. I ended up casting Valerie Perrine who was exceptional in the part, just perfect. I think it was the best work she's ever done except for *Slaughterhouse-Five*. Valerie is one of those beautiful actors who, when given the chance to play a role with some dimension, can deliver a stunning performance. She handles comedy extremely well as she did with her supporting roles in *The Electric Horseman* and *Superman*, but she also has the talent to play more dramatic roles, as she did as Honey Bruce in *Lenny*. Valerie can be very fun too. When we were shooting down in Florida on Valentine's Day, to mark the holiday, Valerie had her pubic hair shaved into the shape of a heart and marched up to Bob Fosse and David Picker and flashed them a happy Valentine.

Jan Miner, who had achieved overnight fame as Madge, the TV spokeswoman for Palmolive dishwashing liquid ("you know you're soaking in it"), was so highly identified with that commercial that it nearly obliterated the fact that she was a talented New York stage actress. Jan gave a fine performance as Sally Marr, Lenny Bruce's mother. I had seen Jan's stage work and had cast her in *Naked City*.

Dustin Hoffman and Valerie Perrine both received critical praise for their roles. *Lenny* went to the Cannes Film Festival, where Valerie received the Best Actress Award. The film received six Academy Award nominations as well as multiple nominations from both the Golden Globes and BAFTA.

In 1975, I flew out to Santa Rosa in northern California to work on Michael Ritchie's film, *Smile*. This was the only time I received credit as an executive producer on a movie, which I shared with David Picker.

The story was about a Junior League beauty pageant for a group of young pre-teenage girls. *Smile* did not go anywhere, despite being a very funny picture. I always felt one of the reasons for its failure was the poster they had for it. The powers that be just didn't know how to market the picture.

Bruce Dern and Barbara Feldon were set to play the leading roles. Barbara was rather well-known as Agent 99 on the television series *Get Smart*, and I was always curious as to why she didn't make more films because she's a very talented and funny lady. Bruce Dern introduced me to his little daughter, Laura; and little did I suspect that she'd become the fine actor she is today.

We took about five or six girls from Hollywood and cast the rest of the girls up in Santa Rosa. There was a Veterans' Hall, which was more like a huge barn where we shot most of the picture. I brought George Roy Hill's daughter, Owens (we called her Ween then), with me. She was about the age we were looking for to play a Young American Miss; and at the time, she was very unhappy and depressed. I suggested to George that I take her up to Santa Rosa to be one of the contestants. The production company had given me a house, and she stayed there with me. I learned that when she flew up from Los Angeles with the other girls, they were all snobby to her, asking what movies she had done; and of course, she hadn't done anything. She never bothered to tell them who her father was. So instead, Ween made friends with all the local girls we cast who were real people and didn't care what her film credits were. When the other girls from Hollywood found out that George Roy Hill was her father, they changed their attitudes, but Ween would have nothing to do with any of them.

Colleen Camp, Annette O'Toole, and Joan Prather were among the girls in the cast. I used Denise Nickerson from *Willy Wonka and the Chocolate Factory* in this movie too. We cast Melanie Griffith to play the part of Karen Love; and Melanie's mother, Tippi Hedren, was there much too frequently. We'd hired a strict woman, who was our official chaperon, whose job it was to check the girls in and out and made sure they were behaving themselves. At six o'clock, when we wrapped each evening, Melanie would run out to where Don Johnson would be waiting for her. Melanie's meetings with Don would result in a big screaming match in the hotel hallway between Melanie and Tippi. I assume Melanie won the battle since she was married to Don twice.

Patricia Mock was hired as the casting director and received credit on *Smile*, but I admit I stuck my nose in and did a lot of the casting. For instance, she was not supportive of casting Barbara Feldon, and she also didn't see what I saw in giving Geoffrey Lewis his earliest comedic role. Geoffrey Lewis was always playing steely-eyed bad guys in the films I'd seen him in before. He came in to see me one day and was so darn funny that I asked him if he'd ever done comedy. He told me that he hadn't, that nobody would ever let him do it. I changed that and Geoffrey, as Wilson Shears, has a very funny speech in the auditorium lecturing girls, where, to his embarrassment, he has to warn them not to throw Tampax down the toilets and plug up the plumbing.

One of my casting coups was the part of the choreographer, Tommy French. I felt that we should get a real choreographer for the part, and Michael Kidd from New York came to mind. I thought he would be a toney, arty guy and was surprised and delighted when, after I got his telephone number and called him, he had an exquisite New York accent. Michael had acted only once before in *It's Always Fair Weather*, a musical comedy with Gene Kelly and Dan Dailey, but he came in and read and was just heaven. He consented to do the role; and considering Michael had choreographed some of the great movie musicals, including *Seven Brides for Seven Brothers*, *The Band Wagon*, *Guys and Dolls*, *Li'l Abner*, and *Hello Dolly!*, it was an enormous contribution to *Smile* that he volunteered to choreograph some of the girls' routines. He worked his ass off teaching the kids their dance numbers. They had some lovely little routines. Michael was a real mensch and did a great job for something he was never hired nor paid to do.

Colleen Camp attempted to instigate a rebellion among the other girls. Unfortunately, she wasn't aware at the time that her creating problems on the set would affect her future in a highly lucrative film series that I was responsible for casting some years later. Colleen told all the girls that we weren't allowed to have any nudity in this picture. At the time of their being hired, I had all the young girls sign a paper acknowledging that there were scenes of undressing since one scene in the script involved the girls in the basement of the auditorium changing clothes as two little boys were peeking through the window. All anyone saw were their backs as they removed their bras. Somehow I got the matter settled. Now that I look back on it, I spent way too much time being a house mother rather than an executive producer.

David Picker granted me permission to cast *The Great Waldo Pepper*, directed by George Roy Hill and starring Robert Redford. The film was only minimally successful; and I always felt that the primary reason was that Susan Sarandon's character, Mary Beth, fell off the wing of a plane and was killed about halfway through the story, and that was a huge mistake. I always believed they should've changed that in the screenplay. George recalls his reason for making the movie and agreed with my assessment:

> GRH: I wanted to make a movie as a tribute to the early aviators. The story of barnstorming in the wake of WWII is not so much about any one character as about the many who chased the sun from town to town in open cockpit biplanes, thrilling people in rural areas who had never seen a flying machine. I asked Bill Goldman to write an outline and we began to work on the screenplay. I didn't take any writing credit on any of my

*pictures except THE GREAT WALDO PEPPER which was
my original story idea and I took a story credit. The script was
good and full of fun and games and lots of laughs about the old
barnstorming days. About two-thirds through the script the story
got dark and it was no longer funny.*

The film revolved around Waldo Pepper, a fictional barnstorming pilot of the 1920s, and included fantastic aerial stunts. George was an avid flyer and had his own little plane, an antique two-seat Waco.

I certainly remember the Waco, for one day he took me out to the airport where he kept it and invited me for a ride. He sat in the rear seat of this beautiful little thing, and I sat in the front seat. I felt like Amelia Earhart. Someone gave me a scarf to throw around my neck, and we took off. This type of plane had one propeller and two seats in an open cockpit. George and I were strapped in, and there was no canopy over us.

As soon as we were up in the air, George started doing tricks—dives, loop-the-loops, all sorts of stunts—I guess to try to impress me. When we landed, I asked, "George, how did you know that I wouldn't freak out or upchuck all over you?"

"You did an old sailor's trick. I could see you following the horizon, and as we turned, your head turned, keeping the horizon in view," he replied smiling.

That was true. As with sailing, if you start to get seasick, watch the horizon, and your equilibrium remains okay. The horizon is the only thing that remains steady.

I hired a lovely young woman named Shari Rhodes to help me cast some of the smaller parts with local people where we were shooting in Texas. Shari finally moved to Hollywood and became a successful casting director and was also an executive producer on *The Man on the Moon*, which introduced Reese Witherspoon to audiences.

The supporting cast included Bo Brundin, Geoffrey Lewis, Edward Herrmann, Kelly Jean Peters, Margot Kidder, and Paul Newman's son, Scott Newman, a very handsome young man who died tragically and much too young only a few years later.

I made a huge mistake in casting Bo Svenson who played Alex Olsson, a rival pilot. He was a total shit on this film. He went around bragging about how he was a great flyer, concocting this whole story. He also told the other actors working on the movie who had to fly that they shouldn't do it, that they should get extra pay for it. I thought he was a friend, but he turned into a terrible troublemaker. George also shared my opinion of Svenson. He was a real pain in the ass and a liar. He told us he'd flown for the navy; and our stunt pilot, Frank Tallman, took him up for a ride in his plane and came down and announced, "He's never flown for the navy." Svenson had been doing secondary roles in secondary pictures, and when he got this role, he suddenly turned star conscious. He would do things like sit in the cockpit and toss his gloves out and say, "I don't like these gloves." He behaved abominably, and George actually fired him during the last week of production.

The air work in *The Great Waldo Pepper* is probably as good as any air work of its kind that's ever been done. It has been compared to *Wings* and *Hell's Angels*, which were, up to that point, the top air work films. *The Great Waldo Pepper* comes pretty close to those films and added a tremendous amount of production to the film. George reflects on some of this part of the film process:

> GRH: One of the most dangerous stunts in the film was when Redford makes a plane-to-plane transfer in midair to rescue Mary Beth (played by Susan Sarandon). Redford actually

climbed out of the cockpit three thousand feet in the air. When I went out on the wing during a test, I wore a parachute. Bob did not wear a parachute. But then he was fastened by a wire that gave him some sense of security. All the wire meant to me was that if he fell off, he would be cut in half by the wire that was around his waist before he hit the ground. It's a scary proposition because in old airplanes you have a lot of very unsafe, violent movement within a short area. You're flying a turkey and you've got to hold on with some tenacity when you get out there. He was very brave and never refused to perform. I would not have gotten out and walked on that wing. For some of the other hazardous stunts and crashes, Frank Tallman doubled as Redford.

The actual plane-to-plane transfer was a highly dangerous stunt and there were no volunteers to be had from the regular Hollywood stuntmen. The stunt involved standing on the top wing of a Curtiss Jenny, feet braced on the cabane wires and climbing in mid-air onto the lower wing of a J-1 Standard being flown alongside. Frank said he knew of a chap named Wiggins who worked as a special engineer at Lockheed that had done some wing walking and he'd look him up. What Frank didn't tell me was that this "chap" was sixty-five years old, so when Ralph Wiggins appeared one day at the office with Frank announcing he would do the transfer, I thought they were putting me on.

Ralph not only wing walked for me, but he insisted on doing it without a parachute that he said would only unbalance him. For the actual stunt I insisted that he wear a specially designed parachute one-inch thick that contoured to his body and, over which he put coveralls. Ralph scoffed at the notion. He claimed if he fell he'd never have the time to get out of his coveralls and activate the chute and he wore it only to humor me. When we shot the stunt, I was flying the camera plane and was in a very nervous state. If you hit a thermo or something like that and the wings starts going down, the whole airplane can go.

Frank Tallman was of that old breed of barnstormers too, but without the recklessness that characterized many of them. His most dangerous stunt in the film was flying below roof level down the main street of Elgin, Texas in a J-1 Standard with about a five-foot clearance off each wing tip.

We discussed that stunt before the picture ever started. In the barnstorming days, the pilots would fly down and buzz the towns to get the folks in the town to come out to the local pasture where they could get five dollars a ride. The airplanes were quite unusual in those days. We wanted to reproduce that and wanted to go a little bit farther than just buzzing the town at a normal level and go right down the Main Street of town.

We had to find a town where we could take all the electric wires and telephone poles and bury them underground. Bummy found a town that would actually let us do that. I began to appreciate just how difficult this stunt was. Frank, one day in a moment of temporary insanity, let me fly his rare J-1 Standard while he flew wing on me in a Stinson L-1. He flew close enough for me to see his grinding teeth as he realized he'd placed his beautiful plane in my hands. I discovered then what a remarkably uncoordinated old bird the J-1 Standard is. It responds with all the alacrity of a three-toed sloth and then Frank later in the filming came roaring down that Main Street with maybe five feet clearance from his wing tips to the edge of the obstructions of the buildings. If he went in and got blown by a breeze or a cross wind coming across some of the streets, there was nothing he could do about it. I knew how much skill and years of experience went into that stunt. There were more than a few corks popped that night.

In filming the crash into the fairgrounds, I had four cameras strategically placed where Frank was supposed to go and then placed a fifth camera down near the end just to cover it from another angle. As Frank came for the breakaway stands, he caught a gust of wind that he could not have anticipated. This didn't help matters much, it meant that he was traveling faster across the ground. If you watch carefully, Frank heads for the breakaway stands and he ducks down and sails through the first one, through the top of the second one and through the top of the third one. Now by that time he has sailed by all the cameras and has not touched ground yet. The breakaway is made out of balsa and is scored so that it will look good but not be dangerous in the crash. Because of this gust of tail wind, he was not past the breakaway and was heading for a real honest to God plank and a 6x6 plank stand. When he hit, he really creamed himself and the airplane. It was a spectacular crash.

I was terrified that I had not gotten the shot because of where the cameras were positioned. I was, of course, worried about Frank, but I was also concerned about my picture. I went down the line and asked each camera operator if they got the crash and each answered, "No, no, no, no." I finally got to Chuck Short, who was our chief operator, and Chuck said, "Don't worry, I got it beautifully." As it turned out, it was even a more spectacular crash than we could have planned.

I knew Frank was all right because there is an old tradition that stunt pilots do and you will always notice it if you look at any of the outtakes of old air pictures. If there is a crash, the pilot will let you know everything is okay by wiggling the tail of the airplane. After the crash, Frank gave me a little wiggle and that just meant, "I'm okay."

Frank talked about being a stunt pilot, but he was really a precision flyer. He never liked the words "stunt pilot" because what he did amounted to very careful precision work that he planned very carefully. That is how he survived, he was so careful in his planning. Frank was probably the greatest stunt pilot alive or the finest precision flyer for movies and that was a hell of a position to have. The only mishap that occurred during filming was when Frank had to fly under a wire and ended up slicing off some of his scalp flying too close.

A few years later, George remembers Frank's last flight.

GRH: On April 15, 1978, just two days short of his 59th birthday, Frank Tallman was scouting locations for the James Bond film MOONRAKER. There are no mountains between Los Angeles and Phoenix and Frank hated to fly with instruments when he didn't have to. He was a very free spirit. He could fly instruments obviously with the best of them, but sometimes the procedures annoyed him. The weather around Los Angeles was bad and he chose to fly VFS (Visual Flight Rules). Frank failed to clear a ridge in the Cleveland National Forest along the Santa Ana Mountains. His plane impacted at an altitude of 3,100 feet, about 400 feet below the crest. At the time of the crash, Frank Tallman had logged more than 21,200 hours of flying in all manner of aircraft, from hot air balloons to the most advanced, sophisticated jets. I guess there are still a few men like Frank Tallman around that are capable of producing great air work of the old days but they are getting scarcer. Frank had the same spirit of flying that Waldo Pepper had. I mean, he was flying for the adventure, for the fun of it and for the thrill and excitement of it. That is what THE GREAT WALDO PEPPER is all about.

After the movie opened, George was sued by Tony Bill who claimed the idea for the film was his. I offered to go to court with him to testify that George had talked to me way before the guy suing him claimed the idea. George also had shown me his scrapbook that he kept as a kid about various pilots and airplanes. I think Tony Bill just wanted to produce George's movies.

Producers are sometimes my least favorite to deal with. They may be the money men, but in large part, they can do more damage in getting a good film made by their demands or their meddling. In 1974's *The Great Gatsby*, all the elements were there for a first-class production. Jack Clayton directed a screenplay written by Francis Ford Coppola based on the popular novel by F. Scott Fitzgerald.

With Robert Redford as Gatsby, Mia Farrow and Bruce Dern as the Buchanans, along with strong support from Karen Black, Scott Wilson, Lois Chiles, Howard Da Silva, Ed Herrmann, and Tom Ewell, I wanted Sam Waterston for the crucial role of Nick Carraway, Gatsby's friend and confidant.

David Merrick was a highly successful producer of big Broadway productions and handled the producer reigns on *The Great Gatsby*. When word of my suggestion for Sam to play Nick Carraway reached Merrick's ear, I got an almost immediate response that Sam was not the right "class" for the picture. Merrick apparently wanted only high-class people to be in the cast playing high-society roles.

Rankled by another inane command from a producer, I begged to differ with him. I had it in the back of my mind that Sam Waterston's lineage was quite grand. When I contacted Sam, I had it confirmed that he was from an old New York family right up there in prestige with the

Cabots. He had attended a private boarding school, had gone to Yale, and spent a year studying at the Sorbonne.

I also had to check out Bruce Dern's background, and while not as stellar as Sam's, Merrick eventually accepted the "class" credentials of both actors.

Merrick's demands also got to others during production. Director Jack Clayton got into a row with Merrick that resulted in his hurling a chair at the opinionated producer.

The Great Gatsby did well in its release and won several awards for the technical aspects of the production—Costume Design, Art Direction, Cinematography, etc.—from both the American and British film academies. The only acting award recognition came in the Golden Globes where Bruce Dern, Sam Waterston, and Karen Black received nominations with Karen Black winning Best Supporting Actress.

Slap Shot is an outrageous comedy that follows the struggling Charlestown Chiefs, a minor league hockey team as they try to attract an audience for their games when they discover the team is about to be disbanded. The screenplay was written by Nancy Dowd, whose brother Ned was a hockey player and appeared in the movie as Ogilthorpe.

After reading the script, Pat Kelley came into George Roy Hill's office and threw it on his desk and said, "This is the most obscene script I've ever read, but I think you'll like it." George read the script; and over a late lunch with Pat Kelley and Bob Crawford, *Slap Shot* co-executive producer and associate producer, respectively, he decided to meet with the screenwriter. The next day, Pat introduced her to George by saying, "I'd like you to meet the truck driver who wrote that script."

George found Nancy Dowd fascinating, particularly because this script had been written by a woman and she was such an elegant gal. He could not believe these words were coming from her typewriter. She explained that her brother, Ned, was a hockey player for the Johnstown

Jets, one of the minor league teams, and carried a tape recorder with him recording the hockey team on the bus and in the locker room. Nancy developed the script based on those tapes. Her dialogue was authentic and brilliant. Nancy hung around the team for a good year and became sort of a mascot. She personally got to know all the guys on the team, and these relationships were evident in the script.

George was intrigued by the project and, when Universal bought it for him, gave the script to Paul Newman who agreed to play the leading role.

Paul worked every day of the sixty-eight-day shooting schedule, appearing in nearly every sequence. He practiced for several weeks prior to the shooting and did his own hockey playing on screen, including the rougher aspects of the game. The only time Paul required a double was for the execution of certain intricate stick work beyond his ability or probably anyone but a hockey professional. Hockey player Rod Bloomfield was brought in to play Paul's stunt double.

George and Nancy started rewriting, and Nancy proved to be sensational. She would turn out an incredible rewrite overnight. They were under a deadline that was imposed by the hockey season because they had to shoot inside the arenas before the spring thaw.

George was trying to figure out the climactic sequence and how it should be played. Nancy had a version that was a wild melee; and out of it, for apparently no reason, one of the lead characters, Ned Braden, starts doing a striptease. George was not sure that this was going to work as a payoff to the story and could not figure out what he was going to do with it.

George had a green light from the studio, not really knowing how they were going to shoot the final scenes. There were a few other troubled spots that were unresolved, and in retrospect, this probably paid off in great dividends because it enabled Nancy to stay with the production during rehearsals and continue to rewrite up through the shoot. George and Nancy's biggest worry was the ending. Somehow it evolved naturally from the many hockey scenes that had been already staged. When shooting got close to the final fight in the film, it had become clear to George and Nancy how Ned Braden would resort to stripping as a kind of absurd act of rebellion.

Originally, Universal had a contract for casting with Mike Fenton for the movie. Mike was an important casting person in California who founded the Casting Society of America (CSA). After some time, George did not agree with Mike, so he hired me and gave me billing as a talent coordinator. Thankfully, once again, David Picker had no objections to my working on *Slap Shot*.

We read Michael Ontkean with a number of good actors when casting the part of Ned Braden. However, from the readings, George had pretty much decided he wanted Nick Nolte for the part. We then sent out an open call for actors who could play hockey to audition at the ice arena in Burbank. Dozens showed up, but they all turned out to have weak underpinnings.

Nolte was absolutely straight about his not being able to skate but was gung ho for getting the part. He worked with a private skating instructor for a couple of weeks, trying to perfect his skills. During the skating auditions, they mixed him in with hockey players, and his skating was so obviously amateur George could not see how he could film around it. There was too much riding on the character of Ned Braden's championship ability to try and get away with faking it or using a double. George felt badly about not being able to give Nolte the role after the risk and effort he had gone through. As an actor, he could have been a powerhouse in the role.

George had even more guilt when Peter Strauss came out for the audition and skated pretty well in one direction but could not stop and really creamed himself on the boards. He wound up breaking an ankle. Fortunately, Michael Ontkean had played for a professional league and became our choice for Ned Braden.

However, getting Michael, who was a good hockey player, to work at choreographing a striptease was not easy. He was shy about stripping, particularly in front of a thousand Johnstown steel workers who had been recruited as extras in the audience. The production was lucky in finding a professional figure skater who assisted with the choreography and gave Ontkean the confidence to perform a striptease with style.

In the supplemental material from the DVD, Michael, who'd been a hockey player with the Toronto Maple Leaf's farm club and for semipro teams in Quebec and Vancouver, was quoted as saying, "I was scared to death for months. I would wake up and say to myself, 'I am going to run away.' But I had great encouragement from Paul Newman and George Roy Hill. I used to get up in the morning at four thirty and work out this routine on ice—the choreography—before starting work. By the time I had to do it, I had surrendered to the character, so it wasn't me doing it!"

There was a role of the guy who broadcast the games, Jim Carrey, a guy who became so excited that his toupee falls off in a scene. Fenton had cast an actor named Michael McGuire who was not a romantic-looking guy at all but considered himself a leading man. He was having hair plugs put in his scalp because he was balding, so I told George about this. I warned George that he was not going to do what the script called for involving the toupee, but George told me that Fenton had him sign and that he would. In point of fact, Fenton had forgotten to have McGuire sign a contract, and the weekend before the scene was to be filmed, I received a frantic phone call from George.

"This part works on Monday, and this guy has backed out! What'll I do?" George asked when he reached me at my home in Bayshore on a Saturday.

I reminded him that I'd warned him about this but immediately set about finding someone. Thank goodness I had a Players Guide with me at home and looked through it. I thought of a guy who would be wonderful for it; and fortunately, he was in the book and also had his telephone number listed there, which was very unusual. I called Andrew "Andy" Duncan, and he was available.

I called George back and told him about Andrew and his availability and offered to get him on a plane to Johnstown, Pennsylvania, where they were shooting. "You can read him tomorrow and see if you like him. If not, just sent him right home, and we'll think of somebody else," I told him.

George told me to just book him and get him on the plane. I didn't want to do that before George read him, but he insisted, so I sent Andy to Johnstown, and George loved his work so much he ended up expanding Andy's part. Andy turned out to be so great in it, and he's one of the few actors that George let improvise lines. He was so natural at it, and his improvising seemed better than the dialogue that had been written so George went with it.

The one thing that Mike Fenton did do was go up to Minnesota or had an assistant go and interview people for the hockey players. These were the three crazy hockey-playing brothers called the Hansons in the script. Fenton found three real brothers, Jeff, Steve, and Jack Carlson, up near the Iron Range in Minnesota; and they all played hockey. Just before filming, Jack Carlson accepted an opportunity to play with the Edmonton Oilers and was unavailable for filming.

David Hanson, also a minor league hockey player, was pulled from his role of "Killer" and was given a pair of thick-lensed black-framed glasses to become the third Hanson brother with his original role taken over by Jerry Houser. The Hanson brothers are hilarious in the film, and I had nothing to do with their casting.

The supplemental material on the DVD recorded that the Carlson brothers and Dave Hanson all played for the Johnstown Jets. The Carlsons were distinctive because of their long hair, thick glasses, and their consecutively numbered jerseys (16, 17, 18). All the Carlson brothers and Dave Hanson had lengthy hockey careers after the filming.

I also didn't have anything to do with the casting of Jennifer Warren, the estranged wife of Paul Newman's character in the movie. I didn't like her for the part; she was okay but not great.

Colonel Kurtz's daughter, Swoozie, appeared in a small part as one of the hockey wives. We cast Brad Sullivan to play Wanchuk, and Brad had become a born-again Christian and balked at saying some of the raunchy dialogue that was integral to his hockey player character and the situations in *Slap Shot*. He finally accepted the part and ended up being the hockey player with the foulest mouth in the group! Strother Martin played the original team owner who was selling the team and had worked with George and Paul on *Butch Cassidy and the Sundance Kid*. Another favorite of mine, M. Emmet Walsh, played Dickie Dunn, rounding out the supporting cast.

I remember going to a rink in New York near the Hudson River and seeing people skating. The darling little kid that I had used so many times named Matthew Cowles was there. He was not a very good skater, but we liked him so much that we cast him as the water boy, Charlie.

When principal photography was finished, George knew that editing was going to be a challenge. As he explains:

> *GRH: I knew when I went into the picture that the editing*
> *would be fast cutting and difficult. My first choice was Dede*

Allen and she was available. I sat with Dede and looked at the footage on film and I'd say, "That's a good take," or, "I don't want to use this part of that take, but that's a moment I like. That we can use." I gave her a general plan of what to do, but then I don't want to mess with her. I only tell her, "I've given you the plan and that's the way I shot it, and if that's the way it falls together for you, fine. But if you come up with another way to do it, for God's sake try it." It's like hiring a writer. If you hire the best writer and then write it for yourself, there isn't much point in it. If you hire the best editor and don't give the editor the chance to make editing decisions and be creative, then you may as well hire somebody who will sit down and cut the film with a pair of scissors to every frame you suggest. If you're going to hire talent, you've got to use it and bring their perspective to it.

Is it any wonder that creative people loved working with George Roy Hill?

Slap Shot was chosen as the closing film for the thirtieth Cannes Film Festival in 1977.

Reaction to *Slap Shot* upon its release was anything but tepid. The film is a wonderful comedy, and we thought it was a lot of fun, but the critics tore it apart. One critic who had always been nice to George said that he should have his mouth-washed out with soap because the word "fucking" was used so much that you finally became inured to it. In actuality, George knew that you can't make a film about the behind-the-scenes of football or hockey without using their language, and their language is almost exclusively "fuck this" and "fuck that." No American film had used that kind of language before, and it was automatically given an R rating.

One of Paul Newman's lines is "You know your oldest kid looks like a fag to me. You better get married again 'cause he'll have somebody's cock in his mouth before you can say Jack Robinson." Jack Kroll from Newsweek called this line "the single most profane sentence ever uttered by a major American actor." Arthur Knight wrote an article that really took off on the film and how disgusting it was.

The critics were quick to attack the film as being pure exaggeration, but they are the people that really don't know hockey. For instance, players really do go up into the stands and fight with the crowds!

George took the criticism until he read a statement that considered the film as "the epitome of the irresponsible film, and that is was paving the way for a takeover of the country by fascism." In a letter he wrote to the *Los Angeles Times*, which was printed in the Calendar section, he noted (and rightfully so):

> At one point late in the comedy, SLAP SHOT, a hockey game has erupted into a free-for-all on ice. One of the players, an infamous brawler named McCracken, chances to look up from a drubbing he is administering to an opponent and spots another opponent skating about the arena in his underwear. Deeply offended by the sight, he skates over to the referee, points out the culprit and in a high moral dudgeon screams: "Make him stop that! That's disgusting!" Audiences viewing the picture roar with laughter at the absurdity of a professional goon becoming morally outraged by anything much less a man skating in his underwear. The fellow's values are all cockeyed and audiences recognize it instantly.
>
> Well, in their reviews last week, two critics of the Los Angeles Times have pointed to SLAP SHOT and in their own

ways have screamed, "Make him stop that! That's disgusting!"
That's pretty funny too.

What on earth can have offended them so? The violence, they
say. It's ultraviolent! Really? A film that has no guns, no knives,
no weapons of death or torture, no rapes, no killings, no broken
bones and in which no one expires even in bed - is ultraviolent?
And this from two critics who have admired recent releases that
have featured amputations, guts spilling out, stranglings, kids
burned to death, mad women impaled by flying knives and so
on? True, there are a lot of fisticuffs in SLAP SHOT, but the
most serious damage sustained by anyone in the entire course of
the movie is a split lip that requires a couple of stitches. Was that
the ultraviolence that so unnerved them?

Was it the language? I am virtually certain that neither
of them learned any new vile words from SLAP SHOT. I am
equally certain that if they walked into a locker room and
heard the same language they wouldn't be in the least shocked
or even mildly surprised. Why are they shocked now? Who are
they protecting, the women in the audience? The notion that
women as a group apart are so delicate and fragile that they
must be sheltered by the men from bad words is not only archaic
and sexist, it's just plain silly. So what are they really protecting?
A convention, that's all. Ever since the movies introduced sound
there has been a convention that since profanity could drive
away some potential customers, it was not to be used, regardless
of the actual ambience in which the film was placed. So for as
many years as we can remember we have had celluloid soldiers,
jocks, construction workers, all talking perhaps with colorfully
mangled grammar, but with a purity of tongue that an evangelist
might envy. Classics were bowdlerized, great issues arose over

single words, remember David O. Selznick's well-publicized fight to let Clark Gable just say, "I don't give a damn?"

Of course no one ever seriously thought for an instant that soldiers, for example, talked in life the way they talked in the movies. But it was, and remains today a deeply ingrained convention, dictated, as most conventions are, by box office consideration. Our friend, McCracken, has certainly seen men in their underwear without shock, just as our two critics have heard language without shock. It is their sense of place that is offended; a convention has been flouted. To McCracken, a hockey rink is a place for brawling and a little hockey playing, not for skating in one's underwear, just as to our critics language acceptable in a locker room is simply not acceptable on the screen. In SLAP SHOT all we did was decide (at a commercial risk as one of the critics pointed out) that if we were satirizing a particular subculture in our society, we should use the language of that subculture. Simple as that.

McCracken, in his rage, continues to the referee, "Make him stop! This is a serious game, not a freak show!" And in so saying, he probably comes closest to explaining his and our two critics' outrage. Violence is a serious business with them and not something to be laughed at. The films they admire contain plenty of violence, but it is treated solemnly, almost reverentially. Action is slowed down so that we can savor the blood gushing from fatal gunshot wounds. Massacres become gory ballets. Decapitations, stranglings are dwelt on in loving detail and solemnly sanctified as art. Well, it may or not be art; I can't tell, because in most cases before I could relish the full effect of these goings on I was impelled out of the theater, not by moral outrage, but by a queasy stomach. SLAP SHOT also may or may not be art, but in contrast its "violence" is neither terminal nor causes serious injury, but instead is treated as outright farce. Far from being revered, it is poked fun at, and this may be what infuriates McCracken and our two critics most. They like their violence slow and serious, not fast and hilarious. Laughter is the one thing violence and super macho cultists cannot withstand. And laughter is what SLAP SHOT is getting, lots of it.

There is no question but what our two critics' moral outrage, like McCracken's is perfectly genuine. But alas, like McCracken, if they haven't got the joke by this time they probably never will.

In the end, *Slap Shot* has become a kind of cult classic with a loyal following. *Slap Shot* also has the distinction of being rated "One of the Top Ten Sports Movies Ever!" by Sports Illustrated, ESPN.com, and The Sporting News.

During the filming of *Slap Shot*, David Picker was offered the position of President of Paramount Pictures. David accepted the offer and disbanded our company, Two Roads. Simultaneously, he told me that he wanted me to move out to California and be head of talent at Paramount. While I felt I was concealing my marital problems from the people I worked with, it was obvious that David knew how unhappy I was in my marriage. His job offer meant a chance for me to live in California and escape from my married life, if I would take that chance.

I accepted David's offer again and set about making plans to leave Bobby without announcing that I wanted a divorce. I was aided in my decision, I am sure, by losing the brownstone. I'd informed the owner that I wanted to buy the property if they ever sold it, but one day I received a call saying the house had been sold. It went along with other properties on that block for a large development of some sort. Considering I had completely reconstructed and restored the house from the slum it was when I first rented it, I considered that move on the owner's part a really shitty thing to do.

I began hiding away clothes in one of my closets when my husband was not around until I was ready to move. Then one of my nieces came with her big car, and we just dumped as much as we could into her car. She drove everything back to my younger sister's home, which was the family farm that my parents had bought. She had a lot of extra space, and for several years, many of my clothes remained there. Assuming that I was simply going out to California to work on another film project, I remember Bobby saying when I left, "Well, you're taking an awful lot of clothes." Shortly after my arrival in California, I called Bobby and told him on the telephone that our marriage was over.

"No, there's no way. I'll never give you a divorce," Bobby told me. In reality, he was now going to lose his gravy train as well as his identity, and he was unbalanced as it was.

Fear is a very strong emotion, and I was full of it. I had to get three thousand miles away from Bobby. I was too much of a sissy to confront him in person and call our marriage off. Whether that would have ended in a very dangerous scene or not, I'm not sure, but I did not have the guts to chance it, and I am ashamed of that. I hope I am a stronger person now.

I didn't let Bobby know where I would be staying for fear that he'd come out "to get me." I'd arranged to sublet George Roy Hill's apartment in Marina Del Rey as he'd moved to a rental house in Malibu for the summer with his family. When the sublet ended, thanks to David Picker's friendship, he arranged for me to get a loan from Paramount so that I could buy a house in Pacific Palisades.

Bobby knew that I was working at Paramount, and David Picker gave a picture of Bobby to all the guards at the gates, telling them that this man was not allowed on the lot. I was known as Marion Dougherty, and the guards didn't know the connection.

I continued to pay for all the household expenses in Bayshore for two years. For some strange reason, I thought that my leaving would force him to contribute more financially. Bobby eventually found out where I was staying and started phoning me with all types of harassment, including threats a step up from just physical abuse. I never found out for sure how Bobby found out where I was, and it really doesn't matter now. The most alarming thing occurred when I heard through Virginia Raymond that Bobby was looking for apartments in the neighborhood where I bought my house. Virginia's husband had finked out on her, and she was left with four daughters to support.

Bobby did come out to California; and thankfully, I was in Japan, trying to sort out problems on *Mastermind*, a troubled picture starring Zero Mostel. I soon found out that Bobby went into my house in Pacific Palisades, claiming the door was open. Since I never had any reason to believe him before, I'm sure he broke in because I never would've left the house unlocked, especially with my being out of the country. I found out he'd been in the house when he mentioned in one of his phone calls that, "I see you left Muriel money in your will." Muriel was our West Indian cook that was very close to me and helped me through my back surgery in Hawaii. The only way that he could've gotten that information was to have gone through my desk at home.

I began to spend more and more time looking over my shoulder. In California, I had grown a little less concerned with Bobby showing up. However, I was so concerned in New York when I came back for work, that I'd walk on the streets where cars came from behind me. I was afraid that he just might be in the city and that he'd spot me. I was uneasy at all times in New York. George invited me for a long weekend to stay at his house at Saltaire on Fire Island, and I was scared to death because we had to take the ferry from Bayshore where our house was.

My divorce was finally granted, and Bobby pretty much admitted defeat. I hadn't removed my furnishings or any personal items from the house when I'd first made the escape to California. As part of the divorce settlement, I'd prepared a list of items that were mine and that I wanted to retrieve, which was agreed to by Bobby and his lawyer. After the divorce, I went back to our house in Bayshore and removed my things on the approved list, at least some of them; many of the things were missing. Bobby came up with this lame story that there had been a burglary at the house. I don't know if he was smart enough to have actually filed a police report, but when I came in to get my things, I had little time to pack because I had to catch a plane back to California. Of course, Bobby arrived late and said he'd been at a meeting with his lawyer. A friend of mine, who had a pickup truck, agreed to help me take the stuff out of my house and get it to a freight company that would ship it all to California.

I knew that there'd been some silverware that was given to us. His parents would give us a few pieces on occasion, and my parents would do the same. There were also things that I had gotten from my family that were not there. I said something to Bobby about the missing items, and he reminded me about the burglary. When I was leaving the house, I happened to glance over at a partially hidden box underneath a sofa in the corner of a room. I went over and pulled it out and discovered my silver.

"Oh, that's where that went. I guess they were leaving in a hurry," Bobby said, referring to the burglars.

When I left, the only thing I wanted to do was to get on with my life and try to forget about a most unpleasant marriage. I don't spend a great deal of time thinking about my past marriage or ex-husband.

Even if I hadn't had a thriving career and great friends and family that allowed me to escape relatively unscathed from an abusive marriage, the one thing that I am eternally grateful for is that I never lost sight of the woman my parents raised. I never fell into that trap where someone could not only physically abuse me but could also convince me mentally that I had done something, anything, to deserve it.

No one ever deserves to be physically abused. It's particularly heinous that the abuse occurs by someone who supposedly loves you. I was extremely fortunate that I emerged from the marriage in one piece and that I found Gary Kleinman to take care of my personal business.

So with a nod to Ethel Merman, on to the next chapter, please.

Paramount Pictures and the Reign of Michael Eisner

As Vice President in charge of Talent at Paramount, I handled the primary casting of many films but rarely received on-screen credit for them. One of the first films I cast there was *Won Ton, The Dog Who Saved Hollywood*, a comedic homage to Rin Tin Tin, who virtually saved Warner Brothers studios in the 1920s with a series of films that kept the studio afloat through rough economic times.

David Picker produced, but unfortunately, an Englishman named Michael Winner directed the film. He was an absolute horror and humorless to boot—what a waste for this was such a good comedic script!

Bruce Dern and Madeline Kahn played the leads, with Art Carney and Phil Silvers costarring as the Fromberg brothers who ran the studio. Terri Garr and Ron Leibman had significant roles, and there were countless smaller parts to be cast.

There was little pay for these smaller parts. I don't know how or why she crept into my head, but I thought of Alice Faye for one of these tiny roles. I wondered if she'd possibly consider doing the minuscule part of a secretary at the studio gate just for the fun of it.

When she agreed, the wheels started rolling in my head, and I started to get greedy. If I could get one star of the magnitude of Alice Faye for what amounted to a cameo, maybe I could get more. And since this was a story of old-time Hollywood, just imagine the possibilities. What fun to get performers who had been big names in the earlier days!

Perhaps one has to be of a certain age or maybe just a true cinephile, but to me, Alice Faye was a movie star! I have significantly helped many actors on their career paths who are considered stars today, but "movie star" in my experience meant those wonderful faces I saw stretched across the movie screen in my childhood.

Once I got started, it became a fascinating and fun game to see who we could get for all these bits, and the performers seemed to enjoy the game also. I cast a multitude of actors who had been stars and audience favorites all the way back to the silent film days. I would phone an agent to ask about someone I had thought of, checking their availability, willingness, etc. Before hanging up, I would ask if they knew anyone else who might be interested in doing a cameo for me. By the time I was finished, I had not only assembled a slew of Hollywood stars but also managed to cross over a bit into Broadway and threw in a few early radio and television icons too.

From the movies, I had people like Joan Blondell, Rory Calhoun, John Carradine, Cyd Charisse, Broderick Crawford, Yvonne DeCarlo, Gloria de Haven, Stepin Fetchit, Rhonda Fleming, Sterling Holloway, Billy Barty, Tab Hunter, Dorothy Lamour, Peter Lawford, Victor Mature, Virginia Mayo, Ann Miller, the Ritz Brothers, Ricardo Montalban, Aldo Ray, and Rudy Vallee. Jackie Coogan and Carmel Myers (who was a D. W. Griffith ingénue) dated from the silent film days.

I even had the temerity to ask Walter Pidgeon to play a butler for a day. Walter only had a tiny bit to do, but I got the chance to sit and talk with him in a beautiful house overlooking the ocean that served as the home of Grayson Potchuck (Bruce Dern). Walter was quite elderly then and chewed gum constantly. I knew nothing about Hollywood and these people when I was a kid; but to me, these were stars, and there was something terribly exciting about meeting them face to face.

From Broadway, I cast Ethel Merman, Jane Connell, Nancy Walker, and Patricia Morison (the original Kate in *Kiss Me Kate*) along with Edgar Bergen, Milton Berle, Dennis Day, Louis Nye, and big band singer Dick Haymes. In total, I'd assembled over seventy stars of Hollywood and Broadway's Golden Age together in one film.

It was terribly sad that the director had to be the worst type of British shit. He was a horrid man from day one. A typical Michael Winner story from the filming of the movie occurred one day at the old Egyptian Theater on Hollywood Boulevard.

Hollywood was somewhat seedy during that time, well before it was cleaned up with the old theaters being renovated and restored. Next to the Egyptian Theater was an empty parking lot. There were not many good places at which to eat in the immediate vicinity, so Michael had a tent set up in the empty lot, with tables set with linens, silver, centerpieces, and had a butler serving a gourmet lunch that included wine. In true gentlemanly fashion, Michael invited no one but Madeline Kahn, Bruce Dern, and Art Carney to join him for lunch. He invited me, but I was so appalled at his inelegant gesture that I could not bring myself to attend. I would join the hoi polloi.

In contrast to Mr. Winner, Louis Malle was a lovely man. *Pretty Baby*, released in 1978, was the movie that brought Brooke Shields to the attention of the movie-going audience. Brooke, with those large doe eyes and angelic face, had appeared in media ads for Ivory soap as a child.

Brooke's appearance in *Pretty Baby* generated a fair amount of controversy since she was only twelve at the time. She played Violet, the daughter of a New Orleans prostitute played by Susan Sarandon, who in the course of the film becomes a prostitute herself. She is abandoned by her mother, who goes off to marry and finally leaves the whorehouse, and is supported by a lonely photographer (Keith Carradine). Bellocq, the photographer, eventually marries Violet; and before their married life really begins, Violet's mother shows up with her husband. They take her back to St. Louis with them where she'll receive her first formal education and live a somewhat normal family life for the first time.

The final look on Violet's face as her new father photographs his family leaves the successful outcome of that happy family scenario highly questionable.

The film garnered Louis Malle a Technical Grand Prize from the Cannes Film Festival and certainly launched Brooke Shields on a film and television (and now Broadway) career that has kept her in the public eye ever since. In other less gifted hands, the nudity and story would have been managed with much less taste and class than Louis Malle had.

The movie's supporting cast featured Frances Faye, Barbara Steele, Seret Scott, Mae Mercer, and Gerrit Graham. From earlier films I had done, we cast Antonio Fargas and Matthew Anton (from *The Bad News Bears* films); and of course, Susan Sarandon had played Mary Beth in *The Great Waldo Pepper*.

Making her feature film debut in *Pretty Baby* was Diana Scarwid. As one of the prostitutes, Diana chose to use a German accent that was not required in the screenplay. She was lovely in her first feature and went on to catch audience's attention in movies like *Mommie Dearest* and *Silkwood*.

Brooke's mother, Teri Shields, created quite a stir of her own with her on-and-off the set antics that at one point I believe landed her in jail.

The second of the four times that I've worked with a woman director happened at Paramount when I cast *First Love*. Joan Darling, who had begun her career as an actor, did many guest appearances on television and was a series regular on Arthur Hill's series *Owen Marshall: Counselor at Law*. Joan played Frieda Krause, his law clerk and secretary, in the series that ran from 1971 to 1974. She had begun directing in her television days; however, *First Love* was her feature film debut as a director. Susan Dey from the television shows *The Partridge Family* and *LA Law* and William Katt, the son of Barbara Hale (Perry Mason's Della Street), starred in the film.

We also cast Beverly D'Angelo, Robert Loggia, and Swoozie Kurtz in supporting roles; and this was one of the few times I've offered a leading role to an actor and had been refused, in this case, for an insecurity I thought actors usually overcame. I had originally offered the role of Elgin Smith that Bill Katt played to John Heard.

John would not do the role because there were scenes where the character appeared partially clad, and John didn't think his body was in good enough shape. Fortunately for John, I considered him too good an actor to lose for the project, so I cast him as David, the second male lead, instead. Either John hit the gym after *First Love* or he overcame some of his insecurities, because he eventually did doff all in the remake of *Cat People* where he starred opposite Nastassia Kinski.

First Love was a critically well received film that did not do well at the box office, which was a pity because Joan is a very good director, and she was confined to directing television projects after that.

Richard Gere came to my attention that same year. Based on Judith Rossner's novel, *Looking for Mr. Goodbar*, Richard Brooks wrote the screenplay and directed this tense drama about a school teacher who pursues pleasure in the wrong places and pays the ultimate price. What a guy Richard Brooks was! Richard was especially crazy about protecting the contents of his scripts and insisted that no one see the script he was working on outside his presence. He had a paper shredder in his office and also on the set, so that when people came off the set, he would grab their sides from them and put them through the shredder.

When I was first allowed to read his screenplay of *Looking for Mr. Goodbar*, Richard made me read the entire script for the film as I was sitting in his office with him watching me like a hawk. Every time I smiled or made a frown, he'd interrupt and ask, "Where are you now? What are you reading?" I told him he was distracting me.

About a week later, I came back and told him that I needed to read the script again. He asked why since I'd already read it. I explained that I'd thought of some people and wanted to see if they were right for the script, so he agreed. He sat there smoking his pipe the whole time, watching me read until I told him, "Please let me turn around. You make me very nervous."

I think Richard sort of dug me because I wasn't as afraid of him as the other people were that he dealt with. He was an equal opportunity intimidator though, I will say that for him. He even made Barry Diller, the CEO of Paramount Studios at the time, read the script in his office.

The film's plot revolved around Theresa Dunn, a young woman played by Diane Keaton, who was searching for her own identity and trying to balance her sexual desires with a career as a teacher of the deaf and also dealing with a dysfunctional and stifling Irish Catholic family life. After an unsatisfying affair with a married professor, her search for love continued to careen out of control as she entered the "free love" and drug scene in New York City and ultimately lost her way entirely.

Richard Gere had done two smaller film roles prior to *Looking for Mr. Goodbar* and nearly missed out on the opportunity to play the role that brought him to a much wider audience. He'd just finished filming *Baby Blue Marine* in northern California and was ready to fly back to his home in New York when I contacted his agent to suggest an audition for the role of Tony. He refused the audition as he was so homesick that he didn't want to stop in Los Angeles, but I contacted his agent again and told him he could easily fly out of Los Angeles and should just come in to discuss the role. Richard did and got the first of several roles that would broaden his visibility to the movie going public. Gere's hyperkinetic Tony, a hustler and user, created a sexual charisma that sometimes obscures the fact that Richard is a very good actor. His energized bouncing around Keaton's apartment in just a shirt and jockstrap remains one of the enduring images of the film.

While Richard garnered a considerable amount of attention in *Looking for Mr. Goodbar*, he cemented his stardom in *American Gigolo*, one of the films that I helped cast at Warner Brothers. The work he did following *Looking for Mr. Goodbar* in *Days of Heaven*, *Yanks*, and *An Officer and a Gentleman* set him on his path to the fame he so richly deserved.

Looking for Mr. Goodbar also offered Tom Berenger one of his earliest high-profile roles, although a supporting one, as Gary, a young man not comfortable with his sexuality that led to tragic consequences. I had to pass up the chance to use Tom in 1977 for *Slap Shot* because he just looked too much like a young Paul Newman in those days. I was happy to see Tom overcome that career hindrance, since there was little he could do about his appearance without plastic surgery, but I would have dearly loved to have been there to hear him tell a plastic surgeon, "You've got to change my face. I look too much like Paul Newman." To my knowledge, Tom has had the good grace not to mess with the great face God gave him.

The strong supporting cast also included Richard Kiley (a lovely man whom I had used on *KRAFT*) as a tyrannical Irish Catholic father, William Atherton as a milquetoast suitor, and Tuesday Weld as Diane Keaton's flight attendant sister who seemed totally dependent on having a man in her life to define her existence. Weld received an Academy

Award nomination for her role of Katherine in the film. Brian Dennehy, who would move on to starring roles, made his film debut in the movie in a tiny part as a surgeon in one of Theresa's fantasies.

Looking for Mr. Goodbar was a film of its time. Sexual freedom and widespread use of recreational drugs in the late 1970s, before the advent of AIDS, was perfectly captured in Richard Brooks's film. If you lived through that time, then the film resonated a strong reality, but to the younger audience, it probably seems a bit contrived and unbelievable.

Barry Diller gave the go-ahead for *Heaven Can Wait*. The film was a 1978 Paramount summer release that was codirected by Warren Beatty and Buck Henry, with both also acting in the movie. Written by Elaine May and Warren, the film was a reworking of the 1941 classic, *Here Comes Mr. Jordan*, starring Robert Montgomery and Claude Rains. I oversaw the casting, while Pat Mock got the actual credit.

The role of Joe Pendleton was originally a boxer in *Here Comes Mr. Jordan*. Warren first offered the part to Cary Grant who turned it down. Warren then wanted Muhammad Ali to play the lead; and when Ali's schedule prevented him from doing so, Warren, who couldn't box but played football, changed the lead role to a football player.

Kate Jackson was Warren's first choice for the role of Betty Logan. Mary Steenburgen and Leslie Caron were also considered, but the part was finally given to Julie Christie.

One day during preproduction, Warren Beatty phoned to ask me to come over to his office for some question on a casting choice. I dutifully walked over to his office on the lot and sat and cooled my heels for quite a time. Finally, I told his secretary that I had work that I needed to be doing. She buzzed Warren on the intercom and told him that I'd been waiting in the reception area for quite a while.

Before I knew it, Warren came bursting through his office door, picked me up, and threw me unceremoniously over his shoulder without saying a word. He carried me into his office where he turned me toward the men he was meeting with—Barry Diller and Buck Henry—and said, "I believe you know Marion."

Let it never be said that Warren Beatty cannot sweep a woman off her feet.

Heaven Can Wait was nominated for nine Academy Awards and took home the Golden Globe for Best Picture (Musical/Comedy). Oscars were given for Best Actor (Warren Beatty), Best Actress in a Supporting Role (Dyan Cannon), and Best Actor in a Supporting Role (Jack Warden).

Charles Bluhdorn was the CEO of Gulf & Western and had purchased Paramount Pictures in 1966. He hired Barry Diller in 1974 when Diller was only a 32 year old television executive. Charles was Austrian born and had a very thick accent that everyone imitated. We'd have weekly executive meetings at Paramount and every so often Charles would attend. For some reason, he and I really kind of hit it off. Sometimes he'd come back to my office after the meeting and we'd sit down and smoke a cigarette and he'd say, "So, tell me about who you're casting." He enjoyed talking about different actors and the casting process. He was a powerful guy and his secretaries would start calling my office asking to speak with him and he'd say to tell them he was busy.

At another one of these meetings, Barry Diller pulled me aside and told me he wanted me to meet someone. He said that this man was a stockholder at Paramount and was interested in acting. Wally Nicita was with me at the time and we walked over to Barry's office. When we got there and Barry introduced us to this man, he had the oddest looking toupee I'd ever seen and I couldn't stop staring at it. As it turned out, the only thing I had in common with this guy was sailing so we started talking about the mechanics of sailing. I told him about "wig waving" and he told me he didn't know what I was talking about. "Wig waving, everyone who sails knows about wig waving." I said. I looked over at Wally and she was sort of giggling. As we were walking back to our casting offices, I said to Wally, "You know I saw you laughing at me. That was kind of rude." Wally then explained that I had my eyes fixated on this man's toupee and kept saying "wig waving" instead of "flag waving." I just burst out laughing. In the end, we were both certain that the guy was no stockholder at Paramount but someone Barry Diller was trying to help out.

Escape from Alcatraz was directed by Don Siegel and produced by Clint Eastwood. Don Siegel had directed Clint previously in *Dirty Harry*, which was a huge hit that spawned four sequels. This was the first time I met Clint.

Don Siegel did not have the career Clint had as an actor; but for whatever reason, he shared the same trait as Clint in that they wanted me to see and hear the actors read and then introduce those that I thought would be right for the part, so I prescreened the actors for them and only had the ones I thought would be good for the role to *meet* them, not read.

Clint, to this day, still will not read with actors because he had such a trauma when he first began to act and to see a director just freaked him out. Nowadays, most actors submit demo reels for casting. In the late 1970s, we didn't have that capability, and VCRs were just starting to come into use. As far as I'm concerned, the arrival of VCRs, with regard to casting, was not a positive step. There is simply no substitute for the casting director reading with the actor in the same room with the director.

Ann Brebner is a wonderful lady in the San Francisco Bay area whom I hired to introduce me to the local actors. It was not only that she knew the actors; she really knew acting and was a tremendous help to me. She introduced me to Jack Thibeau, who played Clarence

Anglin, and another gentleman, who made his feature film debut in the movie in a small part as an inmate. That gentleman, Danny Glover, and another terrific actor, Carl Lumbly, who also played an inmate, have both gone on to become really fine actors in much larger parts than I could offer them on *Escape from Alcatraz*.

French Postcards, a 1979 Paramount release, was directed by Willard Huyck, who cowrote the screenplay with his wife, Gloria Katz. The film was a very pleasant comedy about a group of American exchange students in France. It starred Miles Chapin, Blanche Baker (Carroll's daughter), David Marshall Grant, Lynn Carlin, and George Coe. Mandy Patinkin played one of his earliest film roles as Sayyid, and for the French characters the Americans interacted with, I cast the exquisite Marie France Pisier and Jean Rochefort who was so funny as Monsieur Tessier.

My big find for this movie was a beautiful young woman named Valerie Quennessen who had just graduated from the Conservatoire National d'Art Dramatique de Paris. She went on to featured roles in *Conan the Barbarian* and a starring role in *Summer Lovers* opposite Darryl Hannah and Peter Gallagher. Retiring for a time to start a family, she was tragically killed in an automobile accident in France.

Debra Winger also had a significant supporting role in *French Postcards*. She had done two films before this, *Slumber Party '57*, which was unsuccessful, and *Thank God It's Friday*, a disco-era story that had a cast so huge that she was practically lost among them.

Debra's second film for me was *Urban Cowboy* and would catapult Debra to stardom in her role as Sissy opposite John Travolta. Several other actors read for the part of Sissy, including Sissy Spacek (who had a falling out with Travolta), Rene Russo, and Michelle Pfeiffer (who producer Robert Evans was fighting for). Finally, director James Bridges threatened to walk unless Debra was cast. Evans complained that Debra wasn't attractive enough for the role. The studio executives finally gave in, and Debra was set.

The film struck a chord with a large chunk of the movie-going audience at the time of its release in 1980. It was at the height of a strong Texan and country western music influence in America that included line dancing and riding a mechanical bull. Bonnie Raitt, Johnny Lee, Charlie Daniels, and Mickey Gilley all had cameo roles.

Urban Cowboy was highly popular with a supporting cast that included Barry Corbin, Brooke Alderson, as well major supporting roles going to Scott Glenn and Madolyn Smith. We cast Jerry Hall and her sister Cyndy Hall in their first film roles as the "sexy sisters."

Alan Shane was an old friend of mine back in the days of *Kraft Television Theatre* when he was an actor. I wasn't at all surprised to receive a phone call from him, even though he was now head of the television division at Warner Brothers. I was surprised, however, that instead of calling to catch up on things, he invited me to breakfast at the Polo Lounge. Alan then hinted as to whether or not I might be interested in talking about a position in casting for Warner Brothers. That was the first and last time I was invited to the Polo Lounge for breakfast, very spiffy, I thought.

Interestingly enough, there was a man at Paramount who was a friend of Michael Eisner and also mine. He'd come to me one day not long before Alan's phone call to suggest that I ought to look around for other job options because Michael Eisner, who was now head of Paramount movie division, had plans to replace me. David Picker left a year or two after my arrival to partner on a few films with Steve Martin.

I told this very nice man that it didn't surprise me because Michael and I were not often on the same wavelength when it came to casting ideas. Michael used to hold meetings on Monday morning, and the first thing he would say was, "Now we must find something for Suzanne Somers."

My response was always the same.

"Why? She's overexposed already, and she can't act."

When I finally did receive a call from Michael to come and see him, I'd already met with Bob Shapiro, President of Warner Brothers Worldwide Theatrical Production division. He was very nice to me; and once he agreed to my terms of being able to refuse casting any project I was not interested in, he told me there wasn't anything Warner Brothers wouldn't try to do for me. I was also allowed to bring my assistant with me, and it was a very good financial deal.

With the Warner Brothers deal already under my belt, I went up to see Michael, who'd already gotten wind of my offer. Michael was seated at his desk, and I sat in a chair beside it. To my surprise, Michael got off his chair and got down on his knees and held my hand while he begged me please to not leave him and Paramount.

Sincerity was not Michael's hallmark at the time since I knew he was going to fire me. I quickly realized that while Michael wanted to get rid of me, he did not want me going to a competitor. He merely wanted to spoil my Warner Brothers deal by keeping me at Paramount for just a little while longer so he could drop the ax at the appropriate time. I would've given anything to have that particular scene on camera!

Warner Brothers Waiting—
And the Best of Days

In mid-1979, I began my tenure at Warner Brothers as Vice President of Talent, a position I held until 1998 when I was made a consultant. My association with Warner Brothers lasted another two years when I became semiretired in 2000 and moved back to New York City.

Warner Brothers Studios are located in Burbank and had perhaps an even more stellar reputation and a greater importance in the history of filmmaking than Paramount. This was due primarily to Jack, Sam, Harry, and Albert, the Warner brothers, and the stars who continued to work there, whether under contract or not, like Errol Flynn, James Cagney, Bette Davis, Olivia De Havilland, and Humphrey Bogart.

Steven Ross purchased Warner Brothers in 1969, and in 1972, he formed Warner Communications. Ross was CEO, President, and Chairman. When I arrived at the studio, Ted Ashley was Chairman of the Motion Picture Division in California, and Frank Wells was the Vice Chairman. Mark Rosenberg was the Vice President of Production, and Mark Canton arrived the following year, both working under Robert Shapiro.

Coincidentally, George Roy Hill left Universal over a disagreement with Sid Sheinberg about the same time I arrived at Warner Brothers, and George made his own deal with the studio. The film under dispute was *A Little Romance*, and George made a deal with Arthur Krim and the newly formed Orion Pictures to produce the film and with Warner Brothers to distribute.

A Little Romance was one of George's sweetest and most charming movies. The puppy love romance of the title belonged to Lauren, an intelligent thirteen-year-old girl living with her mother and stepfather in Paris, who is smitten with Daniel, a roguish Parisian with a penchant for American movies and film stars. Their romance is abetted by Julius, a larcenous con man who helps the young lovers make their own romantic magic by escaping to Venice, Italy, to create an unforgettably romantic memory.

The script was written by Allan Burns (of *The Mary Tyler Moore Show* fame) and was based on Claude Klotz's novel *E=MC2 Mon Amour* (Klotz using the name Patrick Cauvin). Again, I found myself searching for two exceptional young actors as the two principal leads who were both thirteen years old, an American girl and a French boy.

I've cast many children in various films and often cannot find the right quality from those submitted by agents. I'm particularly wary of young kids who have appeared in a television series or commercials. Mostly they have no training in theater or have agents who aren't interested in developing their careers. I prefer kids who are not show-offs, but not too shy, ones who are open and interested in talking to you.

Child actors are usually very good or very bad; they are seldom in the middle. When they get to the point where their parents are taking them out on auditions, you not only have to deal with children; you also have to deal with the parents. Parents often make the mistake of coaching the kids on how to act, and that is what comes across when you meet them, little monsters that are phony as hell. It isn't their fault; it is their mother or father who has decided that they know how to act the part and have briefed their kids. They read them without knowing what the part is really about and give them a preconceived notion about how to play it.

Actually, some of the best child actors I've cast have had no experience in acting; therefore, no bad habits, and they're bright and very well adjusted to just being themselves. The director has a terribly important role, and I wanted to include George's thoughts on this:

> *GRH: A director can supply children with a technique and that's not difficult. What is difficult is to cast children who have natural talent, for whom acting is just making believe. I try to tell them to fool me, to pretend that they are the character. Kids are marvelous actors, and when you have kids of your own you know that they're acting half the time to get what they want and they can be very, very convincing. Acting is merely pretending and using your imagination to elaborate on the pretense. You do not have to have any special technique in working with children as opposed to adults, at least I'm not aware of one. You adapt yourself to what you believe are the actors' needs. Every actor has different insecurities that you try to overcome by whatever method that works. Children have different needs than adults, so you give them different supports to use whether it be a line reading or a specific piece of business.*

I found Diane Lane in New York City where she was in *Runaways*, a Joe Papp production in association with Elizabeth Swados. They had been developing *Runaways* for some years, and it was running at the Public Theater, and they were thinking of taking it to Broadway.

Diane was fourteen at the time, which was the age the kids in the film had to be. I told George about Diane, and he called her in to meet with him. He was smitten; we had our Lauren right away.

We were in Paris when George wrote Joe Papp a lovely letter saying he wanted Diane to do the picture, and Papp responded with a curt answer and told him that no one ever left his shows; and if she did the movie, she would never work again in the theater. Fortunately, he was very wrong. Joe Papp was a greatly talented man. Other than his reaction to Diane's leaving his production, I have every respect for the man who has done so much for theater and actors in New York City.

We had to find a boy to play opposite Diane and looked all over Paris. George had been in Paris and found that Margot Coppelier was considered the best casting director in Paris. "She has a face that looks like a map of France and is much older than you and probably very opinionated, so I hope you can work with her," he said to me.

Well, I fell in love with Margot immediately, and we became great pals. We also had wonderful lunches together with plenty of fine wine. Years later, if I interviewed actors who were going to Paris, I always asked them to give my love to Margot, who continued casting and falling asleep in theaters.

Margot brought a lot of kids in to read for the part of Daniel. Most of them were too pretty, and George continually was saying no to her selections. Finally, one day I spotted a kid playing soccer in his front yard. He was a funny-looking kid and was just darling, not pretty; and George loved him.

Thelonius Bernard (his father named him after jazz pianist/composer Thelonius Monk) had been taught English and understood it, but you could not understand one word that came out of his mouth. His pronunciation was from outer space.

George and I brought Thelo back to California after we had cast the movie, and he stayed at George's house in Malibu. George's daughter, Owens, spoke French; but they would not allow Thelo to speak French. Owens could, however, help him interpret some of the lines.

Diane came out to California so she and Thelo could get to know each other. As it turned out, they could barely abide one another. Thelo was at an age when he had no time for girls, and Diane was a young professional.

Diane stayed at my house for about two weeks of rehearsals that I don't think the studio would have allowed, but they didn't know that we had brought them to Los Angeles. I can remember Diane's father was a real character. He sort of acted, or so he said, and he wrote as well. Burt Lane was his name, and he drove a taxi in New York City for a living.

Burt called me and informed me that he thought Diane might be starting to menstruate for the first time. He asked me to talk to her and explain what that was all about. Diane's mother lived in Florida and was not really available to Diane.

I can remember driving back from Malibu with Diane after the kids had been rehearsing at George's house. I began my talk with Diane by telling her she probably knew a lot more about this than I do but offered to answer any questions she might have. She was very sweet, and we talked about it a little bit. I was right; she knew all about it.

As mentioned, George had already set in motion the production before receiving final approval of a budget and a green light from Sid Sheinberg at Universal who had reservations about the screenplay. George was in Paris, scouting locations with Bummy, when he got word that Sheinberg had rejected the movie. George made several calls to various studios and one to Mike Medavoy who was Senior Vice President of Production at the newly formed Orion Pictures.

George caught the next flight to New York and left Bummy in Paris, asking him to keep the company together by hook or by crook. Bummy kept them all together. They had a great time waiting for George to get back, courtesy of Yves Rousset-Rouard, one of the French producers of *A Little Romance*. On George's flight, he saw Arthur Krim, one of Orion Pictures Cochairmen, sitting on the plane with an empty seat beside him. George went over and sat next to him and brought him up to date about the situation, and Krim agreed to back the picture right then. In fact, Krim approved the budget for four and a half million and wanted the picture to get going as soon as George could get back to France. Krim asked George to consider Laurence Olivier for the role of Julius, the old con man. George said, of course, he would consider Olivier and had the distinct impression that Krim might pull his backing without Olivier's involvement in the project.

George went to London to see Laurence Olivier, and Olivier did not really want to do a film. However, he liked George and the script so much that he relented and decided to do it. Bless him, he was not in great health at all.

We started rehearsals in Paris in a big rehearsal hall, and Olivier got along very well with the kids. Diane seemed to be just walking through her part and was not putting a great deal of emotion into it because she did not want to get too close to Thelo. After about a week, George went up to her and said, "Look, I appreciate that you don't like Thelo, that you are embarrassed, but I've got to see the performance. I can't just have you walk through this part. You have to find something in the playing of it that you can hold on to."

"Can I do it just once?" she asked.

"You can do it just once during rehearsal, and then you don't have to do it again if you don't want to until we shoot," George assured her.

She agreed.

As of then, there hadn't been a real performance from her. We had another run-through of the script, and she just knocked the socks off it; she was so good it stunned George. He never asked her to do it again until they got in front of the camera.

George got along very well with Olivier, and the two enjoyed working together as George explains:

> *GRH: Laurence Olivier had magnificent technique. He came on the set with all of his lines learned and he was pushing eighty. He would do things that seemed so spontaneous and when he would do them again he would do them absolutely the same way, having them timed the same way. It reminded me of when I was acting with Sara Allgood in JUNO AND THE PAYCOCK and she was going out the door and her hand touched the doorknob in exactly the same place with the tears rolling down her face at the exact same moment each night. Olivier was that way too. He would do something that seemed wildly improvisational but in actuality it was very studied and very thought out and only looked improvisational. Each take was the same performance unless I asked him to alter something and then he would alter it, but I didn't very often ask him to alter anything. Larry had a concept of the role and brought it in and showed it to me and I was ecstatic with it. I gave him minimal interference and just kept the other actors from running into him.*
>
> *I don't know exactly what his technique was because I think the training in the English theatre is a lot different than it is in the American theater. In the English theatre they work on such things as projection and movement so that they are able to build a technique. In the movies you don't have to have a*

technique, the director can supply it for you and if you've got any instinct at all, well then the instinct will lead you into some disasters at times, but if you have confidence in a good director to guide you, then instinct alone can be enough to deliver a very good film performance. I didn't discuss acting with Olivier, we discussed just about everything under the sun. He was a great conversationalist and it was a very happy time directing him. There was something wonderfully simple about him; he didn't agonize over the role. Probably the most difficult scene to direct occurred at the cul-de-sac after the bicycle race when Lauren becomes disillusioned with Julius and the three characters unmask themselves. It's a long scene that took all day to film. It was really Diane's scene and she was required to sustain high emotions for something like eight or nine hours. It was wonderful watching Olivier remain absolutely still while giving her the scene.

Olivier was in a weakened condition that kept him from doing anything particularly physical. There was a scene where he was supposed to ride in a bicycle race so they had the grip department build a platform so that it had outriggers on it and he could climb up on the bike without losing his balance. When the time came to do the bicycle sequence, Olivier suggested that we do it the next day. That afternoon, he and his driver, along with a couple of production assistants, went up into the hills above Verona; and Olivier got on a bike to see if he could ride it. He didn't want to be seen trying to ride it in front of everybody. He got on the bike and rode it just fine. During the actual shooting of the scene, he looked kind of terrified, which was good because that was in character. He rode the bike, and they didn't use the platform at all. He was a very gutsy man, he liked doing physical things, and he did a great job riding that bicycle. George was highly nervous when he was on the bicycle; one spill and we might not have finished the film. However, he exhibited such confidence that George took the risk and got wonderful shots as a result.

I needed a girl to play Natalie in the film who would be a friend of Diane's character. The character was a somewhat silly girl. For some unknown reason, I told George we'd find her in England. I just knew what she should look like. She would have braces on her teeth and be gawky. She was always saying "Oooh, gee" in the script. Diane's character was the same age but much more hip to everything than her friend was.

George and I were both in London; and through a friend of mine, we were invited to a party that friends of theirs were giving at their home for this school class, whichever class it was when you're fourteen in England. None of the kids were told who we were.

We went to the house, which was about four stories high, but very, very narrow. George and I just wandered around upstairs, and we saw this girl dancing with a boy. We nudged each other and watched them dance. The way they were dancing was just sort of hugging each other and rocking back and forth. It was very sweet, and George used this dance style in a scene in the film.

The young lady's name was Ashby Semple. Isn't that a lovely name? A short time later, we wound up in the living room on the first floor where Ashby was at the piano, playing "Raindrops Keep Falling on My Head," the Academy Award winning song from *Butch Cassidy and the Sundance Kid*.

"That's an omen," I said to George.

We decided that we would try to get Ashby for the movie so I called her mother. Her father was head of the London Bureau of the *New York*

Times. Her mother was not about to let her little daughter go with a Hollywood director to Paris to do a movie.

I told her that George is a very lovely man with his own children who all attended very fine prep schools in New York. I told Ashby's mother what George had done, and upon hearing that he'd directed *The World of Henry Orient,* she told me that she'd gone to the Brearly School herself. That film credit of George's got us Ashby for the film.

George returned to Paris; and I stayed in London to interview a kid who had his own television program in England, Graham Fletcher-Cook. He was as Cockney as ever could be. Graham was quite a known performer in London and was absolutely perfect for the part of Londet, Daniel's friend in the film. He had on this fedora hat, this little kid, thirteen or fourteen years old. He tickled me so much.

I told George I'd found the perfect kid for this part, but he's terribly Cockney, and he has to be Parisian. I had him come to Paris to meet George who loved him too, so we cast him. If you've seen the movie, the lines you hear coming from his mouth were dubbed by a woman in France because the character spoke in French with a French accent. The snappy fedora was Graham's, however, and that became part of his costume.

Sally Kellerman and Arthur Hill played Diane's parents with the adorable David Dukes portraying a clueless egomaniacal movie director who directs the movie being shot during the course of the film. Broderick Crawford had a good time playing himself in a wrap party scene.

George and the writer, Allan Burns, used to argue about Pauline Kael, the film critic for the *New Yorker* magazine all the time. She didn't love George's films and criticized the sound in *Butch Cassidy and the Sundance Kid,* a very sore point for George as he had to contend with filming much of the movie on outdoor locations as well as unexpected noises as on the day they were shooting in a field when the neighbor from the adjoining property began blowing a trumpet to disrupt the shoot. A bribe eventually passed between them to shut him up.

George also criticized Kael's sentence structure. George was a man who liked to win arguments, so while working with Burns on a wrap party scene, he inserted a direct quotation from one of Kael's critiques. Burns read it the next day and complained about it, saying that the line did not make any sense at all and wasn't even grammatically correct. Score one for George; they kept Pauline's line in the movie.

George did not usually like actors improvising—stick to the script—but Broderick Crawford, who was playing himself, enters in the wrap party scene; and his line was "What the hell, free food, free drinks, and I figure I might get laid." Sally Kellerman improvised a line, "He's such a delight!" George liked that line and left it in.

Anna Massey did a lovely little part for us playing Ms. Siegal. She ordinarily wouldn't have played such a small role, but she had known and liked George; and I had once known Raymond Massey, her father, as had George.

Andrew Duncan, who had saved the day for George in *Slap Shot*, and Claudette Sutherland played an American tourist couple who were first charmed then alarmed by their encounters with Laurence Olivier's Julius.

We filmed in the Chateau Vaux Le Vicomte, an extraordinary palace outside Paris. I knew the history of it at one time. It was built for an Exchequer of France and was such a gorgeous palace that the king got angry with him. The king was building Versailles at the same time, and the poor guy never got to move in to this palace because the jealous king had him done away with. The palace hadn't been used in films very often, and we soon found out why. Getting permission for several of these locations was a delicate matter that Bummy and our unique production manager, Madame Ludmilla Goulian, managed to arrange using diplomatic arts unseen since Ben Franklin was our ambassador to Paris.

We wound up shooting at Longchamp Race Track on the outskirts of Paris and then moved our cast and crew to Verona, Italy. George has always tried to take advantage of the location by his staging of scenes, and this is evident with the scenes overlooking the city of Verona.

In Verona, Bummy found a law office with a courtyard and turned it into a small cafe. We received letters and phone calls following the film's release from people wondering where that charming restaurant was located.

We left Verona for Venice, and the most difficult scene to shoot was the two kids "kissing" at sunset under the Bridge of Sighs. In a scene reminiscent of one of Turner's Venetian sunset paintings, it required a gondolier to be pushed by Thelo into the canal, and we couldn't find anyone to do it because the beautiful canal water was so foul. We finally found a gondolier willing to take the dive.

A Little Romance was entirely shot on actual locations in France and Italy, with the exception of one scene in the beginning with Thelo and his father in their apartment. We shot this on a set Bummy designed at Biancourt Studios in Paris. Filming on actual locations saves construction costs and studio rental; however, it often means shooting out of continuity. George completed the film on budget and managed to complete principal photography on location in sixty days.

George Delerue received an Academy Award for his original score of the movie, and Allan Burns's screenplay received a nomination from the Academy as well as the Writers Guild of America.

A Little Romance was a sweet picture; actually, it still is.

Robert Redford, with his directorial debut *Ordinary People*, called to let me know he was having problems finding two kids that he liked for the roles of Conrad Jarrett and the girl he had a crush on, Jeannine

Pratt. I found out that Elizabeth McGovern had been submitted, and the casting director would not see her. The same casting director had also rejected bringing in Tim Hutton to read and meet with Bob. So I suggested them both to Redford.

Both Tim and Elizabeth were cast in the movie, and both gave powerful performances. Tim's was met with broad critical praise, and he became a full-fledged star with *Ordinary People*, winning the Academy Award for Best Supporting Actor. Bob also took home the Award for Best Director.

Clint Eastwood was directing a lot more frequently when I arrived at Warner Brothers. I cast *Any Which Way You Can* and *Bronco Billy* for Clint in my first year at the studio. In my career, I did three more movies for Clint: *Honkytonk Man, Firefox*, and *Sudden Impact*. Clint is a dear man whom I always loved to razz, telling him, "I think you're even cheaper than I am!"

Paul Schrader's *American Gigolo* was one of the earlier films I did at Warner Brothers. Released in 1980, the movie firmly established Richard Gere's stardom and sex appeal for the movie-going audience in his playing the part of Julien. Christopher Reeve and John Travolta were both offered the role, and Christopher turned it down. Travolta went back and forth with Paul Schrader, and they couldn't agree on several issues, and I was very thankful that Richard Gere was finally cast. The supporting cast included Nina Van Pallandt, Bill Duke, Brian Davies, K Callan, Carole Cook, Carol Bruce, and Frances Bergen (Candice's mother). The part of Michelle was offered to Meryl Streep early on, who turned it down, and also to Julie Christie and Lauren Hutton. Hutton was eventually cast with Hector Elizondo in strong roles, which posed an interesting dilemma for the director. Lauren and Hector both have very pronounced gaps in their upper front teeth. Do you get one of the actors to have the gap filled temporarily for the movie? If so, which actor? Schrader opted for the natural approach and let both actors retain their "gaps," but I did enjoy teasing Hector and Lauren about it.

Honkey Tonk Freeway was a 1980 comedy directed by John Schlesinger that had all the makings of a hit, but never quite pulled together in the final cut and did not do well at the box office. While it did not make much money, it did mark the last time I had the pleasure of working with John, and it had a talented and unusual group of performers for such a silly script.

Juliet Taylor handled the East Coast casting, while I took care of the West Coast. John was so concerned with getting people mixed up that he asked Juliet and me to send him Polaroids of the actors we were considering, so he could keep them straight.

The film's several great moments of comedy were handled by a stellar cast that included Beau Bridges, Beverly D'Angelo, William Devane, Jessica Tandy, Hume Cronyn, Howard Hesseman, Terri Garr, Geraldine Page, Daniel Stern, and Deborah Rush. *Honky Tonk Freeway* is a wild story about a Florida tourist town bypassed by a new freeway. After having bribed a government official for an off-ramp that did not happen, the townspeople take matters into their own hands to bring the tourists back. This dark, offbeat comedy included everything from a water skiing elephant to a massive freeway accident to a loved one's cremated remains being mistaken for cocaine.

Private Benjamin was a big hit for Goldie Hawn in 1980, and was the first of four films that I worked with starring Goldie. Directed by Howard Zieff, Wally Nicita and I cast the movie about spoiled Judy Benjamin (Goldie) from a wealthy family who, when suddenly windowed, finds herself enlisted in the army. Judy Benjamin travels through a journey of self-discovery, eventually becoming her own woman or, as the army likes to put it, being all that she can be. The movie was so popular that it produced a television series shortly afterward.

We cast Eileen Brennan from *The Sting* to play Doreen Lewis, a diehard army captain, who butted heads with Goldie's character quite frequently. Both Eileen and Goldie received Academy Award nominations for their roles, with Eileen repeating her role in the television series. Armand Assante, Craig T. Nelson, Hal Williams, Barbara Barrie, Sam Wanamaker, Mary Kay Place, and Albert Brooks were also in the cast.

Robert Webber replaced Dabney Coleman as Col. Clay Thornbush after Dabney dumped his role at the last minute because he got offered a better job in *Nine to Five*. The production company sued Mr. Coleman and won the case, taking him to arbitration. And yet another actor joined my list of "never get around to seeing."

Armand Assante played a romantic lead in one of his first lighter roles as Henri Tremont. Armand was so good in the film, but I'm not sure we did him any favors. So convincing as the romantic Frenchman in the movie, complete with a French accent and continental charm, this New York City born actor of Irish and Italian ancestry had to contend with everyone thinking he was French for years afterward.

Following *Private Benjamin*, I found myself once again working with the team at George Roy Hill's company, Pan Arts, to cast *The World According to Garp*.

George had purchased a coop apartment at 920 Fifth Avenue and invited me to live in the second master bedroom whenever I was working in New York. It was a spacious and beautiful apartment on the ninth floor, overlooking Central Park at Seventy-Third Street. Gloria Swanson, the silent film star who once had an affair with Joseph Kennedy Sr., happened to live on the first floor.

With George's direction of Steve Tesich's (one of my brownstone tenants) screenplay, T. S. Garp leapt from the pages of John Irving's best-selling novel, replete with quirky characters, wild situations, and all the comments on society (violence, feminism, parenthood, etc.) onto the screen in a widely acclaimed film that scored heavily at the box office and was well remembered during awards season.

The film follows Garp from his infancy through his unusual childhood with his formidable mother into his adulthood, becoming a loving family man and successful writer (though still in his mother's shadow), and continues right up until his death. Garp's path through life is one of constant searching for meaning and making sense of it all.

Casting *The World According to Garp* created some real challenges based on the unusual characters that populated the screenplay (and novel); but central to everything was, of course, finding T. S. Garp. George and I discussed the possibilities of several actors to play Garp. We strongly considered Dustin Hoffman. When George had a breakfast meeting with him, his comment was, "Doesn't the older Garp come in a little late?" Dustin wanted to cut the whole first part of the script; and, of course, that would've made it a different picture, not the picture George wanted to make. We had read an awful lot of people for the role, including the wonderful Bill Irwin, when Robin Williams came in to read. After George met Robin, he decided this was probably the person he would like to have play the part.

I don't recall how his name came up; he was a comic, and he hadn't done any dramatic roles. Could he handle a dramatic role with all the baggage he was carrying around with "Mork"? George and I were afraid that if we used someone like Robin Williams who is known for a certain role, then they are always remembered for that role. Robin had this insane kind of character that he played on television, and I was afraid that in the serious scenes during the film that people might not take him seriously.

Robin had just gotten off the *Mork and Mindy* television series and spoke in just rapid-fire, rapid-fire. If you've ever met Robin, he gushes, he's so brilliant. As much as George may have wanted Robin, neither of us were sure we could get him to do anything but the silly stuff he did on the television show. We had Robin read with me for a whole day from sun up to sun down at George's home out in Malibu.

We read the script repeatedly, with George pacing him on the script. Robin had things he would say, interjecting things into the script that he should not have done, but he was always doing that. George proved just as tenacious as Robin as he halted Robin's reading and made him eliminate his additions and stick to the lines of the script. At the end of the day, George knew we had found our Garp.

Even after Robin was given the role of T. S. Garp, George was constantly on top of Robin's line readings, proving his tenacity and matching Robin's brilliance with a bit of his own. I remember one day we were on the set and about to go on with a scene.

Knowing George was a pilot, Robin pretended he was going through a pilot's checklist: flaps down, wings up, etc. In Robin's version, it became: Don't say Mom, don't be too fast. He would break everybody up; he would be so silly on and off the set. While he was training himself, he was joshing George about it. The minute Robin stepped in front of the camera, however, he would get into character, yielding to George's will. Robin delivered a fine-tuned performance that I think surprised many people.

It is to Robin's credit that he was able to reign in his improvisational genius and become T. S. Garp. George loved what Robin was doing and was very pleased, but still would remind Robin to keep a tight rein on everything he was doing occasionally. George seemed to have gotten Robin in a frame of mind from the very beginning of the film and be a tamer Garp. All this started that one day in Malibu, that entire day that we read through the script.

Robin went on to bring more tightly reined performances in his career with *Awakenings*, *Moscow on the Hudson*, *Dead Poet's Society*, *One Hour Photo*, and his Oscar-winning performance in *Good Will Hunting*.

The role of Jenny Fields, T. S. Garp's eccentric mother, was a gem for any actor to play and as important in casting as Robin. I have always felt, however, that every role requires careful casting, from the starring roles down to the very small supporting roles.

The World According to Garp was Glenn Close's first film. George and I went to see her in *Barnum* one night on Broadway. I knew there was this woman in it that was supposed to be good. Juliet Taylor's husband, James Walsh, was general manager of the play.

In the opening scene of the play, Glenn's character, Charity Barnum, is up in a loge box on the side of the theater, looking down at the action on stage. She was so still that both of us thought that it was a mannequin up there. Finally, her stillness broke, and she delivered a line.

"Anybody can do that. We'll have to see," George told me.

We first brought Glenn in to read for the role of Helen, the wife of Garp. Then we decided to try reading her for Jenny Fields, Garp's mother, although she was too young for the older Jenny and did a rather odd reading. Nevertheless, George thought that Glenn had a focus and intensity that worked better as Jenny Fields, rather than Helen, a focus that he had noted in Glenn's Charity Barnum. We both agreed that she was an exceptional talent.

Glenn remembers her agent describing Jenny as a "young Katherine Hepburn." She figured that since Charity Barnum was a straight-backed New Englander, she had a shot. I never send out descriptions like that or any type of general breakdowns (descriptions of characters being cast) to agents, handling most of my contact with them verbally.

Glenn had heard about George that "his casting director knows who he wants more than he does." She thought I was formidable, brilliant, and self-effacing (her words, not mine). During her reading, Glenn recalls being nervous and trying desperately to do justice to Katherine Hepburn, "an impossible proposition," in Glenn's words.

Glenn received an Academy Award nomination as best Supporting Actress for her first film. It did not go unnoticed by critics and audience alike who bothered to find out that Glenn convincingly played Robin Williams's mother when, in reality, she was only five years older than Robin.

To this day, she credits me as the "mother" of her movie career and George as her "father," which I think is just lovely. When Glenn's "father" had become friends with her, he confessed that he thought her audition in the style of Katherine Hepburn was, as Glenn recalls him saying, "one of the most hideous readings he had ever been obliged to sit through." Glenn also recalls that it was George that was such a big help in adapting her acting technique from stage to film.

When Glenn was having problems memorizing lines in a difficult monologue, she eventually decided it may be the writing. She summoned up her courage to ask George if he would mind if she worked on the monologue with screenwriter, Steve Tesich, rewriting it so that it flowed more easily to become a monologue she could memorize.

George told her to go ahead, and she approached Steve, telling him that she was having difficulty with a particular monologue (how Garp was conceived, she believes it was) and that George had told her it would be okay to work on it with him. She was greeted by a burst of laughter from Tesich who promptly told her she was having difficulty with the one monologue that he did not have anything to do with. George had written that particular speech!

The part of Helen Holm, who eventually becomes Garp's wife and the mother of his two children, still needed to be cast. When we were reading people for the part, I called Mary Beth Hurt. She did not give a good reading at all, and that surprised me very much. I was talking to her and discovered that her favorite pet, an old dog of hers, had died the night before.

I told George that she's perfect, but he disagreed. I tried to defend myself and Mary Beth's poor reading by telling him that her dog had died the night before, but he was unswayed.

Eventually, we had a script read through in New York with several of the actors that we'd already cast. John Irving asked if he could come and listen to the read through, and George didn't really want the author there, but he couldn't say no to him.

I set up the reading one morning, and we served coffee and doughnuts. Everybody was just milling around when George came in and saw that I had Mary Beth reading the part that he said he did not want her for. He looked daggers at me. He then asked me to introduce everyone, despite the fact that he knows I sometimes have a terrible time with names. I can't even remember the names of my own family when I'm under pressure. I introduced everyone around the table and was reading all the roles that hadn't been cast yet. George wouldn't even look at me.

We had a break about an hour into the reading, and John Irving made a beeline to Mary Beth Hurt. He told her she was exactly what he had in mind when he was writing the novel. George was not amused. I got more daggers. Eventually, Mary Beth got the part, and George came to love her performance.

Neither George nor I knew that Mary Beth and Glenn Close were best friends. The morning after the infamous table reading, Glenn Close recalls receiving a case of wine delivered from George to her apartment. She remembers waiting a while to summon up the nerve to call Mary Beth and see if she also was sent a case of wine.

When Glenn talked to Mary Beth, she found out that she'd received the same case of wine and wondered what it all meant. As Glenn put it to Mary Beth, "Are they kissing us off? How classy is that? Or are we being congratulated?"

Glenn's agonizing day, as she puts it, ended when her agent heard from me. Glenn recollects being so thrilled to have her first film role that she didn't even care if she had to play Mary Beth's mother-in-law.

Another important supporting character in *The World According to Garp* was Roberta Muldoon, a transsexual former football player who was a close friend of Jenny's and a doting godmother to Garp and Helen's children. George did not want to cast a woman in the part. If he had, we would have cast Christine Lahti, whom we did see. But George insisted on getting closer to the real thing. We interviewed a couple of transsexuals in California and then went to New York to interview more.

To accomplish this, we had to get hold of a doctor who performed the sex change operations, which was not that easy. He said he would help us and then called some of the people he'd operated on.

There was one lady who showed us a picture of herself as a sailor. She was a dancer in a strip joint on Forty-Second Street and made us promise that we would never tell anyone about it because no one there knew that she had once been a he.

We had screen tests for Roberta in a large empty space next to Lincoln Center on the Upper West Side. We tested four actors who included Bill Hurt, John Lithgow, Jeff Daniels, and Victor Garber. The screen test consisted of George talking to them impromptu about how they felt about their operation, why they did it, how painful it was, what people thought, etc. Then we wanted to make sure that they could handle the scene where Roberta is throwing a football to one of Garp's children. George said he wanted to make sure the actor he cast would run like a man and not a woman.

At first, George had mixed feelings about John Lithgow because he's quite tall, and Robin Williams is on the short side; but I sort of insisted on it. When it came time for John to test, the football was thrown to him at the far end of the stage, and then he was supposed to catch it and run back toward the camera. When John was in position, George threw a football to him, and it happened to hit John in the chest. John grabbed his "breast" and said, "Ow!" It was such a natural reaction. That did it. John got the part.

In the opening scene in the film, Jenny Fields comes in with baby Garp to her parents' house (a large home we shot in on Fisher's Island) and Hume Cronyn and Jessica Tandy, who played Jenny's parents, did the film as a favor to us. They were so funny. They worked for scale plus a contribution to a retreat for an artists' camp they supported.

One of the reasons I got Hume and Jessie was a friendship I'd formed with Jessie. Abel Gance's *Napoleon* was playing at Radio City Music Hall, and Jessie and I went to see it and sort of got friendly. Hume was a darling but really loved money, and we didn't have much in the budget for the minor roles. I'm sure that Jesse talked Hume into saying he'd do it.

There is a very good example in this film of the old saying, "There are no small parts, only small actors." Ellen James was a character in the film who'd been violently raped and had her tongue cut out. This act inspired a whole following of Ellen Jamesians who figure prominently in the film and Garp and his mother have many arguments about Ellen and her followers. Though she is talked about often in the movie, the character, Ellen James, only has a very brief scene, not more than one minute on screen; and she has no tongue.

We cast Amanda Plummer as Ellen James, and she played out a scene at a memorial service for Jenny when she runs with Garp across the street to help him escape a mob of angry women. There is one little motion with her hand pressed against her chest that she makes when she turns around to send him on his way. That gesture is so moving and might have been all of eight or nine seconds on screen, but it was just more than any words could have said. Amanda is such a wonderful actor coming by her talent via parents, Tammy Grimes and Christopher Plummer.

There is a scene in the film where Garp and Helen are looking for a house to buy and are taken by a real estate agent, played by Kate McGregor Stewart, to look at a house. Suddenly, a little biplane comes swooping down and crashes into the house right in front of them. The pilot climbs out of the plane on the second story of the house, checks to make sure everyone on the ground is all right, and then asks, "Do you mind if I use your phone?"

I told George, "You should play the part of the pilot since you're a pilot."

"Absolutely not." He refused.

Unfortunately (actually fortunately, I think), there was just something so appealing about the idea that I could not let it go.

I spoke to George's producer, Robert Crawford, and Bummy and told them I thought George should play the part. They thought it was a good idea too. Even Jim Appleby, who was the stunt pilot, agreed.

We were on location somewhere, and it came down to the day I had said I had to fly back to California. The following day, they were shooting this particular scene so George asked me who's playing the pilot. I told him I couldn't find anybody. George expressed his disbelief at that statement and told me to just get somebody, that the actor only had a couple of lines to say. The crew was all in on this by now; and of course, Ann Roth, our costume designer, had an old-time aviator suit and helmet that she knew would fit George.

So the next day they filmed the scene, I pretended I had left a message that I couldn't cast anyone to play the pilot so George had to do it. The scene only lasted for a couple of minutes, but it is very cute. It was also great to see George on screen in only his second film appearance since *Walk East on Beacon* in 1952.

I think he was really delighted to be in his own film and finally did forgive me for the trick, but he told me, "The day came along where Ann Roth put me in my old flight jacket, and I felt my old stage fright tightening up in my throat, and for the next nerve-racking couple of hours, I sweated out a couple of lines, and we got a wide and medium shot. I think I probably got through it because Mirek Ondricek (the Director of Photography) was directing, and I could not understand a word he said, but the way he did it was so reassuring."

Besides the wonderful performances George elicited from his cast of actors and the strong story, thanks to John Irving (who also did a cameo as a wrestling coach) and screenwriter Steve Tesich, George framed the story beautifully using a "flying baby."

The World According to Garp is one of my favorite films that I cast. I thought the cast we put together was wonderful, especially getting Swoosie Kurtz to play a prostitute hired for Garp by his mother. Another great scene in the film was the meeting between Swoosie's prostitute with Glenn and Robin. If anyone is curious about casting an actor as opposed to having someone who just looks right for the part should watch Swoosie's performance in that scene. She was so funny and charming in the role that George expanded it and had her character show up a couple of more times later in the film, which was not in the original script.

David Shire scored the film and composed an original piece for the "flying baby" sequence at the beginning of the film, but George had his mind set on using music by the Beatles. Luckily, his friend, Ted Ashley, knew Yoko Ono; and he was able to secure the rights to use "When I'm Sixty-Four." When the movie was previewed with David's original piece and then the Beatles, the reaction was overwhelming for "When I'm Sixty-Four" so George had to go with the Beatles.

The World According to Garp has always been a special film to me. The fact that as often as I read the script and saw the film (and still occasionally view it), I cannot keep from crying as a wounded Garp is flown away at the end. I am forever grateful to whatever little burst of imagination that came into my head to insist that George play the pilot. It is lovely to see him looking so handsome and vital.

During production of *The World According to Garp*, I flew to Germany to cast Clint Eastwood's *Firefox*. It was being filmed in Austria, Greenland, and also in the States. Mary Selway helped me cast the film out of Munich and London.

Clint starred as Major Mitchell Gant, a Vietnam veteran haunted by images from the war, who is pulled into a government plot to steal Firefox, a Soviet stealth air weapon that flew several times faster than the speed of sound. Firefox was equipped with a nuclear arsenal and had its weapon systems guided by the pilot's thought control.

Mary Selway came up with some great British actors like Freddie Jones, Ronald Lacey, Kenneth Colley, and Nigel Hawthorne. I cast some top-notch American actors like David Huffman, Warren Clarke, and Stefan Schnabel. I also cast Dimitra Arliss, who several years earlier had done such a great job in *The Sting*. She played a small role of a scientist who helps Major Gant. One of Germany's most popular actors, Klaus Lowitsch, played Soviet General Vladimirov for us.

As lovely as Munich was and as good as the film *Firefox* was, the thing I remember most was flying from Munich early one afternoon to London and then onto New York via the Concorde. I had no sooner gotten into the apartment when George called me from the set on Fisher's Island where they were wrapping up *The World According to Garp*. He told me to go down to the Forty-Eighth Street heliport immediately, and I found myself flying to Fisher's Island a short while later via helicopter. Arriving at Fisher's Island, I was a little discombobulated when I realized I arrived there earlier in the afternoon than when I had left Germany that same day.

Harold Ramis's *National Lampoon's Vacation* became a huge summer box office hit in 1983, and spawned three sequels and also a made for television movie. With Chevy Chase attached as the star portraying Clark Griswold, casting his wife and children became a matter of matching the actors to the material and also to Chevy.

The character, Ellen Griswold, needed to be played by someone who was both adept at comedy and attractive. I auditioned several actors for the role; and when I heard that Matty Simmons, the producer, wanted Colleen Camp for the role, I immediately vetoed that suggestion. No way was I going to have Colleen instigate another foolish rebellion among the cast like she did on *Smile*. I was able to circumvent Matty's choice by relying on one of Chevy Chase's.

Chevy was in the office, listening to the three or four actors we thought were best for the role of his character's wife. I had recently cast Beverly D'Angelo in a comic role for John Schlesinger's *Honky Tonk Freeway*, and I felt she had everything the role called for and more. Beverly had already proven her dramatic and musical talents in films like *Hair* and *Coal Miner's Daughter*, but she was so funny in Schlesinger's quirky comedy that I favored her over the other actors we were reading.

Matty Simmons did have Colleen Camp involved in the readings with Chevy, but I saved Beverly for the last of the auditions; and when she walked in wearing a form-fitted white jumpsuit, she just looked great and Chevy's eyes popped right out of his head. Beverly was set and appeared in all four movie editions of *Vacation* and was a beautiful and comedic gem in each of them.

Imogene Coca was the other favorite of mine from *National Lampoon's Vacation*. As Aunt Edna, she was as obnoxious a relative as any one of us would ever hate to have in our family, but she delivered an unforgettable performance as the disagreeable relative who gets foisted off on the Griswolds, complicating their trip to Wally World when she dies en route. Unable to bear riding with a dead body in the car, Aunt Edna is unceremoniously tied to the roof of the Griswold station wagon, abandoned in the middle of a rainstorm, and left propped up in a lawn chair in the Phoenix backyard of the Griswold's cousin Norm when they discover he was away for the weekend.

Imogene's appearance in *National Lampoon's Vacation* nearly did not happen because she was unsure of her ability to play a character that was so unlikeable. Luckily, she overcame her hesitation and created a whole new generation of fans, most of whom probably never knew that she had created one indelible comic character after another on Sid Caesar's *Your Show of Shows* in the 1950s.

Phyllis Huffman and Susan Arnold handled the casting of the supporting roles that included Randy Quaid and Miriam Flynn as the Griswold cousins (they also became part of the *Vacation* franchise). Anthony Michael Hall and Dana Barron, who created the roles of the Griswold children, Rusty and Audrey, ended up being recast for each addition of the film series. Smaller roles and cameos were given to Brian Doyle Murray, Eddie Bracken, James Keach, Eugene Levy, Christie Brinkley, and John Candy.

Protocol, written by Buck Henry, Nancy Meyers, Harvey Miller, and Charles Shyer, was a comedy about Sunny Davis (Goldie Hawn), a cocktail waitress who finds herself thrust into the political arena when she unwittingly saves the president's life. The film was directed by Herb Ross. I found some very good actors for the film: Andre Gregory, Chris Sarandon, Cliff De Young, Gail Strickland, Ed Begley, Jr., Kenneth Mars, Jean Smart, Keith Szarabajka, and the wonderfully funny Joel Brooks.

Herb could be a bit of a prima donna at times. We did some casting in New York; and one day at lunchtime, I ordered in for Herb, myself, and the secretary. A fairly healthy check arrived, which I paid, then later turned it over to Herb's secretary along with two tickets to a play that Herb had asked me to get. It was one of those plays that was almost impossible to get tickets on short notice, but I pulled a few strings and got them for him. He reimbursed me for the tickets but refused to pay for the lunch. Well, who should pay then? The secretary who gave up her lunch hour? The casting director who had to cancel her lunch date to accommodate Herb's schedule? I call that ungracious and cheap.

Herb was not nice to the smaller people, particularly the women. I got phone calls from four women in tears after their first day on the set. I told them after the day's shooting that he was probably just having a bad day. He was not nice at all to the "little" people.

Yet I have to love Herb because he later directed one of the funniest roles with one of the funniest ladies—Margaret Whitton—in *The Secret of My Success*. I had nothing to do with that film, but it was only one film later when I got to know Margaret. She had one of the funniest scenes I'd ever seen in that film as an oversexed executive's wife trying to seduce Michael J. Fox. In one seduction scene, she is in hot pursuit of Michael's character and jumps over the back of the couch to corner him. The move was Margaret's idea, a very funny one, and Herb let her play it that way.

On the other hand, Jonathan Demme was a terrific director to work with, one I wanted so much to work with again. We'd worked together previously on a film called *Citizen's Band*. Jonathan's *Swing Shift* starred Goldie Hawn as Kay Walsh, a sailor's wife, who in 1941, joins the ranks of the working women in an airplane manufacturing factory while her husband is off fighting in World War II.

We had a good time casting it and got a great supporting cast that included Kurt Russell, Fred Ward, Ed Harris, Susan Peretz, Sudie Bond (I loved her), Holly Hunter, Lisa Pelikan, Charles Napier, Patty Maloney, and Stephen Tobolowsky.

The role of Hazel, Goldie's best friend, which Christine Lahti played, was difficult to fill. We read many different type actors for the part. The readings took place in the producer's office, which was very roomy; and we had the actors come in and read with Goldie, reading one scene where they were marching along to go into the airplane factory. The women were all lined up to go in on their first day at the factory, and they were adlibbing.

Goldie, five-foot-six, was doing the scene with Christine who is very tall and towers above Goldie. They were improvising, and I recall Christine saying, "Come on, shorty, get a move on. I haven't got all day!" When that improv was over, Goldie came up to me and threw her arms around me and said, "Oh, thank you for giving me somebody that I can really work with!" Once cast, Christine's five-feet-ten-inch height was increased by the forties hairdo her character sported in the movie. She was so good in the part that she was nominated for an Academy Award for Best Supporting Actress.

Of course, this was the film where Goldie fell in love with Kurt Russell, who played Lucky, a leadsman at the airplane factory, and thereby hangs a tale. Goldie wanted Kurt's role larger and Christine's role smaller. Go figure! It altered the film story considerably from the original; however, all in all, it was a well-received film.

Holly Hunter was in the cast in one of the first movies that she did. I cannot take credit for her, because Jonathan Demme knew her. She did a small but very moving part as Jeannie, a soldier's wife who also works in the factory.

Swing Shift was a lot of fun to work on, and as I said, I'd have done another film with Jonathan Demme in a heartbeat.

One of the most delightful collaborations I had while working at Warner Bros. resulted in a lifelong friendship with a very talented, very sweet man. Our friendship really began in 1984, when I again met Richard Donner who was directing *Ladyhawke*, a romantic fable about two lovers under an evil priest/sorcerer's curse. Dick, like George, was lovely to work with.

My first meeting with Dick was many years earlier when he directed an episode of *Route 66*, titled *A Bridge Across Five Days*, which starred James Dunn and Nina Foch. It aired in November 1961.

I cast *Ladyhawke* along with Mary Selway and Francesco Cinieri, who handled the British and Italian (it was filmed in Italy) casting, respectively.

The lead role, Phillipe Gastone, the Mouse, was a gem; and we saw many actors including Sean Penn and Dustin Hoffman before casting Matthew Broderick. I had known Matthew's father, James, a fine actor that I'd cast in *Kraft Television Theatre*. Phillipe is a roguish, affable character that besides addressing the audience directly, a convention most associated with the stage, wins its affection by assisting the tormented lovers Navarre and Isabeau, who are played by Rutgar Hauer and Michelle Pfeiffer. Dick originally wanted Rutgar to play the evil captain and Kurt Russell to play Navarre, but Kurt decided not to.

Phillipe is aided in helping the lovers reunite by a monk, Father Imperius, wonderfully played by British actor Leo McKern. One of the joys of the film is watching veteran McKern interact with relative newcomer Broderick. There was real comic chemistry there, and they delivered plenty of comic relief to the film and contributed much to the poignancy of the story.

Matthew had two hits behind him when he played Phillipe, *Max Dugan Returns* and *War Games*. He would go on the following year to become a full-fledged star in *Ferris Bueller's Day Off*.

Michelle Pfeiffer had already created notice with her earlier appearances in *Grease 2*, *Scarface*, and *Into the Night*. She was absolutely lovely as Isabeau and further convinced the audience of her beauty and acting talent. While I was convinced of her potential, I don't think I fully realized her talent until I saw her performance in the 1992 release of *Love Field*.

John Wood, Alfred Molina, and Ken Hutchison also added to the fantasy story, providing the villainy.

The following year, *Wildcats* was released. In this film, Goldie Hawn played Molly McGrath, a divorced woman who desperately wanted to coach football. She is given the chance coaching a team in an inner city Chicago school. Her work there makes a big impact on the players she coaches and also herself as she becomes her own woman.

I surrounded Goldie with Swoosie Kurtz, Robyn Lively, Brandy Gold, James Keach, Jan Hooks, and M. Emmet Walsh in her family circle. Nipsey Russell played the principal of Central High where Goldie's character coached, and Bruce McGill was the football coach from Molly's former school and provided the primary villain to the story.

Among the football players were several actors who were making film appearances early in their career. Two of the actors I found made their film debuts in *Wildcats* and went on to become leading actors.

I'd heard about Woody Harrelson acting in a play in San Francisco as an understudy and that he was very good. I brought him down to Los Angeles and immediately cast him in the role of Krushinski. Soon afterward, Woody was cast as the bartender on the television sitcom *Cheers*.

I also had some very jazzy African American actors in *Wildcats*. Wesley Snipes made his feature debut as Trumaine, the ladies' man of the team. An interesting note about Woody and Wesley is that they later teamed up for another box office success, *White Men Can't Jump*.

Mykelti Williamson, Tab Thacker, and Rodney Hill were early in their film careers; and LL Cool J had a sort of cameo in his first film and also wrote the title rap song. Rounding out the football players were Jsu Garcia (Nick Corri at the time), Albert Michel Jr., Eddie Frescas, Willie J. Walton, and Lindsey Orr.

About ten years before she came back into the public eye in a big way with *Titanic*, Gloria Stuart played a small bit for me in the private girls' school scene with another character actress stalwart, Ann Doran, whom most remember as James Dean's mother in *Rebel Without a Cause*.

When the director Michael Ritchie and I were in New York auditioning actors for *Wildcats*, a memorable thing happened. We were in the office reading people, and one of the actors reading was Ving Rhames. There is a scene in the picture where Goldie Hawn goes into the men's locker room for the first time and faces the guys on her new team. As a prank, they have all kept only their jerseys on and hold their helmets strategically placed until they announce they are suited up and ready to play, all putting their helmets on at the same time.

Into my office comes Ving Rhames dressed in a porkpie hat, sawed-off T-shirt, tattered shorts, and sneakers, no socks. The minute he walked in, I had a sneaking hunch that he was going to do something unusual. He did. He started reading the scene; and as he was reading it, he first took off his hat, then took off his T-shirt, then down came the shorts with no underwear beneath them.

Michael Ritchie did not help me one bit. Here Ving was, this great big African American actor with absolutely nothing on but his sneakers. I did not blanch; I just let him go through the scene with me.

When he was finished, we thanked him for his reading. He didn't get the part, but I did admire him for his . . . guts. I looked at Michael afterward and told him he was a big help on this one. Michael told me he thought I was very cool about it.

I didn't meet Ving Rhames again until quite a few years later when I was casting *Rosewood*. We were down in Florida because Ving and someone else we were interested in casting were working on a film down there. So I came face to face with Ving once again. By this time, he was quite well known. And I thought I knew him fairly well too.

I must say that neither of us made any reference at all to the earlier meeting. Maybe he didn't remember it, but I sure as heck did.

During the filming of *A Little Romance*, George Roy Hill went to visit a doctor and was diagnosed with early stages of Parkinson's disease. He decided not to say anything to anybody, not even his family, for the fear that word might get out and hurt his career. After completing *The World According to Garp*, George met with Robert Daly and Terry Semel who were the Chairman and CoChairman at Warner Brothers and confided in them the fact that he had been diagnosed with Parkinson's. They were both very decent and told George that they would promise to keep it among themselves, and George was able to direct two more films.

In 1984, John LeCarre's successful novel, *The Little Drummer Girl*, was adapted for the screen by Loring Mandel with George Roy Hill directing; and, boy, did I love casting that film. The only thing bad about it was that it was not terribly successful when it was released.

John LeCarre is a pen name used by David Cornwell, a very handsome, charming man. I really had a good time with him as he was on the set quite a lot. I was in Europe for so long working on *The Little Drummer Girl*, that I had to turn over my casting for Clint Eastwood to Phyllis Huffman, who was one of my associates at Paramount Pictures that I brought with me when I came to Warner Brothers. I miss Clint; I loved working on his films. Phyllis worked with Clint until she passed away from a brief illness in 2006. I miss Phyllis too.

We traveled all over Europe when casting *The Little Drummer Girl*. I was scooting between London, Paris, Tel Aviv, Jerusalem, and Munich, where our studio was. I had clothes scattered in the different cities because I was going for quick trips all the time to one place or another.

Diane Keaton starred as Charlie, and the movie was really her story; the character was based on David Cornwell's half sister in real life. Before I arrived in England to do some casting, I was told that David's half sister, Charlotte Cornwell, who is a well-known actor, was terribly upset because it was her story.

I felt badly about it, though it was not my fault. The studio wanted an American star. It had been talked about on British radio and television a good deal. Finally screwing up my courage, I invited her to lunch. What I thought would be a very tense get together turned out to be about a three-hour lunch with quite a bit of wine at L'Escargot. She's a wonderful lady, and I've now seen her in several plays in the States. I was so glad that we got our relationship squared away.

George, as with *Hawaii*, where he wanted all true Polynesians, wanted real Israelis and real Arabs in the parts in the film so I had to see many actors who were unknown to us. I met a lot of very interesting people. They had no casting directors; and Levia Hon, Rodika Alkalay, and Perry Kafri were the only three agents in Tel Aviv. I'd been warned about them, because they were very tough dames whom I was told were not going to like me coming in; but the three of us became great friends.

The climate was very tense in Tel Aviv when the movie was made. I learned a great deal about the tensions between the Arabs and Israelis. Every time I flew into Tel Aviv, I was practically strip searched because it was such a scary time.

There was a man named Slomo Mograbi, and if ever a name was perfect for its bearer, it was this guy. He worked for our production company in Tel Aviv, but a thief is what you'd call him in the States. I would make the deals for the actors and then the checks for them went to Slomo. He was supposed to take out the taxes and return the money to the agents for the actors. Now sometimes this would take months and months. Meanwhile, Slomo would deposit the money, earn the interest on it, and eventually give it back to these three lady agents. *Mograbi.* It was a wonderful name for a guy like that.

I went to Paris to see an actor I'd heard about named Sami Frey, who was very big in the theater in France. He took a bit of talking to, because he was so busy in the theater, but we finally worked it out so that he played Khalil, a very important part in the film.

It was then too that I found Yorgo Voyagis. He was a Greek charmer and was coming back to the States to do a job. He was there at the first reading we had in New York. Diane Keaton just lit up like a Christmas tree when she saw him, and they became very friendly during the shooting. In fact, once we started shooting, the chemistry off the set between Yorgo and Diane was much more exciting than it was on camera. It seemed the minute the camera started rolling, Yorgo lost his radiance and was impassive. Yorgo just became dead on camera where personally he was very engaging. He's a great guy, but at times, it was also a bit difficult to understand his English.

Michael Cristofer played Tayeh in the film and was awfully good as were a group of Israelis who played the gang. There was a part in it, Kurtz, the head of this group who was German. Klaus Kinski became our Kurtz despite his agents' insistence that he wouldn't read. Now everybody said he was the worst person in the world, that he did terrible things to people, like throw things at them or even hit them. I was also told I'd never get him to agree to play the part. It just so happened that he was in England at the time; and I asked him to come to Munich to talk to George, just talk with him, since obviously we knew that he wouldn't read.

George was so clever, though. We sat in the hotel room, and George very gently was telling him the story and talked enthusiastically about a scene in the script and started to read that scene. Kinski was, after all, an actor and couldn't resist and started to chime in; and before you knew it, he was reading the part. Good actors usually want to experience and experiment with a meeting or reading so they can judge the director's bent and he theirs.

For the first rehearsal, we had to have all the kids brought from Israel to Munich. All the Israeli girls were just so beautiful and very sweet. I noticed that Klaus was really making quite a play for a couple of them, so I went to the girls and told them that Kinski was a star and a woman chaser. They were told that they didn't have to accept any advances from him at all, that it wouldn't affect their employment; and, in fact, we did not want them to become involved with him. They were all crazy to get the job because they desperately needed the money, and this was a big deal for them, but I let them know they did not have to feel obligated to play footsie under the table with Klaus Kinski.

Klaus was very sweet throughout the whole project. I think he probably hated me, although I'm not sure if he ever knew what I did. I think we became friends one night at dinner when he offered me a cigar, and I actually smoked it all the way down.

In Munich, the company was living in a rundown old hotel. Loring Mandel (the screenwriter) was there, and LeCarre (David Cornwall) came and spent a good amount of time on the set. At night, the three of us used to go out for dinner. We'd then come back to our flea bag hotel; and Loring would go up to his room and write, while David and I would go to this little sitting room and have schnapps and talk.

David is one of the most attractive men I've ever met, also one of the funniest with a wry humor. I went out to visit him at his home on the heath with his wife and his two whippets in Cornwall, England. We were sitting there one night, and he talked about a critic at which point both dogs started to howl. David had taught them to howl anytime the word "critic" was mentioned. We got caught on the heath in a rainstorm at one point, and I had to take off all my clothes and put them into a dryer, wearing David's clothes, while mine dried so I could go back to my hotel.

We were traveling around so much that a whole group of us from the movie were at the Athens airport about to separate and go in various directions when we ran into David. He was a very mysterious guy, and nobody knew where he was going, maybe it was to Panama to write *The Tailor from Panama*. David wrote all his books in longhand and never made a copy of anything. My flight was called, and my baggage was taken and put on a cart, and I headed off to another part of the airport.

When they were unloading my bags from the cart, I recognized one of them was not my bag, but remembered it as David's briefcase. I knew the briefcase had the only copy of the book that he was writing at the time. Since I couldn't go back or I'd miss my plane, I tipped my driver and told him he must get this back to where he'd picked me up. I instructed the driver to have David Cornwell paged immediately and give the briefcase to him. I have never been sure, but I may have saved a John LeCarre novel.

We had a costume designer on the film, if you could call her that, who looked like she had just come out of a butcher shop with her butcher shop clothes on. She had absolutely no taste and spoke not a word of English. This woman had gotten some clothes together for an important final scene for Yorgo that were the worst clothes I had ever seen in my life.

I knew I wasn't allowed to do this because of the union, but I told Yorgo, "Let's go shopping. We can't allow this woman to put you in what she has selected for you."

George was not very cognizant of costumes when he's in production because he's always working on the script, so I took Yorgo to a store in Munich and selected some clothes for Yorgo's scenes.

When I realized Yorgo was the same size as George, I thought that what I'd do is select something that Yorgo would look good in and also George. Then when the film ended, I would buy the clothes for half-price and give them to George as a Christmas gift. That was one of the only times I think I have been a wee bit dishonest. George wore Yorgo's clothes from that film for years afterward; they were some of the best clothes he had.

Mykonos was a wonderful island. We filmed there for three or four days. I was sick as a dog most of the time, but the scenery was lovely. I had some type of intestinal or stomach upset, and it got even worse when we returned to Tel Aviv. The Israeli agents—Levia, Rodika, and Perry—the ones that I'd been warned about—brought me homemade soup or something that was an old family recipe for soothing the stomach. The food generally, I gotta tell you, at least at that time on a Saturday, was pretty lousy because it was all kosher. I always hated Saturdays, and I would get someone to go with me to a Romanian place or an Italian place so we wouldn't have to eat the kosher food.

Filming at other locations was not so easygoing or as beautiful as George points out:

> *GRH: We were shooting in Jericho nearby a local Palestinian camp. A group came over from the camp to where we were shooting and started throwing rocks at us and tearing down some of our sets. We packed up as much as we could and got the hell out of there in a hurry. They were a militant group and managed to knock the camera over. Shortly afterward, I was directing a scene and noticed several men sitting in the background talking to one another. They were in a square in front of the building I planned to shoot. I thought they were extras in the picture so I walked over there and loudly let them know they were in the background and to get the hell out of the shot. Bummy was standing beside me and the two of us quickly realized that these men were not part of the picture. They were very unhappy with my direction and looked as if they might be ready to kill.*
>
> *There were several dangerous situations. We were lucky we were able to make a comfortable movie in a very tense situation. I do not think anyone was really aware of the powder keg we were sitting on. Janet Stevens, a young American woman who was part of the Palestinian group, was one of the liaisons we worked with in pre-production and we were shocked to learn that she was killed during the US bombing in Beirut.*

Warren Beatty came over to visit Diane Keaton at Christmas time. George was hoping he would get along fine with Warren because when they were casting *Butch Cassidy and the Sundance Kid*, the studio wanted Warren to play Sundance and George insisted on Robert Redford to play the part.

I must say that Warren was charming and helpful to George who was having some kind of trouble with Warner Brothers. I don't know if the studio didn't like some parts of the script or what the problem was. Warren told George that if he could do anything to help, he would speak to the guys back at the studio. He told George they shouldn't do this to him. It was a very nice gesture. Warren's a good guy.

We saved so much money on the budget that the studio gave George a Rolls-Royce Corniche convertible as a bonus. I told George that I certainly earned at least a fender or so of that beautiful car. One day we drove through Central Park in it with the top down, and I felt a bit guilty thinking that passerby who were not that lucky would really hate us, but I was so surprised by New Yorkers who waved at us and gave us the "thumbs-up" sign.

A 1987 big hit for Warner Brothers that launched three blockbuster sequels was *Lethal Weapon*, which brought my friend Richard Donner and myself back together. This cop/buddy film was one of the most successful pairings of two actors in a film for quite some time. In Shane Black's original screenplay, Martin Riggs and Roger Murtaugh were police sergeants recently assigned as partners. One character dealt with personal struggles involved in the loss of his family and his suicidal tendencies with trying to move on; the other involved growing older and having to deal with a large family and this new partner he was just assigned.

American-born Mel Gibson had moved to Australia with his family when he was thirteen years old. He worked in Australian made movies until 1984, when he appeared opposite Anthony Hopkins in a remake of *Mutiny on the Bounty* called *The Bounty*. Until that time, Mel's fame grew out of the many Australian movies he had appeared in, most especially *Mad Max* and *The Road Warrior*. Both films achieved a huge popularity in the United States, but it was not only the futuristic action films that brought Mel to the attention of the American audience.

Two Australian releases from 1981 also gave a strong indication to American critics and audiences that Mel had more to offer than just an appealing, good-looking action hero. *Tim*, a romantic drama about a learning and emotionally impaired Australian laborer who falls in love with an older American woman beautifully played by Piper Laurie, displayed Mel's ability to inhabit a character quite unlike himself. *Gallipoli*, a World War I drama about two friends, fellow sprinters, who are pulled away from their lives in Australia to fight against the Turkish army at Gallipoli, was critically acclaimed and became a prestige Paramount release in 1981.

I was invited to attend a cocktail party on the Paramount lot in connection with the *Gallipoli* release and its two young stars, Mel Gibson and Mark Lee. Now it may seem hard to believe that a twenty-five-year-old Mel Gibson could be at a party in America and not be besieged by fans, studio brass hoping to make a deal, or whatever, let alone those that might have been physically attracted to the stunningly handsome star; but I noticed Mel and Mark standing off to the side, looking around and seeming incredibly miserable. I was surprised to see how shy they were; and being quite shy myself, it was obvious to me that we had that in common, if nothing else.

I went over to talk with them, sensing they were feeling totally out of their element at this big Hollywood gathering. Mel was so shy then, but both he and Mark were such sweet kids; it was impossible not to be taken with them.

After reading *Lethal Weapon*, I thought of Mel Gibson and talked to Dick Donner about him playing Martin Riggs. From what I remember,

Mel was considering giving up acting all together and becoming a rancher back in Australia. We tracked Mel down and got him a script, and he met with Dick. Mel had been working very hard to get rid of his strong Australian accent. With each progressive film Mel made here, he continually improved until he was talking like a real American, which indeed he was. The combination of his strong accent and his emergence in Australian films has always made it difficult for many to believe that he actually was born in the United States. As Dick recalls, "When Marion suggested Mel and was convinced he could get rid of his Australian accent, I thought it was a wonderful idea. And we met. And it was."

We'd discussed many actors to play Roger Murtaugh, but never an African American actor as it was originally written for two Caucasian policemen. What made me think of Danny Glover was a stroke of luck, one of those heaven-sent ideas. I didn't ask Dick or producer Joel Silver what they thought of the idea. One day I just asked them to see someone I had a hunch about. When Danny came in, they were both a bit startled, but it worked! Danny was not an unknown, having had roles in *Places in the Heart*, *Witness*, *Silverado*, and *The Color Purple*; but none were "buddy" films. As Dick recalls, "More important, I now realize how narrow minded I was because it did not say that Martaugh was black. And maybe Marion didn't see him as black either but just as the best actor available for the part, but Marion's adding Danny Glover turned out to be the creation of one of the greatest film partnerships in the business."

This was the film that made Danny a major star, which thrilled me as he is a wonderful, beautiful man. Danny does an awful lot of good work, not only as an actor but also in his charity work, the benefits of which are felt around the world.

Dick knew as well as I did that chemistry between whomever you cast is what makes a film work well in the end. Whether you're doing a romantic comedy or an action movie, there has to be chemistry between the actors for the audience to be really drawn into the story and to care about the characters.

Mel Gibson proved a perfect foil as well as counterpart for Danny. Martin's (Mel) tenuous grip on life is offset by Roger's (Danny) world weariness and relatively calm nature. As Martin becomes acquainted with Roger's family and starts feeling a sense of family again, the audience is pulled into really caring about what happens to the two characters.

Since Martin is attracted to Roger's warm family, it was important to cast a wife and children that would make that seem believable by attracting the audience as well. Darlene Love had made only one previous appearance in an Elvis Presley movie, *Change of Habit*, where she sang in a couple of scenes. The lead singer from a vocal trio known as The Blossoms, Darlene had sung backup for hit singles like Shelley Fabares's "Johnny Angel" and also for Elvis on many of his recordings as well as singing backup for his 1968 television special, *Elvis*. Appearing in all four *Lethal Weapons*, Darlene was a joy as Danny's patient, loving wife.

The three Murtaugh children were ably played by Traci Wolfe, Damon Hines, and Ebonie Smith. They too appeared in all four films.

Gary Busey provided the heavy, and Mitch Ryan and Tom Atkins had featured supporting roles.

Dick Donner always had a big heart. He is always trying to give jobs to friends, people in trouble; he's a very, very generous man. For any fan of his movies, you have been sure to notice some familiar faces that seem to pop up on a regular basis in his films. Some of his "regulars" included Hollywood columnist Army Archerd's wife, Selma; Steve Kahan (Dick's cousin); Paul Tuerpe; Marian Collier; and Mary Ellen Trainor. As with Elaine May's directive when I cast *A New Leaf*, Dick always had a list of people that were to be given parts in his films.

J. Michael Riva was the production designer on three of the four *Lethal Weapons*. I'd met him when he was a baby on Third Avenue in New York when the E1 was elevated. You'd have to stop talking when the E1 came by roaring and shaking the whole apartment. I knew Michael's mother who was Marlene Dietrich's daughter, Maria Riva.

Two years later, Dick did the second *Lethal Weapon*, and the franchise was growing as the sequel grossed over twice as much as the original. An important character in the sequel was Leo Getz, an annoying federal witness, who got pulled into Riggs and Murtaugh's police work. I cannot take credit for Joe Pesci as the casting suggestion belonged to Mark Canton, who was the head of production at Warners. Joe was wonderful in the part, and the character was wildly popular; but Joe drove me crazy, just like his character did Riggs and Murtaugh in the film.

Pesci's agent was a horrible pest, treating Joe as if he was such a great big star (which he was not). He always acted like he was God's gift to comedy, which maybe he was. Who knows? Making his contract was one of the worst experiences I've ever had. You might have thought he was Marlon Brando and Robert Redford all wrapped into one. He had a very high opinion of himself and still does, but I will not deny that he was very good for the film.

I was in London casting *Batman* when I heard what a good actress Patsy Kensit was. She'd been a big hit in *Absolute Beginners*, a musical that she starred in with David Bowie. I contacted her and asked her to meet with me for drinks. Back in the States, when I brought Patsy into read for the role of Rika, not too long after first meeting her, she reminded me that I had cast her before. Not having any recollection of it, I asked her when. Patsy told me I'd cast her in *The Great Gatsby* in 1974 as Pamela Buchanan, the daughter of Mia Farrow and Bruce Dern's characters. Patsy was only four years old at the time, and I told her that really made me feel old.

Rika Van Den Hass was introduced in *Lethal Weapon 2* as a love interest for Mel's character. By the end of the screenplay, Patsy's character was killed off. It was an unfortunate move since I know that Dick Donner would've preferred to have brought her back for future sequels.

Lethal Weapon 2 had another strong villain of the series, Arjen 'Aryan' Rudd. I cast an English actor Joss Ackland in the role, and he was highly memorable as a diplomat involved in all kinds of crimes who every time he was caught in the act cried, "Diplomatic immunity."

Since *Lethal Weapon 2* had been a huge success and partly because of the addition of Patsy as a love interest for Mel's character, for the second sequel, three years later, the screenplay added another female character for Riggs's love interest.

Rene Russo was discovered at a Rolling Stones concert by John Crosby, an agent for ICM (International Creative Management). With Crosby's encouragement, Rene signed with the Ford Modeling Agency and wound up on the cover of *Vogue*. I had met her on a general interview sometime before casting *Lethal Weapon 3*, but had never read her, so I thought why not see her again.

We called Rene in to read for Lorna Cole. She really did not give that great of a reading, but she tried so hard. We saw a lot of actors for the role but eventually offered Rene the part. After she got it, she went out and really learned all the kickboxing moves her character, a police officer working in Internal Affairs, would do in the movie. Rene got so good at it that she was able to do most of the stunts herself.

Rene had done a few movies before, such as the girlfriend of Tom Berenger in *Major League*, but her Lorna Cole was a breakthrough film role for her. She came back for *Lethal Weapon 4* and hit it off with Mel well enough that she also played his wife in Ron Howard's movie, *Ransom*. Perhaps it was more that she had gone to school with Ron in Burbank than it was Mel's influence that got her into the movie, but Rene's become a respected actress who works quite a lot and is a lovely lady to boot.

Dick's wife and frequent producer, Lauren Shuler Donner, made an appearance in *Lethal Weapon 3* as a nurse, along with Dick's regulars in the cast. The second sequel produced box office results, which nearly matched the first sequel.

To invigorate Danny Glover's storyline for the third sequel, stand-up comedian Chris Rock was added as a police detective who had secretly married Danny's character's daughter, again played by Traci Wolfe.

With the return of Mel, Danny, Rene, and Joe, *Lethal Weapon 4* again had a strong villain character named Wan Sing Ku. One of the successful elements of the series had always been a strong villain. *Lethal Weapon 3* had used a slight twist when the villainy was provided by British actor Stuart Wilson, totally believable as American Jack Travis, a former police lieutenant who had gone bad. With *Lethal Weapon 4*, the villain returned to the more exotic variety . . . foreign, mysterious, powerful, menacing.

Jet Li had become a wushu champion by the time he was eleven in his native China. He would win the gold medal in the sport (which is something like a performance version of various martial arts) four more times, becoming an instructor and then getting into the movies and creating a boon to the kung-fu-type movies in China. He later relocated to Hong Kong and continued to make movies.

When it came time to cast *Lethal Weapon 4*, one of the producers suggested Jet Li. His name had been outside my frame of reference since he'd never done an American movie, and I was not a fan of Chinese kung fu movies. We cued up some of Jet's Chinese movies since I didn't even know who he was at the time. I dutifully contacted his agent, checked to make sure he spoke English, and informed the producers and Dick. We did have a list of Chinese actors for the role, but the producers were already pretty much set on Jet Li so he was cast as Wah Sing Ku. Everyone knew he was going to be big, and they wanted to tap into the huge foreign audience Jet Li had already to watch this film, his American debut.

When Jet Li showed up at the studio ready to work, apparently, the agent I'd spoken to had misunderstood the word "English," as whatever language Jet Li was speaking, was not English. We soon discovered that Jet had almost zero knowledge of English, but the producers were certain that he could be taught to learn his English dialogue. I certainly hoped so because Jet's character had a ton of dialogue!

Joel Silver, one of the producers, and Dick Donner were trying to sell the studio on Jet Li; but Lorenzo di Bonaventura, a production executive from Warner film division, said that they needed to test him first. We assigned a Chinese actor to work with Jet on his English and then had him film a screen test opposite Mel Gibson.

While Jet Li's screen test posed problems because of the language barrier, you could see that he had the right look and showed considerable charisma. The producers, however, knew that if they were going to use him, he wouldn't be able to speak much English; so they created another part for Jet, who spoke only in Chinese.

The role of Benny Chan became the secondary villain. Much of the dialogue that Jet was supposed to have spoken was transferred to the Uncle Benny character. We flew Kim Chan out from New York to meet Dick and Joel.

I remembered Kim because almost thirty years earlier, I had cast him as the theater cashier in *The Owl and the Pussycat*. Kim read for

Uncle Benny and auditioned with the dental office scene, which was one of the funniest in the entire series. To get information out to the crime lord, the three policemen (Danny, Mel, and Chris) arrange to interrupt Benny's dental exam; and alone in the room with him, they use nitrous oxide (laughing gas) to induce him into revealing secrets. If Mel, Danny, Chris, and Kim were not having a good time doing that scene, they certainly didn't let on to the audience, because it was quite irresistible, providing the audience with some very big laughs while also advancing the plot.

But Jet Li is what everyone remembers after they've seen *Lethal Weapon 4*. They recognized his great look; he was evil, menacing, and is a great martial artist. His villainy was entirely accomplished without the use of a gun, but as diabolical as he came across in the final cut; if the audience had seen the screen test, they would probably have laughed. Jet has gone on to great success in other American movies like *Romeo Must Die* and *The One*.

Auditioning always has its fair share of memorable moments. Actors who are dead set on getting a part or at least doing everything they can to get a part are constantly full of surprises. When I was reading actor Everett McGill for the role of one of Jet Li's henchmen, Everett added to the reality of the scene he was doing when he whipped out a real switchblade, as the scene called for, and held the blade to my throat as we continued reading the scene. Dick was there and Joel Silver too, but there wasn't a sound in the room, and I kept on reading. Everett was certainly menacing enough in his reading as he's shown in villainous roles in movies like *Silver Bullet* and *License to Kill*, but the decision was made to cast all the henchmen as Asians, eliminating Everett's chance for the role.

Another memorable character from *Lethal Weapon 4* was Ping, a half-pint-sized Chinese boy with only two words of dialogue, both in

Mandarin. While he didn't have lengthy dialogue, the character of Ping was integral to one of the escapes from disaster that befalls Riggs and Murtaugh.

I realized we would have to do an open call to find a boy that spoke Mandarin, so we held a casting session for the role of Ping at a school in Chinatown during the holidays, while Dick was taking a break in Maui.

I've never been an advocate of cattle calls of any type and was a bit apprehensive at what the session might bring. We walked into the gymnasium, and there were over two hundred people there. The room was filled with mothers and fathers and children. We had to find a little boy and a little girl (the girl was cut from the final release), and of course, we had to go through everybody. I never liked to turn people away, so everyone got their chance.

The children auditioning had a line to say, and one was worse than the next until suddenly this one little kid came in. He was so darling and smart and just got everything right. His name was Steven Lam. He had a front tooth missing and, when he smiled, was just adorable.

Steven could have made a lot of money doing commercials, but his family was old-time Chinese who did not speak English. It was a niece of theirs whom we talked to, but the family wouldn't allow him to continue with a career, despite our bringing in an agent specializing in children and pointing out to the parents through an interpreter that their son could make a lot of money for his college education if he wished to continue acting and doing commercials.

For all the action, car chases, fights, incredible stunts, etc., that made the *Lethal Weapon* franchise so successful, its ultimate success was rooted in the relationship between the characters, Martin Riggs and Roger Murtaugh, that Mel and Danny played. Without it and the incredible chemistry between them, the franchise would have been much more run-of-the-mill.

There are those that would argue that as successful as the films were with the additions of Joe Pesci, Rene Russo, and Chris Rock, with each successive *Lethal Weapon* film, the time and story taken away from that core relationship pulled the audience's attention away from what really mattered most in the series. While it was necessary to have the characters of Riggs and Murtaugh develop as the franchise continued, I think there are many who thought it unnecessary to keep bringing back the newly added characters.

With compelling stories and some sense of development of the lead characters, Mel and Danny alone would have been enough to continue making the franchise a successful one; but such is the nature of Hollywood that when sequels are made that the powers that be do not want to veer too far away from what made the last installment successful. I think it underestimates the intelligence and taste of the movie-going audience, but nowadays that is the way things seem to be done when making sequels.

Knowing that *Lethal Weapon 4* would be the last sequel in the series, Dick decided to have credits at the end of the picture and wanted to put photos of those of us who had worked on all four films. He asked me for a snapshot he could use for the end credits, and just as a joke, I sent him one where I was in my office pouring a martini from a very large pitcher. I knew he'd recognize the pitcher as one he'd recently sent me (full of martinis) for my birthday. He had other snapshots to use; but imagine my surprise when, at the premiere, there I was in the credits holding a pitcher of martinis!

Warren Beatty asked me to come over to London when he was casting *Reds*. I was already doing some of the casting in the States for his production that had several casting directors. When one of his English casting directors was having problems recognizing the right American accent for one of the scenes where Diane Keaton, playing Louise Bryant, goes back home to Oregon, I came over to fine tune that part of the casting.

While I was in London, Warren asked me to go to Paris with him. He wanted very much to get Simone Signoret for a part in *Reds*. I didn't think it was right for me to go since we both knew that she was ill, but he insisted that he wanted to talk with her about the film. I really think Warren just wanted me to go because he wanted company. In Paris, we were staying at the George V Hotel. There was a rumor floating around that he was there with his sister, actress Shirley MacLaine, so the paparazzi buzzed around Warren and whoever was with him, in this case, me.

Now a long time ago, people thought that I resembled Shirley. I think it may have been because we had the same haircut at the time. As we left the hotel to make our way to a waiting car, we had to maneuver through construction barricades with cameras snapping endlessly as we did so. Once inside, Warren, for whatever reason, immediately assumed a bent-over position to prevent a photographer from getting a shot of his face.

As he sat bent-over, with only the top of his head showing to a paparazzo who jumped onto the hood of the car and clicked away, I commented that he must have the most photographed bald spot in the business. I don't think he liked that comment too much, but Warren has always been very sweet to me and is such a talented man. Considering my faux pas in mentioning his hair, I thought he may have liked me because I reminded him of his sister.

When Maureen Stapleton was cast as Emma Goldman in *Reds*, she had a foible in that she refused to fly. It was the dead of winter when the production was under way and the Queen Elizabeth II was not crossing the Atlantic. We finally figured out a way to get her to England for filming on a tramp steamer down around Africa and up to Europe where she then traveled by train to the location. Maureen went on to win the Academy Award for Best Supporting Actress.

I found myself in England several times over the years and always enjoyed my time spent there. In 1983, I started looking for actors for British director Hugh Hudson, who was starting the production of *Greystoke: The Legend of Tarzan, Lord of the Apes*. Ultimately, Patsy Pollock did most of the casting of the movie and has the screen credit, but I began looking for Hugh early on with the help of Glenn Daniels who began to work for me.

Greystoke was the only production of the Tarzan tale to ever concentrate on the balance indicated by Edgar Rice Burroughs's novel. It detailed how John Clayton's parents were killed after a shipwreck in the jungles of Africa, leaving behind a baby that was adopted and raised by wild apes. Upon his discovery by British explorers many years later, Tarzan is returned to the England home of his relative, the sixth Earl of Greystoke. The film is divided between Tarzan's being acclimated into a society of wild animals and then existing and trying to make a place for himself in civilized British society.

The key element of casting *Greystoke* was obviously to find an actor who could portray a man with a tragic past, raised by animals, and struggling to find his own true identity upon being introduced to his British roots. The concentration would be on a very talented actor who could evoke all the different facets of John Clayton's life rather than finding some muscle-bound athletic actor who looked great in a loin cloth swinging on vines.

I met a young man in New York that I thought had potential and flew him to London to meet Hugh Hudson. No one in the industry had heard of Viggo Mortensen in 1983, nor had I. Viggo does strange things as an actor; he is a strange thing, but undeniably, he is a fascinating actor. At that time, I correctly guessed that he would be around for a long time.

Hugh did tests with Viggo and a young French actor who'd been brought in from Paris, Christopher Lambert. I watched the tests of them swinging through the trees in the studio in England; and while Viggo tested well, Christopher was very interesting because he had this unsettling look in his eyes. He had suffered from myopia as a child; and even as an adult, it gave him an unusual look that Hugh loved and definitely fit the strange "ape man" who would be returned to British society.

Hugh cast Christopher, and Viggo was sent back to the States where the following year he would make his feature film debut in *Witness*. Viggo has worked ever since and has enjoyed great popularity in Peter Jackson's *Lord of the Rings* trilogy as Aragorn.

Christopher ended up being the perfect choice to play Greystoke, capturing the character's intensity, charisma, and untamed nature. An interesting footnote, Christopher later married one of my earlier discoveries, Diane Lane. They had a child together but were later divorced.

For the role of Jane Porter, Hugh really wanted French actor Isabelle Adjani for the part. Isabelle spoke very good English and was undeniably a beautiful woman who was also a talented, Academy Award–winning actress. The studio, however, nixed her casting, saying they didn't want two French actors in the leading roles. That, unfortunately, was the undoing of the casting for the role of Jane, because Hugh eventually, after seeing many people, selected Andie MacDowell because she looked the most like Isabelle, which was a really lousy reason to hire any actor for a part.

We met Andie, a terribly sweet woman, in New York where she was a model at the time. She was selected for one quality only but continues to work, although I really don't know how. As an actor, she has an emotional range from about A to B; it always seems the same to me. Perhaps *Four Weddings and a Funeral* was the movie that most closely captured Andie's real-life charm and appeal, but I knew the role of Jane should have been cast differently.

When we saw the first dailies sent to us from London, it was crystal clear that Andie could not act her way out of a wet paper bag. Something definitely needed to be done to salvage the role of Jane Porter.

Glenn Close had been dying to play the part. She was a tad older than she should've been for Christopher, but she even went in on her own and did a screen test. It was very kind of her. When Glenn heard of the difficulties we were having, she graciously offered to dub Andie's lines. The physical beauty on screen is Andie's, but the heart of Jane Porter is pure Glenn Close. Not every actor would do what Glenn did, which is one of the reasons I love Glenn.

The supporting cast was peppered with some very fine English actors. Ralph Richardson played the sixth earl of Greystoke. I fell in love with Ian Holm's work, a lovely, lovely actor, who played Capitaine Phillippe D'Arnot. Ian Charleson, who was so good in *Chariots of Fire,* and later died of AIDS, was in the cast as Jeffson Brown. David Suchet (who I also used in *The Little Drummer Girl*), James Fox, Nigel Davenport, Cheryl Campbell, and Richard Griffiths rounded out the cast.

Perhaps one of the most indelible memories I have of my time spent in London was in 1989, during the filming of Tim Burton's *Batman.* While we cast most of the lead roles in the States, I cast all the remaining roles of *Batman* in London while we were filming. My accommodations in London became much more deluxe than a hotel room when Tim Burton, who had been provided a nice two-story flat near Holland Park for his stay during the filming, had a falling out with his girlfriend who lived with him in the flat. Tim didn't want to be reminded of her, so the production relocated him; and since they'd already paid rent on his Holland Park flat, I moved in there.

It was a bit strange at first since Tim had left behind many of his paintings. If you've ever seen a Tim Burton movie, then you probably already know that Tim has an imagination unexcelled and surrounds himself with his own artwork of skeletons, ghosts, weird-looking creatures, etc. He probably could be really scary to some people who have never had the chance to meet him only to discover a forever-young man with an abundantly fertile imagination and a youthful, impish charm. Tim has aged some since that first time I met him, but I would wager quite a bit that he is still blessed with that wildly creative streak that makes him such a unique and incredible person.

Eventually, Tim removed the rest of his things, and the flat became less strange. I fell in love with the location. Every morning I'd go out with my pockets full of peanuts, bread, and carrots and walk to Holland Park where I'd feed the various animal residents. There were lots of squirrels, and the rabbits got so used to me they began taking carrots right out of my hand. With swans nearby, it was just a peaceful place to spend time each morning.

Tim had already set Michael Keaton to star as Bruce Wayne/Batman. He liked Michael's eyes; and if you've seen the movie, you may recall Tim featured them heavily, particularly in the cowl that Batman wears. I had no problem with Michael starring as I'd cast him the year before in the drama *Clean and Sober*, and Tim had previously directed Michael in his last film *Beetlejuice*. Michael had the ability to give Bruce Wayne/Batman the vulnerable human quality that was required and also the bravado, athletic and otherwise, to make his heroic feats believable, while having to be fitted and spend a lot of time in a heavy black rubber suit! What became so surprising was the amount of letters

Warner Brothers received from people objecting to the casting decision. The other actors who were strong contenders for the role of Batman were Alec Baldwin, Tom Hanks, and Bill Murray.

The coup of landing Jack Nicholson as the Joker had nothing to do with me. He was the first choice of both Tim and the producers, but in the beginning, he wasn't that interested. I actually wanted Robin Williams who we'd cast in *The World According to Garp*. Tim Curry, William Dafoe, and David Bowie were also in the running. Warner Brothers actually offered the role of the Joker to Robin, and he accepted. When Jack Nicholson got wind of Robin's acceptance, he suddenly changed his mind. Apparently, he'd just seen Tim's film *Beetlejuice* and had a change of heart. Robin was released by the studio, and that really kind of pissed me off. It also created tension between Robin and the studio as he demanded an apology, which he so well deserved. This was the only film that I worked on with Jack Nicholson, who was very nice, and we talked quite a bit on the Pinewood Studios set.

We began with Sean Young as Vicki Vale, the film's leading female role. We hadn't been in England very long when she was rehearsing a scene and fell off a horse, injuring her shoulder in the process. While she was not injured badly, she made a big fuss about it; and when she backed out of the film, it forced us to recast the role. One of the ironies of filmmaking is that the scene in which Sean was injured was eventually cut from the movie.

Producer Jon Peters had been having an affair with Sean; and once she'd been replaced on the film, she promptly moved into Jon's place, the penthouse of the St. James Club. She was there for weeks until Jon eventually had to kick her out.

When Kim Basinger was cast and arrived in London, she replaced Sean both in the film and in Jon's apartment. Kim was a very sweet lady, but I did not think very much of an actor at the time. She was brought to England and set as Vicki without my knowledge, as I know I wouldn't have cast her. I believe she divorced her husband shortly thereafter.

I cast Michael Gough as Alfred Pennyworth, the butler. He happened to be in the States at the time I was casting. What a sweet man! I'd seen him on stage in *Breaking the Code* in New York a year or so earlier. Thank goodness he stayed in New York long enough for me to be able to cast him in something. Gough made quite a run on playing the character in several of the subsequent *Batman* films. I think it was a godsend for him as he was quite elderly.

There were an awful lot of small parts in *Batman*. Mary Selway, the best casting director in London, helped me out there. She was aghast, however, at my chutzpa in having people read for me for such small parts. It was not done that way in England.

I also took Polaroids of the people I read. There were way too many people to call in to meet Tim, so I took photos of them for him to look at. Mary also thought that this was just terrible. I told her she had to forgive us; we were just colonialists and didn't know any better. I told Mary to just blame it on my being a dumb Yank; but I added that it was her landsman, John Schlesinger, who'd taught me to take Polaroids so that he could match them up to the roles. The British people were very cordial to me; I didn't have a thing to complain about in the way I was treated.

For some roles, I decided to cast actors, who along with talent, also resembled real-life counterparts. There were no real-life people in the film obviously, but fictional Gotham City has elements of New York City so it was fun to cast Lee Wallace as Gotham City's mayor. Lee looked very much like the New York City mayor at the time, Ed Koch. As DA Harvey Dent, I sought to match the charisma and looks of a Rev. Jesse Jackson-type politico and cast Billy Dee Williams.

In principal supporting roles, Pat Hingle as Police Commissioner Gordon was cast. Like Michael Gough, Pat has continued to play the character in other *Batman* installments. William Hootkins, a friend of mine who lives in London, I cast as Lt. Max Ekhardt. For the small but pivotal role of crime lord Carl Grissom, I ran into Susan Smith, my agent friend who was in London at the time; and she talked me into letting one of her clients, Jack Palance, play the role. I never would've thought of Jack Palance for I knew he was too expensive for my budget; but Susan, whom I dearly adore and respect, is also a helluva businesswoman and convinced me that I could somehow find a way to hire him. Tracey Walter, a good luck charm and friend of Jack Nicholson's, played the Joker's first henchman, Bob the goon. Tracey appears in many of Jack's films.

Jerry Hall, who we'd previously cast in *Urban Cowboy*, played Alicia Hunt, a mistress of the Joker's. Jerry was quite flashy. I remember riding with her to see Tim at the studio; and, my goodness, you might have thought she was going to meet the president. She applied her makeup the whole hour's drive out to the studio, but she sure wowed the guys once we got there.

Another friend and a very sweet man, Robert Wuhl, was cast as Alexander Knox, a newsman on the trail of the mysterious Batman. Robert brought his wife over to London with him during the filming. One night, when we went to dinner, as we entered the restaurant, there was a large group of people from the cast and crew of another movie filming in London at the time, *Family Business*. They invited us to join them; and their director, Sidney Lumet, acted as host and introduced people up and down at the table.

When Sidney came to introducing me, he asked if any of the assembled group knew Marion Dougherty. Dustin Hoffman promptly got up from the table, walked over to me, and kissed me. He told the group that I gave him his very first job in television and then set him up for *Midnight Cowboy*. That meant a lot to me.

There were many small parts in *Batman* that required British actors to speak without British accents. I was very proud of the fact that I worked with them quite a bit to get their lines right. There was this one man, however, who had one word, "armor," that he could never get exactly right. When we saw the first sneak preview of *Batman*, everybody sounded just fine except that actor and the one word he never quite managed. I just winced when I heard it, but no one else seemed to notice.

Believe it or not, *Batman* was a very hard sell to investors. It was a huge financial risk for Warner Brothers, and they had to prove to their investors that Tim Burton's vision of *Batman* was indeed a marketable one. Even with the financial success of Tim's *Pee Wee's Big Adventure*, investors were eager to see the gross receipts from *Beetlejuice* before committing to this new "gothic" take, which was inspired by the darker Batman stories of the day. At one point, the studio actually asked Tim to help create a short film about the project so they could screen it for their investors. It is important to realize that Tim is the one responsible for creating this incredibly cinematic dark superhero.

Every executive at Warner Brothers seemed to be walking on egg shells and thin ice prior to the film's release date. There was a lot of tension in the air at the studio. It was a tremendous investment and risk for this being really the first film to bring a super comic hero to life. Basically, *Batman* was either going to be a huge success or a huge failure. It all paid off when *Batman* became the highest grossing film of 1989, and one of the ten top grossing films ever released up to that point. Of course, all the protest against casting Michael Keaton as *Batman* turned to praise right after it opened.

Batman was a fun picture to work on, and I enjoyed it so much that when Tim asked me to cast the first sequel, *Batman Returns*, the only sequel that Tim would direct, I readily agreed. In the sequel, which was filmed back in Los Angeles, Batman battles not one but two arch villains from the comic book series, the Penguin and Catwoman.

No one quite understood why Sean Young, who'd already had the chance to be in one of Tim's *Batman* movies, was so set on getting the part of Catwoman. She actually dressed up in a Catwoman suit and came to the studio in an attempt to track down Tim. He was as horrified as I was at the notion and hid in his bathroom until she was asked to leave the studio by security.

From what I recall, there were so many names that were discussed for the role: Lena Olin, Jodie Foster, Bridget Fonda, Ellen Barkin, even Madonna and Cher. The role was first offered to Annette Bening, and she accepted; however, she soon learned that she was pregnant and had to turn it down. The lovely Michelle Pfeiffer, who was a much bigger star by this time than she was when I first cast her in *Ladyhawke*, then accepted the role when it was offered to her and ably performed the dual role of Selina Kyle/Catwoman with appropriate feline grace. She was very active in creating one of her few villainous performances.

Again, for the role of the Penguin, many actors' names were brought up in our preproduction casting discussions. Dustin Hoffman, Marlon Brando, John Candy, Bob Hoskins, and Christopher Lloyd were all talked about; but Danny de Vito was Tim's vision of the Penguin and, indeed, looked very much like some of Tim's sketches. After Danny agreed, Tim asked Paul Ruebens and Diane Salinger to play the Penguin's parents. They had starred in Tim's first feature, *Pee Wee's Big Adventure*.

One of my favorite memories of *Batman Returns* was a visit I made to the set of the Penguin's lair that featured an entire flock of live penguins. The studio was lined with huge air conditioners that kept the temperature so cold inside that I had to borrow a winter coat to wear for my visit. I got to meet some of the real penguins and pet their incredibly soft feathers. They truly are a sweet animal. The penguins used in the film were imported from a couple in London who raised them from eggs they had retrieved on the Falkland Islands where it was illegal to remove live birds.

As penguin "parents," this couple talked to their impending arrivals through their eggshells. When the chicks hatch, they associate the voices they have heard with their parents and become very attached to the trainers.

Another of the villains Batman faced in *Batman Returns* was Max Schreck, and I suggested Christopher Walken to Tim. Tim, who had a penchant for death figures and all kinds of weird imagery in his drawings, immediately said, "Oh, oh no, Christopher Walken . . . I'm afraid of him."

"Well, that's silly. He's an awfully good actor," I said and sort of insisted on bringing in Christopher to meet with Tim.

Now I meant to go over to the office to introduce them at the meeting, but something happened that prevented me from getting there until later. Christopher was in Tim's office with his back to me as I entered, and I said, "Hi, Ronny!" Tim looked at me as if he thought I'd lost my mind.

Christopher was very sweet to me because when he was a child, he and his brothers, Glenn and Ken, were hoofers on a Broadway show. I knew him as a child when he was using his real name, Ronny. That sort of broke the ice, and we cast him as Max Schreck, and Tim got over his fright of this gifted actor. He apparently came to appreciate Christopher's talent as much as I did as Christopher would soon work with Tim in *Sleepy Hollow* as the headless horseman.

Batman Returns was another huge financial success for Warner Brothers and again set new records for a film on opening weekend.

Unfortunately, that was the final *Batman* installment that Tim directed. Being so successful, the franchise was now a super-powered machine; and Warner Brothers wanted a new director, bigger supervillain characters with the film having a lighter and more colorful look.

When production began on *Full Metal Jacket*, I found myself working with the great director Stanley Kubrick. I believe Stanley called me first and I spoke to him several more times on the telephone, which surprised the studio executives as he was so reclusive.

What Stanley wanted from me were cassettes of male actors for the parts I would be casting. As long as I am able to meet and read the actors in person, I have no problem putting them on videotape to pass along to the director. But instead of putting a number of actors on one cassette (most audition scenes would only be a couple of minutes in length), Stanley asked that for each actor I was submitting, only one actor should be put on each tape.

Somebody told me that Stanley wanted to build up his supply of videocassettes so he could record over them without having to pay for them. That may sound a bit farfetched for a successful film director who could well afford to purchase as many cassettes as needed, but there did not really seem to be any other logical reason for his request. It was his little eccentricity.

That foible I could have lived with, but when I called one agent of an actor I was interested in and was told that another casting director, Mike Fenton, had already asked to put the actor in question on cassette for the same movie, I called Stanley's lawyer in Los Angeles to find out what the heck was going on. I told him I wanted to put an actor on tape and was told that Mike Fenton was doing it. Some friend of Kubrick's apparently had been talking to him about casting and asked if he had tried Mike Fenton.

My involvement with the project ended there, as I had no intention of working in tandem with Mike. The final credits had six names credited for casting, including mine. I must admit it's sort of nice to be listed in the credits of a Stanley Kubrick film, although I don't know whether I was actually responsible for anyone being in the cast or not.

Guilty by Suspicion was a film directed by Irwin Winkler that I was particularly interested in casting. It concerned the blacklisting in the 1950s, a time in which I had strong feelings about, having lived through that very dark period of history that, unfortunately, I don't think we are immune to living through again. It was a very interesting script, with the casting pretty much a combination of Irwin's and mine.

The film starred Robert De Niro, Annette Bening (I thought she was awfully good), George Wendt (of *Cheers* fame, proving he is a terrific dramatic actor as well), Patricia Wettig, and Chris Cooper (in his second feature film). The cast also included Sam Wanamaker, Luke Edwards, Ben Piazza, Gaillard Sartain, Tom Sizemore, Barry Primus, and Brad Sullivan. Martin Scorsese did one of his rare acting performances in the movie. Producer Gene Kirkwood, who had executive produced Irwin's *Rocky*, also acted in the film as Gene Woods.

The movie follows De Niro's career-minded Hollywood film director, David Merrill, as he tries to get on with his work amid the growing very real threat of McCarthyism that is destroying those around him until it begins to deeply affect his life, his family's, and his career.

Back in my days at *Kraft Television Theatre*, Joseph Welsh, the counsel for the U.S. Army in the McCarthy hearings, appeared on one of our shows that was about law schools. On *Omnibus*, a television series that presented everything from dramas and musicals to documentaries,

Welsh had met and immediately liked Dick Dunlap, one of our directors, who invited him to appear on *KRAFT*.

Mr. Welsh agreed to come on *KRAFT* and speak during three minutes at the end of the show that Dick had saved for him. He had everything carefully written out that he wanted to say.

Virginia Raymond, the assistant director, who worked with me on *KRAFT* for all those years, was there and spoke with him about how he became involved with the McCarthy case.

Welsh's law firm was in Boston at the time of McCarthy's reign of terror, and he was home with a cold one day. Bored, he turned on the television and found himself fascinated and appalled at the House Committee on the Un-American Activities hearings being aired. McCarthy's knowledge of the law (he was supposed to be a lawyer) was so bad that Welsh decided that if ever he could get this guy, he was going to do it.

It was Joseph Welsh who was largely responsible for bringing down McCarthy. This occurred after the then President Eisenhower had finally felt McCarthy had gone too far when he assailed a military man in the hearings. The bombastic senator was finally on the receiving end of the questions, and Welsh asked McCarthy the question most difficult for him to answer.

"I think I have never really gauged your cruelty of your recklessness," Welsh told McCarthy. "Have you no sense of decency, sir, at long last?"

Joseph Welsh also asked Virginia if she wanted to know what was in McCarthy's briefcase. During the hearings, he always made a great gesture of pointing to his briefcase, indicating that he had the evidence right in there. Welsh told Virginia that the "evidence" was actually his liquor bottle and a gun.

Senator Joseph McCarthy was not a very bright man and was looking for a political football. Roy Cohn, working for him at the time, had been instructed by McCarthy to find him something that would get him attention. He definitely accomplished that.

McCarthy succeeded in becoming one of the great villains of the twentieth century. He was eventually censured by the Senate in 1954. It is interesting to note that, besides all the careers and lives he destroyed, not one person who was questioned by the Committee ever went to prison.

Craig Zadan and Neil Meron produced a trifle titled *If Looks Could Kill*. Fortunately, they didn't let it slow them down, however, and lately have been responsible in a very large way for reviving the American musical on both television (*Gypsy, Annie, The Music Man*) and on film with the Academy Award-winning musical *Chicago*.

We were holding readings at Craig and Neil's place in Los Angeles. They'd just bought this place, and it wasn't fully furnished so we held the readings in a sun room, and the actors had a stool to sit on, and I conducted the readings while sitting on the floor.

Richard Grieco was a heartthrob of the teenaged set at the time because of his television appearances in the series *21 Jump Street*, and the spinoff series developed for his character, *Booker*. In true hot shot fashion, Richard arrived for his audition on a motorcycle, wearing a pair of torn shorts with holes all over them, particularly in the butt.

Richard came in and sat on the stool with me on the floor in front of him. From that vantage point, one could see right through to Sunday up his shorts, which was very distracting. Imagine coming in to read for a fairly well-known casting director and two producers who were very well thought of in just shreds of clothing. I was quite disgusted with his appearance and not particularly impressed with his reading; but Richard was given the lead role of Michael Corben, a charming slacker who flies off to France with his high school French class only to be mistaken for a spy and, separated from his class, becomes involved in international James Bond like intrigue.

It was an unsuccessful movie and failed to launch a film career for Richard. I was much happier with the supporting cast that included Gabrielle Anwar (in her first feature film) as Richard's love interest, Linda Hunt and Roger Rees as the wonderfully over-the-top villains, and Robin Bartlett as a mild-mannered French teacher who becomes almost a commando to protect her students.

In retrospect, not that it particularly did his career any good, it seems that perhaps Richard chose what he wore to the audition to make an impression on the producers rather than me. When dressing for a particular audition, it does not hurt to wear something vaguely appropriate for the part one is reading. In California, T-shirts and shorts are frequently worn by actors to auditions. However, if you know it's a part of a CEO and you have a suit or at least a sports jacket and tie, that might help your image. For ladies coming in for a sexy part, it obviously doesn't help to wear a burlap bag, but you don't have to wear see-through blouses either. I would say that most directors do like to look at good figures, that is, if you have one.

I don't think you have to come in with a dirty face if you're up for a coal miner. Let the director use his imagination a bit. And, ladies, don't cut those long tresses when up for a flapper; you may not get the part and may need your hair for the next interview. Let the studio give you the appropriate haircut after you are hired.

The first movie of Mel Gibson's that I cast besides the *Lethal Weapon* franchise was *Forever Young*, which was released in 1992. Mel played a test pilot, Daniel McCormick, who in 1939, asks a friend experimenting with cryogenics to freeze him for a year so that he doesn't have to endure the love of his life's coma. When Daniel is released from his cryogenic freezer by two precocious boys, not one, but fifty-three years later, he finds himself in a new world and time. The film's supporting cast included Jamie Lee Curtis as Claire, the mother of Nat, one of the little boys who releases Daniel. Nat was played by Elijah Wood who nicely made the transition to an adult actor and now is a big star playing Frodo in *The Lord of the Rings* trilogy.

Forever Young was a sweet movie released just before Christmas, directed by Steve Miner and written by Jeffrey Abrams, and did quite well at the box office.

Isabel Holland's novel, *The Man Without a Face*, was translated to film in 1993. With a screenplay written by Malcolm MacRury, the film marked Mel's first film directorial effort and was a very special film for several reasons.

The Man Without a Face is the story of a reclusive man and former teacher who lives in a remote house on the ocean outside of a town in New England. The man, Justin MacLeod, is physically and emotionally scarred from an automobile accident some years earlier. A troubled adolescent is caught on MacLeod's property; and despite his fear and initial revulsion, Charles Norstadt, the boy, becomes emboldened enough to ask MacLeod to tutor him so that he can pass the entrance exam to a private school.

Since the bulk of the story revolves around Charles Norstadt and his uneasy relationship with Justin MacLeod, it was very important to find a young actor that was physically just on the verge of puberty. It was also necessary to find someone who could handle a range of demanding dramatic scenes, yet be likeable enough for an audience to identify with and care about.

I felt like I'd seen every kid in California before I heard of some young man who was supposedly very good performing in one of the theaters down in Texas. I asked a casting friend of mine down in Texas to look him up and put him on tape in a scene from the film.

After having gone through I cannot tell you how many kids, I viewed his tape; and suddenly, it just hit me. He was so good and so right. There was a point in the reading that he even had a little tear that came into his eye, and it was perfect.

I hurriedly called Mel Gibson and told him he would not believe it, but I had finally found the boy to play Chuck. I urged him to get over to my office as soon as he could. He came over right away, and we watched the tape together. Mel was as impressed as I was with eleven-year-old Nick Stahl's video audition. We contacted Nick and had him fly to California the following day.

Nick had done a couple of television movies prior to *The Man Without a Face* and worked spottily after the film until 1998, when he had his first breakthrough role as an adult in *Disturbing Behavior* and *The Thin Red Line*. His appearance in the movie *In the Bedroom* and the blockbuster *Terminator 3: Rise of the Machines*, which starred Nick in the role of John Connor opposite Arnold Schwarzenegger, seem to indicate Nick's steady rise to bigger roles in high profile movies; but Nick's Charles Norstadt in Mel's first directing effort was a terrific performance.

Mel, of course, selected the hardest thing in the world for his first directing effort. He not only directed but played the lead as well in a role that required him to go through three or four hours of makeup every morning to become the facially disfigured Justin MacLeod.

Mel does not like to read people; he's like Clint in that respect. He likes to meet them and see what they've done. As it was his first directing job and my not really knowing him as a director, I was extra careful to make him comfortable and give him many choices, so I brought in quite a lot of actors for the role of Catherine, Charlie's mother. Much of the information that explains Charles's situation comes from the character of his mother who has been married multiple times and struggles to keep her family going while she deals with her neediness to have a man in her life.

We started meeting actors in California and then went to New York to see more. While I was in California, I saw an actor from New York who was there doing a pilot for a television series. I thought I'd never met her so I arranged for a general interview. This was not someone I thought of originally; but the ingénue in her pilot, Robin Tunney, said she should go and see me about a film with Mel Gibson. She wasn't too anxious to meet me, and I was just so-so about meeting her, but we arranged to meet anyway.

Usually, I see people for about ten to fifteen minutes, but I remember she came in at ten in the morning. At ten forty-five, my secretary buzzed me and asked if I wanted to be rescued. I asked her why, and she said we'd been in there for over forty-five minutes gabbling like two teenagers. I told her it wasn't necessary. There was some spark that just passed between Margaret Whitton and me. We didn't talk a whole lot about the film, but we got to talking about baseball.

Margaret is an avid New York Yankees fan and knows more about baseball than any man I've talked to. Of course, I hadn't seen a game in a stadium since the Dodgers left Brooklyn. I was so pissed off at them when they went to Los Angeles that I didn't follow them. Margaret said she had a box at Yankee Stadium and asked if I would like to go to a game. I told her that I would. It was at that Yankees game that Margaret reminded me that the fascinating young girl that I had sent to New York to meet the director of *The Heart Is a Lonely Hunter*, way back in 1967, was the rabid Yankees fan seated next to me. All these years later, Margaret Whitton remains my closest and dearest friend.

Margaret and I had both wondered what on earth got into our heads. Margaret normally would never invite a "suit" out (I'm the suit), and I would never accept an invitation from an actor. We have laughed a lot about that. Anyway, I arranged a meeting with Mel to see Margaret in New York since we were scheduled to go there the following week and Margaret would be there too.

Despite his aversion to it, when we had Margaret in, I told Mel that this time we've got to read for him, because I think this is definitely an actor who may be right for the part of Catherine. So we did read Margaret, and then Mel and I had to go back to California to meet with another five actors.

We'd seen over a dozen people by this time, and I remember the last person to see us was Helen Mirren. I thought to myself, "Oh god, Helen's been getting a lot of publicity and doing a lot of good things lately, and this is it. Mel's going to cast her." Helen didn't read; she just came in and met. My dismay had nothing to do with Helen's talent as an actor. She was wonderful then and continues to be so, but that magic that clicked between Margaret Whitton and myself made me want her to get the role. However, I wanted it to be Mel's choice.

After it was all over, I said to Mel, "That's it. You've seen at least a dozen of the best actors I could find. Which one do you want?" By this time, I thought he might have forgotten about Margaret because he was acting kind of strange in the meetings in New York. He was fidgeting around like crazy. We had a very small couch (sound familiar?), and he was trying to get comfortable on the couch, and I thought he wasn't paying too much attention.

"I think Margaret Whitton," he answered.

I was so happy that I jumped up and hugged him, which I think scared the hell out of him. Margaret is such a wonderful actor, and I was terribly glad about her getting the film, particularly since the role of middle-class Catherine with her lack of self-confidence is not usually the type of role Margaret gets the chance to play. I wish I'd had a more glamorous part for her to play. She is quite a stunning lady; and in retrospect, it was probably an opportunity she had to let the fans know that she didn't always have to play the rich, gorgeous bitch.

We shot *The Man Without a Face* in Maine, and upon my arrival there, I still had many small local parts to cast. We were all stationed in this large motel kind of housing. It was really kind of grim, and the food was pretty bad too.

Margaret, ahead of time and sight unseen, had rented a house to stay during filming; and after I'd been in the motel for a week, she asked if I'd like to come and share the house with her. I gladly accepted; and once again, we wondered why on earth she asked me, a suit, to come and stay with her and why I, who very much respected, but didn't generally hang out with actors, accepted. We stayed in this house and went out each night to dinner at a club. Margaret even joined me on an overnight visit to a dear friend mine from the Cleveland Playhouse days who lived in Maine.

In the film, Nick Stahl's character had two sisters, Gloria and Megan. Fay Masterson played Gloria, the older sister; and she was a perfect match for Margaret, both of them red-headed and attractive enough to be totally believable as a real-life mother and daughter. Fay ably handled the role of the older sister suffering teenage angst as she tried to deal with growing up in a frustrating family life.

For the younger sister, I cast Gaby Hoffman. I later realized that Gaby was a kid that I'd seen when she was three or four. Her mother was Viva, the Warhol star that we cast in *Midnight Cowboy*. Viva came out to California at one point as I was considering her for another film so we had lunch together at Ma Maison. Viva asked her little type what she would like, and I was just in horror when she ordered caviar. I looked at the menu and saw that caviar was sold by the ounce, and I thought, "Oh geez, what are they gonna say to me about my expense account?"

Sure enough, Gaby ate the whole ounce. She became a wonderful little actor and was very good in this film.

Geoffrey Lewis was cast as the police chief, along with several New York friends like Viva, Jack De Mave (whom I had known forever), and Jeannie De Baer, who all appeared in small roles in the party scenes. I used Michael DeLuise, one of Dom's sons, as Gloria's boyfriend. He shares his father's gift for comedy.

I took very special care to try and bring in people that I knew would be fine with Mel since this was his first directorial project. I didn't realize what a great director he would soon become, able to handle actors well, along with the complications of a huge production like *Braveheart*, for which he won the Academy Award for Best Director. Mel was also able to direct movies with a very sensitive subject matter such as *The Passion of Christ*.

When I returned to New York and was having drinks with George one evening at the apartment, George got a phone call from his best friend, Paul Newman. Paul was creating a marketing poster for his new product, Newman's Own Virgin Lemonade. He asked George what woman he should use to be on the poster with him. George deferred to me, telling Paul that his casting director happened to be sitting next to him.

I had one of those flashes of improbable ideas when Paul asked me what I thought, and I asked him, "Do you know Whoopi Goldberg?"

Paul roared with laughter at my suggestion and replied, "No, but I'll call her tonight!"

Paul did and got the same roar of laughter from her. A few days later, I received a magnum of the finest champagne from Paul, a great thank you for a nutty idea.

A copy of the poster that was created hangs in my hallway and makes me smile every time I see it. Paul and Whoopi are featured in old-fashioned clothing with the name of the product along with a banner proclaiming that Paul's lemonade "Restores Virginity." At the bottom of the poster is the line, "Fine Foods Since February."

Funny Farm turned out to be George's last film. There were other projects he would have liked to have done; but with the onset of Parkinson's disease, while not accepting defeat, I think he felt that he couldn't be certain that he'd be able to give future directing projects his 100 percent, so *Funny Farm* became his last hurrah.

Based on a Jay Cronley novel, the movie was shot in Vermont. *Funny Farm* starred Chevy Chase and Madolyn Smith as Andy and Elizabeth Farmer, a Manhattan sportswriter and his wife, who abandon city life to relocate to the countryside of Vermont.

It was a funny picture, and I think is another case where George's strong hand as a director helped a very large talent like Chevy deliver a wonderful comedic performance. Roger Ebert, in his June 3, 1988, *Chicago Sun-Times* review noted, "Chase is not exactly playing a fresh kind of role here—his hero is a variation of the harassed husband he's been playing for years—but he has never been in a better movie. He has everything just right this time, and he plays the character without his usual repertory of witty asides and laconic one-liners. It's a performance, not an appearance." Ebert said of George in the same review, "George Roy Hill makes it better . . . because he finds the right tone and sticks to it—a sort of bemused wonder at the insanity of it all in a movie that doesn't underline its gags or force its punchlines, but just lets everything develop naturally."

George spoke about directing Chevy in *Funny Farm*:

> *GRH: The style in which the first draft of the screenplay was written was to play on obvious gags with broad slapstick routines*

and Chevy making faces. I wanted to tone down and let him be much more himself and let the situations be funny.

Chevy's background, mostly because of SATURDAY NIGHT LIVE, was all clowning around. His tendency was to mug and to get a laugh. My idea was to approach the comedy in a kind of style that was much more realistic.

I think what made Chevy and I close throughout production was a kind of mutual respect and perspective and sense of humor and where it all sits. For Chevy, humor is ultimately physical having less to do with the delivery of the line, the expression that you give and the expression you get in return. His tendencies were always broad and I'd say, "No, Chevy, down boy!" This led to much laughter on the set. In my eyes, Chevy seemed to relax and he improved as we went along, not as a performer, but as an actor.

I don't play for laughs because I don't believe you should play for laughs. When playing comedy or tragedy you make it believable. If you start sending up lines or commenting on them by saying, "this is funny," it collapses on you. You've got to have a grounding in reality. In farce, particularly, you've got to have a special intensity. You have to play it a little harder to make it even more believable. If your audience thinks for a moment that you think it's funny, you lose them. Playing for laughs is sending up lines. Play it sincere; then it's funny.

We discussed the possibilities of who should play Chevy's wife, and I remember we wanted Kathleen Turner; however, the budget wouldn't allow it. Amy Irving read for us, but she was a little soft. We needed someone who would be able to blow up at Chevy. When I brought in Madolyn Smith, we were both impressed with her reading. She had the look we were searching for, and there appeared to be the right sense of balance when she read with Chevy.

The assorted townspeople in the movie that complicate the Farmers' move to Vermont include Kevin O'Morrison, Joseph Maher, William Duell, Alice Drummond, Dakin Matthews, and Brad Sullivan. Sarah Michelle Gellar made her big screen debut in this film as one of Elizabeth Farmer's (Madolyn Smith) students.

Lest you think it does not bother me to cast someone in a role where they are going to be particularly disliked because of the character they play, I had cast Audrie J. Neenan in Clint Eastwood's *Sudden Impact*. Her character, Ray Parkins, is certainly one of the most truly despicable female characters ever written; and to Audrie's credit as an actor, she performed the role brilliantly. Audrie, at the time, was a comedian on a very popular HBO comedy series, *Not Necessarily the News*. I felt so badly about giving Audrie the role in *Sudden Impact* that would certainly be despised by the audience, that years later I called her and offered her the role of Ivy in *Funny Farm*. It was a much smaller role, but oh-so-much kinder and gentler than Ray Parkins.

Funny Farm was a heartwarming experience as George often surrounded himself with his same creative team, and this was his last film. Once again, he brought together the guys from Pan Arts, Patrick Kelley and Bob Crawford, Henry (Bummy) Bumstead as production designer, Ann Roth as costume designer, Miroslav Ondricek as director of photography, and Elmer Bernstein as composer.

Academy Award–winning screenwriter Brian Helgeland (he shared writing credits on *L.A. Confidential* with Curtis Hanson) made his directorial debut with *Payback*. Based on Donald E. Westlake's novel, *The Hunter*, Brian cowrote the screenplay with Terry Hayes. The story followed a "dead man's" return to get $70,000 owed to him by the man who shot him, Val Resnick, a sleazy hood with a penchant for sadomasochistic hookers.

I handled the casting with my associate, Doug Wright. Jane Haldeman also cast out of Chicago where the film was shot. Mel Gibson was set to play Porter, the lead character beset by problems in getting his money. Brian had one talent as a director that is invaluable. He really didn't know that much about casting and did not make the mistake of assuming he did. I don't know if it was the fact that he was directing his own screenplay or if it was because he insisted on wearing khaki shorts throughout the entire shooting schedule in the frigid winter temperatures of Chicago, but Brian delivered a film that was well-received critically and financially with interesting characters and performances.

As an actor, Mel has never had input into the casting of any of the films I've done that he starred in; but for some reason, he didn't think our choice of Kelly Rowan for the part of Porter's drug-addicted wife was a right fit for the role. Brian had seen her in *187*, a film I'd cast; and Doug and I were looking forward to reading her, both feeling she could handle the role. Mel, however, felt that Deborah Unger, who'd been tested for *Ransom*, the film Mel did for Ron Howard, was better suited for the role of Lynn. Deborah hadn't gotten the part in *Ransom*, and I think Mel just felt sorry for her.

I was not a terribly big Deborah Unger fan, which had much to do with *Crash*, a recent film I'd seen her in that starred Holly Hunter and James Spader. *Crash* was a very strange film, basically all the characters in the film getting off on violence and being in car wrecks and the film featured lots of nudity. It seemed like every other scene Deborah Unger had her clothes off. This was *not* the Paul Haggis film *Crash*, which won Best Picture in 2006; it was a David Cronenberg film from 1996.

I was honest when I spoke to Deborah's agent and said, "You know I saw her last film, *Crash*, and it didn't do anything for me. I didn't really like her performance that much."

When Deborah came in for the audition for *Payback*, she greeted Doug and me and handed me a check.

"What's this check for?" I asked.

"I understand you really didn't like my last film, *Crash*, so there's a check for seven dollars and fifty cents to reimburse you for the movie admission," Deborah responded.

For casting directors reading this, write this down as one of the rules of casting: Never tell an actor's agent anything against their client, even if it's true!

There was a variety of interesting "bad guys" standing between Porter and his money; and Doug and I found actors like Gregg Henry, Bill Duke, David Paymer, John Glover, William Devane, Jack Conley, Kris Kristofferson, and James Colburn to play them.

Along with Deborah Unger, Maria Bello handled the other principal female role connected to Porter. As Rosie, she provided the primary love interest for Mel's character, although it was a very small part of the screenplay.

Certainly, the juiciest of the female roles in *Payback* was that of Pearl, an Asian dominatrix who used every part of her body to help Gregg Henry's Val live out his S & M sexual fantasies. Pearl was also the most difficult role of the film to cast, but not for any lack of Asian actors who could handle the role.

Doug and I originally read Lucy Liu for the role. Lucy, at that point in her career, had done mostly television work. Whether it was from the exposure upon the release of *Payback* or not, Lucy went into the television series *Ally McBeal* after the film, and eventually launched into the thriving film career she enjoys today with her roles in *Shanghai Noon, Charlie's Angels*, and Quentin Tarantino's *Kill Bill*.

From the moment Lucy read for us, Doug and I knew that Lucy would do an incredible job with the role of Pearl. The only real trouble we had with our decision was that the director was good friends of an agent's mother of another Asian actress, Ming Na Wen. Rosalind Chao was also in the mix for the role of Pearl; and callbacks were scheduled for Rosalind, Ming, and Lucy while Doug read the sides (the dialogue chosen from the sections of the screenplay for auditions) opposite our trio of Pearls.

In retrospect, it seems unfair to Rosalind that we did not have someone in attendance who was rooting for her as much as Doug and I were for Lucy and Brian for Ming. Both Rosalind and Ming are actors of sufficient talent to have played Pearl, but in the audition process, it was Lucy who just nailed the role. It was also clearly evident to Doug and I in that Friday callback session that Brian had his heart set on Ming every bit as much as we had ours set on Lucy.

Brian threw a curveball to Doug in the callback session when he announced that he'd like to have the action of the scene improvised, with Doug assuming the role of Val Resnick. Brian and I sat on a couch nearby and watched each of the three readings.

The actors came in to read, one by one; all had their black leather pants on and their various accoutrements of whips, chains, and handcuffs, none of which they'd been told to bring. During Lucy's improv, Doug was down on all fours, with Lucy slapping him, kicking him, and making him kiss her boots. At one point, she even ripped open Doug's shirt, sending the buttons flying. Brian and I were enjoying every bit of the improvised scene. Poor Doug couldn't tell if we were laughing at him getting beat up by Lucy or at Lucy herself, but he and I hoped that the improvised scene would work, whatever it was.

I could tell that Brian was set to offer the part to Ming that day, and Doug and I both stood up to him and told him that he shouldn't do this to the film, that Lucy would be much better than Ming as Pearl. Showing another attribute of a good director, Brian listened to us and agreed to a second callback session the following Monday, with Ming and Lucy reading opposite Gregg Henry who'd been cast to play Val. This thrilled Doug to no end as he wasn't sure his clothing budget could withstand another callback session with him reading Val.

On Monday, Lucy came in with Gregg and Ming Na Wen had bowed out. Brian eventually agreed to trust our judgment and Lucy Liu was a delicious Pearl. The audience loved her performance.

Considering Mel Gibson's very pleasing physical appearance, I think it's terrific that he's been so successful as an actor and filmmaker. It's not often that an actor, first of all, can be blessed with Mel's looks and actually have the acting talent to truly play a character role. It is also almost as unlikely that an actor who looks like Mel would be given the chance by the powers that be in Hollywood to continually choose roles that are quirky, multidimensional, and more interesting than the standard, traditional leading man roles in romantic dramas and comedies that capitalize on the audience fantasizing about being up there on the big screen opposite Mel.

Mel's a smart guy and has been extremely fortunate that the audience has responded as much to his choice of roles as to the way in which he performs them. I always look forward to a Mel Gibson role, just to see what Mel's going to do next. Now that he's added directing and producing to the mix, his projects are even more exciting to anticipate.

Maverick was directed by Dick Donner, and Mel Gibson was set to play Bret Maverick, and Jodie Foster shortly after was signed on as the female lead, Annabelle Bransford. From what I recall, Dick's first choice was Meg Ryan to play Annabelle, and I'm not sure what happened with that. The project was based slightly on the 1950s television series starring James Garner, and it was decided early on that Garner should have a substantial supporting role.

The film told the story of Bret Maverick doing everything in his power to obtain $25,000 in cash to assure him of a seat in a high stakes poker tournament held on a Mississippi steamboat. The game was overseen by James Coburn as the commodore. The big event takes up a good share of the final half of the film with the poker players vying for a pot of a half million dollars.

Since we had James Garner to remind the audience of the original television series, Dick decided it would be great to assemble as many old western stars as possible for small parts or extras in the poker scenes. This brought back memories of *Won Ton Ton* to pull together famous faces associated with westerns that included Dub Taylor, Leo Gordon, William Smith, Doug McClure, Paul Brinegar, Henry Darrow, Robert Fuller, and Will Hutchins. In a slightly larger role, Denver Pyle played a cheating poker player ejected from the steamboat after being discovered.

Another element represented in the faces of the extras was a country-western music contingent that included Clint Black in his first on-screen role. Among the others seen fleetingly were Waylon Jennings, Vince Gill, Carlene Carter, Kathy Matteo, Hal Ketchum, and Reba McEntire.

Since the tone of *Maverick* was often tongue-in-cheek and light, Dick prevailed upon Danny Glover to play a bank robber who has a run-in with Mel in the bank being robbed. Also in supporting roles were Alfred Molina, another British actor who plays villains extremely well, as Angel; Graham Greene as a straight-talking American Indian friend of Maverick's friend, named Joseph; Paul L. Smith as the archduke; and Geoffrey Lewis as the banker who owes Maverick money.

Dick also called upon a couple of friends from past movies to do cameos, among them Margot Kidder from *Superman* and Bert Remsen from *Inside Moves*.

There was considerable chemistry between Mel and Jodie that surprised many people who read the tabloids. One of the scenes required Mel to come up alongside the stagecoach Jodie is riding in and kiss her. The kiss didn't last that long in the film, but anyone watching the dailies of the multiple takes of that kissing scene could tell that Jodie was really getting into it! I think she really dug Mel. No, I know she did.

When I joined Dick Donner's production of *Assassins* the following year, Antonio Banderas and Sylvester Stallone were set for the movie. It was not a memorable movie with the exception that Dick attempted to change Stallone's acting style, and I thought he did pretty well. Antonio was very charismatic, but this was not the film to do it for him.

Finding a leading lady who wanted to work opposite Stallone was not easy. Everyone had previously passed on it, because they did not want to work opposite a wall, but the lovely Julianne Moore took the role and was rewarded with not being photographed as nicely as she should've been.

The year before I did *Lethal Weapon 4*, Dick's *Conspiracy Theory* came out, starring Mel Gibson and Julia Roberts. The story of a highly paranoid New York City cab driver, Jerry Fletcher, who along with a vast array of personality quirks is obsessed with a lawyer, Alice Sutton, who works in the city's Justice Department. *Conspiracy Theory* was a late summer release and a nice commercial hit. Dick, along with his "regulars" in the cast, made an appearance early in the film as Mel's frustrated taxi customers. Dick also made use of an earlier film we did together, *Ladyhawke*, in a movie theater sequence where Jerry is menaced by hordes of SWAT-team-like government commandos out to get him.

Patrick Stewart, who ten years earlier had risen to stardom as Capt. Jean-Luc Picard in television's *Star Trek: The Next Generation*, reminded the audience of his versatility as he menacingly beset Mel's character. Cylk Cozart appeared as Agent Lowry who had the misfortune to constantly be mistrusted by both of the characters, Jerry and Alice, and had the bumps on his head to prove it.

I also cast Jenny Wright in a small role that was filmed, but eventually cut from the final print. Jenny, who'd played the coquettish Cushie in *The World According to Garp* years before, was so funny in the scene; but it was not to be seen by the audience, and I really regretted that.

Dick Donner has been a phenomenally successful director and producer of films. It is one of those rare occasions in Hollywood when a guy who is as sweet and nice as Dick has seen the commercial and financial success that so often eludes them. If you have Dick Donner as a friend, you have something very special in your life, and I am delighted to say that I have the pleasure of calling Dick my friend.

It is inevitable that during a casting director's career you cast someone who has never acted or cast an actor who has never previously been in a film. One of the unparalleled benefits of my job has been in helping an actor's career along. I don't think I have a colossally large ego, and I believe that in almost all cases that true acting talent will be found out. I always felt that if I didn't offer someone their first part in a film, then someone else would in another project before too long.

In the second of the two films I cast for Michael Caton Jones, *Doc Hollywood*, I asked a favor of an actor to whom I had given his first movie role and also introduced an actor who had not been in a film before.

Having previously cast Woody Harrelson in his first film, *Wildcats*, I could not resist asking Woody if he would do the small supporting role of Hank Gordon in *Doc Hollywood*, which starred Michael J. Fox.

Woody did a great turn in a part that was not as large as those he was used to playing once he'd arrived on television's *Cheers*.

The biggest problem in casting Michael J. Fox's leading lady was finding someone both talented and small enough to play opposite Michael. When Julie Warner read for us, Michael Caton-Jones and I both felt she was ready for her screen debut and would make a perfect romantic foil for Michael, which indeed she did.

The previous film that I cast for Michael Canton-Jones was *Memphis Belle*, the story of a bomber flight crew in WW II based on real events. The screenplay required several terrific young male actors and was populated by some of the best, including Matthew Modine, Eric Stoltz, D. B. Sweeney, Billy Zane, Sean Astin, Tate Donovan, Reed Diamond, Neil Giuntoli, and Courtney Gains.

Juliet Taylor and I cast *Memphis Belle* together. Beyond finding terrifically talented actors for the parts, we were also given the added responsibility of doing whatever we could to make the actors distinguishable from one another. Much of the film's action had them suited up for their bombing flight into Germany. With the various paraphernalia that bomber flight crews wore at this time, sometimes all that distinguishes one actor from another were their eyes and mouth.

I don't think Tate Donovan knew that distinguishing one actor from another was part of the casting process for *Memphis Belle*, but he showed up sporting a mustache that simply was not right for his face or for the role. The moment I saw it, I made Tate go into the bathroom and shave it off. He later gave me a little shaving mug and brush holder that on the side read, "To MD from TD."

Perhaps the oddest bit of casting in *Memphis Belle* was finding the right actor to play Sgt. Clay Busby, the farm boy tail-gunner, who dreamed of having his own farm after the war was over. Harry Connick, Jr., was making a big splash in the music industry at the time; and I'd seen him perform in California. The comparison of his voice to Sinatra's was certainly an accurate one, and he was a real showman, putting on a great show.

If you've seen Harry, you know that besides that terrific singing voice, he is very easy on the eyes with wavy hair, large expressive eyes, and a great smile. I don't even know why I made the connection when we were looking for Clay Busby, but we called Harry in to read, and he turned out to be more than competent in his acting debut.

Nancy Savoca's film *Dogfight* starred River Phoenix as a soldier on leave who becomes involved in a contest with his soldier buddies to see who can bring the ugliest woman to a dinner date. I was terribly happy to get Lili Taylor to play River's date who ends up making him care for her more than he ever would've believed. Lili is not an ugly woman by any stretch of the imagination, nor is she a beautiful one. She is a wonderful and fearless actor who will do more than what is required to fully realize a performance.

Aside from the chance to once again cast Holly Near as Lili's mother, the most notable casting to emerge from *Dogfight* is probably the feature film debut of Brendan Fraser. As sailor #1, he did not utter more than a single memorable first line, "How'd you like to eat my shit?" But Brendan was one of those actors whom I felt was destined to be discovered no matter who it was that did the discovering.

The next year, Brendan went on to a breakthrough role in a successful comedy titled, *Encino Man*. We were able to offer him a much more substantial role when Nessa Hyams, from the old brownstone days, cast him in *With Honors*, which also featured Joe Pesci, Moira Kelly, and Patrick Dempsey.

Superstardom came to Brendan with Disney's *George of the Jungle*, followed closely by his most critically acclaimed role in *Gods and Monsters*. Once *The Mummy* dominated the summer box office, Brendan has pretty much been able to work nonstop.

When I was casting Lasse Hallstrom's film, *Something to Talk About*, I wanted to read Matthew McConaughey for the role of Eddie Bichon. Matthew had appeared in *Dazed and Confused*, which was filmed down in Texas where Matthew was from.

The reading became problematic when his agents said no, that Matthew would not read for *Something to Talk About*, which floored me because this was a project being directed by Lasse Hallstrom and produced by Paula Weinstein, not exactly names without influence in Hollywood. Matthew's agents wouldn't let him come in and meet these people, let alone myself!

I really raised the roof and asked them who the hell they thought they were that they would not let Matthew come in for a meeting. I told them in no uncertain terms they were going to ruin him.

Matthew did finally come in and gave a marvelous reading, but he was too young for the part that was eventually played by Dennis Quaid. I thought so much of Matthew's talent that I brought him to the attention of Bob Daly, who was Chairman of Warner Brothers at that time. I strongly recommended that they try and get him a good role in another one of their films.

A Time to Kill came up right after that. The film already had Kevin Spacey, Sandra Bullock, and Donald Sutherland attached so they didn't need another star name; and that became the film that launched Matthew's career. I don't know exactly how much of the favor Matthew knew about, but he's been very sweet in occasionally sending me a card or note.

I always loved it when I got to go to a country where I'd never been and see and meet the people that live there. It felt so refreshing. In Prague, Czechoslovakia, I had a unique opportunity to visit there twice, first in 1971, when George was filming *Slaughterhouse-Five,* and then again in 1994, when I cast Bernard Rose's *Immortal Beloved.*

Prague is a unique city in that its architectural beauty was not marred by World War II like so much of Europe. Many films are shot there because it's possible to find castles, concert halls, residences, etc., that have the same interiors and exteriors as when they were first built along with the original artwork and chandeliers, etc.

There were such gorgeous places that they shot in, and Prague was an amazing city to me because I had seen it before the Iron Curtain was lifted and again nearly twenty-five years later. I remember walking through the main square the first time during production on *Slaughterhouse Five.* It was very drab with just a few people walking by, all dressed in, not rags or anything, but all monochrome, with no joy on their faces.

Well, that same square during the time I worked on *Immortal Beloved* was full of at least five bands, including a dixie and jazz band, among other types of music being played; and it was just teaming with life. Broadly smiling people filled the square in their now brightly colored clothing. There was not a smile anywhere to be found when it was under Communist rule. Prague is an incredibly beautiful city, and it was great to be able to spend time there.

Bernard Rose's screenplay was based on several historic documents that dealt with many lesser known aspects of Beethoven's life, including his gaining custody of his nephew and the mystery of the one true love of his life that has never been solved. The identity of Beethoven's "immortal beloved" is open for discussion, and Bernard's take on whom that might be comprises the structure of the film.

The casting of *Immortal Beloved* began in London. I was able to cast Jeroen Krabbe, an actor I've known for years and years. I'd wanted to cast him in another project a while back, but because of a change of schedules, we weren't able to work it out. For years afterward, when he'd come to see his agent in Hollywood, he'd phone me to say hello and never failed to ask when I was going to repay him for the movie I owed him. Besides being a fine actor, Jeroen is a well-known painter in Amsterdam and an author of cookbooks. I'm fortunate to have one of his paintings in my New York apartment.

Jeroen was very good as Anton Felix Schindler, a lifelong associate of Beethoven's who searches out Beethoven's immortal beloved in the film. Originally, Jeroen was interested in playing Beethoven, and I believe Bernard may have been considering him until Gary Oldman came into the picture. Gary was reluctant to play another historical figure, although those he'd played before were far more contemporary (Sid Vicious, Joe Orton, Harvey Lee Oswald); but his manager talked him into playing the role. Bernard's vision of portraying Beethoven (warts and all) was wonderfully realized by Gary's performance.

For the multiple lovers of Beethoven, we cast Isabella Rossellini as Anna Marie Erdody, a lovely Dutch actress by the name of Johanna Ter Steege played Johanna Reiss, and Valeria Golino was cast as Beethoven's first love, Giulietta Guicciardi. I had met Valeria, a fine actress, many years ago and had never been able to cast her until this film.

Marco Hofschneider, a young German actor, played Karl, Beethoven's nephew. Marco continues to work in his native Germany and has done one or two other American films. The famous conductor, Sir Georg Solti, who was the music director on the film, had a very zoftig daughter, Claudia, whom we cast as Theresa von Brunsvik.

Miriam Margolyes played the little part of Nanette Streicher, the Swann Hotel manager. She'd just won the Olivier (Britain's equivalent to an Oscar) for her work in *The Age of Innocence*. One afternoon in London, we were headed to tea, walking from the Hotel Mayfair, not a terribly chic hotel where I was staying, to the Ritz. Miriam was stopped by many people wanting her autograph. We got into the Ritz to have tea, and they took one look at her dressed in jeans and some sort of sweatshirt and wouldn't seat us. We had to walk out of there and went around the corner to another place where we had tea and crumpets and spent a lovely afternoon.

Barry Humphries was cast in the movie as Metternich. I imagine many a fan of Barry's most famous incarnation, Dame Edna Everage, would have seen the movie and totally missed the fact that he was in it.

Donal Gibson, Mel's brother, played a small role, as did Alexandra Pigg, the wife of director Bernard Rose. Bernard himself even got into the act doing a cameo as did producer Bruce Davey.

When I was in London casting, my room was on the hotel's sixth floor where we were auditioning actors. I became very annoyed by somebody who was playing the piano on the fifth floor. Finally, out of frustration, I called the front desk to complain. They informed me that it was a gentleman who is playing Beethoven in a movie. I didn't know that Gary Oldman was staying in the same hotel. Obviously, I rescinded my complaint. It was amazing what he accomplished.

Gary played the piano before the movie, but if you see the movie, although the piano playing was dubbed; that was Gary's finger work. Bernard decided that if Gary could master the fingering of the most difficult piece performed in the movie, the cadenza from the *Emperor Concerto*, then the audience would buy the fact that it was really Gary playing. With Gary's mastery, Bernard was able to move the camera from Gary's face to his hands and vice versa, revealing that there was no "hand dubbing" being done.

I experienced a lovely surprise on *Immortal Beloved*. After I'd gotten back to Hollywood and had moved on to another casting assignment, Bruce Davey, a producer who's not known for spending a lot of money on budgets, bless his heart, sent me back over to Prague to see the climactic scene of the performance of Beethoven's *Ninth Symphony* and the *Ode to Joy* being performed. It was toward the end of Beethoven's life where he couldn't hear at all, but in the scene, he goes and stands in front of the symphony as they perform. Gary played the scene brilliantly; you could tell Beethoven was feeling the beat of the music with his entire body.

I stood behind this glorious setting in a real theater that was the actual theater where in the 1700s, the first performance of *Die Fledermaus* was performed. It was so wonderful that I just stood there and listed and cried. If I never told you, Bruce, your generosity was one of the nicest things that has happened to me.

Immortal Beloved was not a big commercial success; but the soundtrack, when it came out, was a best-selling CD. I like to think that Bernard's hope that the movie would bring a love of Beethoven to some young moviegoer who had previously been unaware of his brilliance was realized many times over.

Just before leaving London, I learned that Mel Gibson had just checked into my hotel and was staying on the floor above me while he was casting *Braveheart*.

In the course of casting *Immortal Beloved*, I met with a young woman who had just gotten out of drama school. I was not able to find a part for her in *Immortal Beloved* but was so taken by Catherine McCormack that I sent her up to meet with Mel. Catherine ended up playing Murron, the young woman William Wallace, Mel's character, marries.

The second film I worked on with Bernard Rose was *Anna Karenina*, released in 1997. We'd already cast Sophie Marceau and Sean Bean in the leads but needed several English actors for the other important supporting roles. We only had about a week in London to read actors before Bernard was to go to St. Petersburg for a location scout. I was going to stay in London to complete the contracts for the British actors, but Bernard requested that I go to St. Petersburg to find the almost forty Russians we needed to play smaller parts. It was the middle of winter, and I had a lousy cold, but the lure of seeing St. Petersburg got me to change my mind.

My dear pal Margaret Whitton insisted that if I were going to Russia, I should take her mother's old mink coat. As I am a devout animal lover and donate to many animal preservation organizations, I felt too guilty about wearing the coat in London, also afraid that some zealots might throw paint on me, so I didn't wear the mink in London; but boy was I happy to wear it in Russia! Almost all the people on the frigid, wintry St. Petersburg streets were also wearing furs, so I felt quite in the swing.

I arranged my flight, and then the morning before I left, we heard some big news from Russia. There had been a double murder in a hotel in St. Petersburg. The hotel was the Nevskij Palace, the hotel where I'd made my reservation! This was also only a couple of months after another casting director, Elizabeth Leustig, was run down by a car and killed in the streets of Moscow. Despite those two instances, I got on the plane and found St. Petersburg to be a wonderful city. Bernard, however, took great delight in showing me signs of the blood from the murders in my hotel as soon as I arrived.

The next morning, work started at nine o'clock in the "studio." There were these little dinky rooms for offices, but at least we didn't have to bring our own toilet paper as we did in Prague! I was given an interpreter and a file clerk whose job it was to go to the basement and bring me photographs of actors. These were not eight-by-ten headshots with resumes on the back, but little snapshots pasted or stapled on pieces of corrugated cardboard. Some of the photos were taken way back when and were not at all current. If I was searching for someone to play a thirty- or forty-year-old; instead, I'd get a good grandfather type!

The young file clerk was kept very busy that day, bringing me lots of photos, and I selected those who looked a bit like what we could use. The interpreter was very good, and she was more than likely some type of a casting person. She could give me some idea of acting credits, so we set up appointments for the next day. The hours were usually from 9:00 a.m. to 7:00 p.m., six days a week. Lunch was some strange cold cuts that I didn't eat and a big kettle of soup, which I did eat as it was hot, though watery. Coffee was vile so I changed to tea. I learned to eat a big breakfast at the hotel, which was great—a buffet of fruit, eggs, bacon, breads and pastries and caviar, which I really hogged up on (as we used to say on the family farm).

Very few performers spoke any English so I became quite adept at sign language and facial expressions. The Russians were quite jolly and entertained by this strange American woman. But it worked. They understood what we needed for the parts. We worked out of there for a few weeks and finally got a good group of actors together. I couldn't wait to see their names on the crawl (the scrolling on-screen credits at the end of the film) for it would surely give a sense of reality to the film.

There wasn't much time to see the city for I fell in love with the Hermitage, the breathtaking museum at the Winter Palace, and went there three times. Whenever I could get a break, I would try to go; however, it would take a month to see all the fascinating exhibits there.

All the rooms were very large, and the highlights for me were in this one particular room where there was a small statue by Michelangelo that you could walk right up to. They had one large burly Russian woman in each room to guard, but there were no ropes, no glass cases—you could touch anything. This statue was of a nude man bending over, his hands on his feet. I could see all the chisel marks, very faint delicate lines like little scratches. I was so close my nose was almost touching the marble.

There were two paintings by Da Vinci that had never even been seen in art books, and I could stand only six inches away from the brush strokes.

But the real thrill was an exhibition called "Hidden Treasures." This had seventy-four paintings by Cezanne, Carot, Delacroix, Gauguin, Van Gogh, Manet, Matisse, Degas, Picasso, Toulouse-Lautrec, Seurat, Roualt, Daumier, and some others, paintings almost no one had seen before outside Russia.

Some of these gems were hidden away in the Hermitage during World War II. They were only on display for a limited time in the Winter Palace before being returned to their special storage conditions in the Hermitage and then being returned to their original museums or owners. Many were from German collections or private dealers. Most were of the Impressionist and post-Impressionist schools. It was a dazzling exhibit; and as before, you could go right up to the works to see the brush strokes and then stand back and get the full effect.

A group of us from the production would walk to the Winter Palace from the hotel to see the River Neve frozen over with people skating or pulling sleds on it. The buildings were painted soft red, yellow, blue-gray, or off white. You had to be very careful crossing the streets, walking immediately when the light turns green for the streets are three times as wide as ours, and the drivers do not stop for the pedestrians once the light changes. You saw no beggars on the streets (we were in a fancy part of town), nor tourists or litter, just lots of snow and bumpy ice. All the buildings are huge, like the country itself.

We finally finished our "needle in a haystack" search for the Russian parts, and I was about to leave for London when Bernard and crew asked me to go to Moscow with them. Bernard was shooting a skating scene and then a town square scene inside the Kremlin. Well, that I couldn't resist, and I also was to meet a few Russian actors that spoke English.

Nikita Mikhalkov, who directed and starred in *Burnt by the Sun*, which won an Oscar for Best Foreign Language film in 1994, was a big star in Russia and arranged for us to shoot a scene inside the Kremlin.

We took a midnight train from St. Petersburg to Moscow, which is quite an experience and a bit dicey but is supposedly safer than flying Aeroflot. Bernard, the crew, and I met and boarded the train at 11:30 p.m. We were all booked on the same sleeper (for safety's sake) so all six of us stood around the corridor, having vodka before retiring for the night.

We had our own security guard and purchased extra locks for each room. Our rooms were very tiny and very hot, so I decided to sleep in my clothes but had to get up about every hour to discard some apparel. By the time we arrived, I was in the nude and still hot! I took a shower and tried to look less like a mummy. Daryn Okada, the director of photography, and I decided to go sightseeing in Red Square. I felt like I was in a newsreel, and Stalin would pop up any second. I went to the office only to find out that this was some sort of holiday for women so, of course, I didn't get to see any Russian women that day.

The following day, we were allowed into the Kremlin, which seemed quite beautiful. As we were shooting a great scene with horse-drawn carriages, men and ladies in beautiful period costumes, etc., we saw a line of limousines carrying Boris Yeltsin, then the Soviet premier, to his office that was at the edge of this beautiful square. A few hours later, the bullhorns rang out, asking us to leave. It seems we were making too much noise for Mr. Yeltsin.

That was the end of my Russian visit, and I got on a flight back to London. I'd been worried for some time to see if we'd gotten the actors that were needed. I was really fortunate that we were able to get James Fox for Karenin. I lost Sinéad Cusack but got a lovely little lady for the part of Betsy, Jennifer Hall. She was the spitting image of her mother, Leslie Caron, and her father, Peter Hall. Although she hasn't done a lot, the genes are sure there.

I lost Diana Rigg for Countess Vronskaya but found a delightfully funny lady named Phyllida Law, who has a daughter named Emma Thompson. Finally, we finished casting in London with a group of good actors that included Fiona Shaw, Danny Huston (John Huston's son), Alfred Molina, Mia Kirshner, Niall Buggy, plus my forty Russkies. I often recall what a joyous experience that was!

Jon Peters produced *Rosewood* and wanted us to make up an album of photos and bios of all the actors that we saw for the film, whether we used them or not, to be presented to him. I didn't spend any time at all considering his request and told him absolutely not, if we did that, we wouldn't have time to cast the picture.

Rosewood, based on a true story, concerned a small town in Florida that in the 1920s suffered its destruction and the massacre of most of its African American male citizens when a Caucasian woman lies about a crime committed against her by an African-American man when actually it was a Caucasian man. The production of *Rosewood* hinged, to a certain extent, on getting a star name for the role of John Wright, the storekeeper who has an uneasy relationship with the African American population. As he struggles with his morals, he becomes a somewhat reluctant hero and helps Mann, played by Ving Rhames, a wanderer who has arrived in town, to help a group of women and children escape to Gainesville.

There was some conjecture that the film would not be made unless they got a "name." The producers had contacted Jon Voight's agent before I came on board, and he had turned them down after reading the screenplay.

During preproduction, I was invited to dinner by Charles Durning. He then called me the day of the scheduled dinner to ask if I would object to Jon Voight joining us. I, of course, had no objection. Charles didn't know that Jon had turned down the lead in a film I was casting.

During dinner, I told Jon that I had thought *Rosewood* had an interesting script and was surprised that he'd turned it down.

"Well," Jon said to me, "if you're doing the casting, it might be a good film. I'll read the script again."

He overrode his agent's objections and agreed to accept the role of John Wright and ended up giving the film the star name it needed.

Jon Peters wanted us to use Esther Rolle for the role of the family matriarch Aunt Sarah to get another "name" actor in the project. Esther, unfortunately, was in poor health at this point; and John Singleton, the director, had a lot of trouble with her. I had wanted Isabelle Monk to play that role but had to settle for using her in the much smaller role of Emma. It was unfortunate that I was never able to offer Isabelle a greater screen role. She is a very talented actress from Yale drama school who has achieved considerable recognition for her stage work at the Guthrie Theatre in Minneapolis.

Rosewood was a movie that revealed a little-known story in Florida history. It was difficult for some to watch as it exposed the extreme racism in the South in the 1920s. I have always wondered why the studio or Jon Peters asked me to cast the movie. As pleased as I was to be asked and delighted with the cast that we assembled, I thought they would've used an African American casting director. There are some fine ones in California, among them Jackie Black, who endeared herself to me by saying I was the "mother of casting."

Along with Jon, Ving, and Esther, the cast included Don Cheadle, Michael Rooker, Elise Neal, Catherine Kellner, Akosua Busia, Kathryn

Meisle, and two actors that I was very familiar with, Paul Benjamin and Bruce McGill.

The O. J. Simpson murder trial was in its final stages during the casting process. My associate Doug Wright and I had just finished a meeting with John Singleton and immediately turned on the television to listen to Johnny Cochran's closing argument in the trial.

"Damn Johnny Cochran, he's going to get O.J. off," I told Doug.

Doug was frozen speechless when John walked back into the room after we'd thought he'd left the building. Uncertain of how John felt about the murder trial, Doug feared our goose was cooked.

I didn't blink an eye and handled whatever John needed before he left the building without making any comment on our view of the trial. John is a gifted director who achieved fame with his earlier films *Boyz N the Hood* and *Higher Learning* and continues to helm challenging and popular projects. He was in his late twenties when he directed *Rosewood*, and I enjoyed his professionalism and class. I fully expect he will keep making wonderful films.

The Last Boy Scout, a film directed by Tony Scott, was another Shane Black screenplay that featured a pairing of male stars—Bruce Willis and Damon Wayans. It was a less successful venture than the *Lethal Weapon* series that Shane had spawned years earlier, but it delivered a solid action movie over the Christmas holidays when it was released.

Bruce Willis, who was a big star at the time, having come off great big screen successes in the first two *Die Hard* movies among others, decided to flex his muscles despite not having casting approval. We had offered the role of Sarah Hallenbeck, the wife of Bruce's character, to Marg Helgenberger, a talented Emmy-winning actress and a very beautiful woman. Bruce decided that he wanted Chelsea Field to play his wife instead of Marg, after Marg was already told she had the role.

Bruce had invited himself into a casting meeting we were having with the director and producer, something that had never happened to me before nor, I'm happy to say, since. I'm always happy to talk to the stars of a film about the others in the cast, but I've never had a lead actor tell us to recast a part for absolutely no reason except for ego, a foible I find charmless and unnecessary.

Tony Scott was a nice man, but he insisted that everybody be put on tape and asked us to use a VHS-C tape, these tiny little things. He ended up with a stack of tapes five feet high. The odd thing was he never seemed to want them and never did anything with them, but he was worse than Stanley Kubrick in terms of wanting all these people on tape.

Another little eccentricity of Tony's surfaced as I cast the parts of the football players of the fictitious Los Angeles Stallions team that figured prominently in the film. We ended up with some name football players in the cast, and I was very impressed with them because many gave such good readings.

The role of Billy Cole, an overstressed, drugged wide receiver football star, kick-starts the film's action; and Tony wanted an actor with a particular kind of face for the role. Feeling enormous pressure to win a game the Stallions are losing after receiving a threatening telephone call during halftime, Billy Cole adds more drugs to his system and returns to the rain-soaked field and proceeds to catch a pass from the quarterback and heads for the goal line. As the opponents start lining up to take him out before he can score, Billy flips out and pulls a gun from his uniform; and, stunning his teammates and the cheering crowd, he shoots several opposing players as they run at him before he crosses the goal line and ends up shooting himself in the head before the charging police and security men can stop him.

The first day of readings for Billy Cole, I brought in Billy Blanks, who I thought was perfect for the part with his build, talent, and a kind of haunting, troubled look he could bring to his eyes that fit the character to a T. Billy is the founder of a popular exercise regimen known as Tae-Bo, a combination of Tae Kwon Do and boxing.

Tony said Billy was not what he was looking for, so we continued auditioning.

We ran through all the teams on the West Coast; and, not having any success with those I brought in to see Tony, I decided to bring Billy in again because in my estimation he was perfect for the role.

When Tony saw Billy for the second time, he did not recall that he'd already seen him and told me Billy was just perfect, just shows to go ya!

Tony smoked cigars through the whole production and seemed to particularly enjoy my readings with the various football players. While my associate, Doug, ran the camera, I read opposite the football players with some really raw dialogue. It didn't bother me as much as I think Tony thought it did, and we ended up with a well-cast picture.

The Last Boy Scout was Halle Berry's first commercial success in a small pivotal role as Cory, the girlfriend of Damon Wayans character.

Three to Tango was a 1999 film that you'd have to twist my arm to get me to admit that I cast. I was working with a first-time director and a producer who had absolutely no taste. It was last film I worked on for Warner Brothers before retiring, and I asked to have my name removed from the credits, but the studio refused. I've been fortunate enough to usually work with directors who have artistic approval. I have once or twice cast for one who is overruled by higher-ups, which is a disaster as far as I'm concerned.

A Yankee Girl Relaxes . . . a Bit

Many people find it interesting to follow one's "life path." Obviously, it is the most interesting when you are around my age and can reflect on where you were born, what values you got from your family that have stuck with you throughout the years, and ponder all the changes and choices you've made as you travel along this great journey called life. To examine a life, the gathering of friends, lovers, and fascinating people in your circle while experiencing times of joy, sadness, and great emotion is intriguing. I know that I've tried to do my best to get to the end of my life with some dignity and am still working on it, but I have the good fortune to look back on the life that I have led with great fondness and a sense of satisfaction.

The noted psychic Sylvia Browne, whom I have met on more than one occasion through my friendship with Lindsay Harrison, who cowrites Sylvia's books, says that before we are born, we chart a life course for ourselves with lessons to be learned and experiences to be had. If you are lucky, like me, you realize that things remained fairly balanced through the course of your life.

I can't say that I'm thrilled with the creaks and shudders that my body has developed as time goes on, but I have been luckier than most with my health. God knows I enjoy the life I lead and am grateful for all of the experiences I've had along the way.

For a man as vital, stimulating, and interesting as George Roy Hill was, he did not deserve the slow debilitating destruction of his body with Parkinson's disease. George died on December 27, 2002, at the age of eighty-one. He was unique in practically every respect that made him, at times, difficult for many people to deal with, but ultimately made him a one-of-a-kind and gentle man that everyone who was fortunate enough to have known him was personally thankful to have him in their lives. He was not a perfect man but, oh, such a worthwhile one.

In 1984, the University of Oklahoma was host to a celebration of George's films, and in the program for the event, Paul Newman wrote the following:

What is George's special allure? Why do performers tickle his soft underbelly with affection and pick up all the dinner tabs that he never sees? Because they know that they will never be better, that George's 'detached' eye will spot a successful mannerism, an irrelevant gesture, an irresolute intention, a personal comment, stomp it underfoot, and politely ask for something original. In the largest sense, he is insurance (not always "no fault" insurance) but the sweetest coverage around. In the environment of film, where there is so much bad taste, so many berserkers, amateurs, executives, and people 'puttin' on airs,' George is truly a straight arrow. Hollywood tends to corrupt, but one of the least corrupted is George. More and more films tend to be designed for the lowest common denominator, but George has come through all of this with an ethical perspective. He does not simply do things to have a job. He has a thirst to complete something with merit while assuring the title of 'professional artist in residence' and gives it a good name.

For a time in the 1970s, George was the only director to have two films on the top ten box office hits of all time: *Butch Cassidy and the Sundance Kid* and *The Sting*. He was also the first director to achieve that distinction. History will judge George's films and their favor in the hearts of fans from future generations.

George had little use for critics in his life, particularly Pauline Kael, who he referred to as an "idiot." He defined critics as the following: "Critics are the people who show up on the battlefield after the battle is over and shoot the survivors." It was ironic that years later, up in the Berkshires, George would finally meet Kael face-to-face, and they were amazed that they actually liked each other as people. They were both suffering from Parkinson's, and Pauline passed away a few years before George.

Robert Redford described George as "bright, tight, fun, talented, distrusting, and demanding. And I like him. Some people read the funny papers in the newspaper because that's as far as they can get, but George reads them because, for him, they speak of something very much of this country. He recognizes that the way comics are constructed has a lot to do with a comic view of life. People who are militaristic in their style tend to be shut off in their minds, but the thing I respect about George is that, with all of his control and discipline that he demands from the people who work for him, he manages to keep an open and inviting mind to challenge himself and others. I should know because I feel I am very much like that myself."

Paul, speaking at George's memorial service in May of 2003, was also quick to point out that George could be very generous with his time and advice. When Paul was in Oregon starring in *Sometimes a Great Notion* with Henry Fonda and Lee Remick, he found himself having great difficulty with the director until things got so bad that Henry Fonda finally blew up on the set and the director was fired.

Not wanting to shut down production while they hired a new director, Paul decided that, since his company was producing the film, he would bite the bullet and take over the directing chores. He did not relish the task, but felt he had no other choice.

He called George to explain the situation, and without any solicitation on Paul's part, George fueled up his antique Waco biplane and flew cross country to Newport, Oregon. Upon arrival, George promptly locked himself up in the editing room and disappeared for two days. After checking out the footage that had already been shot, George emerged from the editing room and handed Paul a list of shots that were still needed before taking off for parts unknown.

It must have become apparent that George was my favorite director and his films were the highlights of my career. We were the closest of friends and loved each other deeply. On one recent evening, I was feeling chilly and found an old sweater to put on. I realized that it was one George had left at my house a long time ago. When I slipped it on, I felt a wave of warmth and security and the remembrance of one of the dearest souls in my life.

In 1989, the Deauville Film Festival was celebrating their fifteenth anniversary and honored George. He invited me along as his guest, and that was the last trip we took together. We had a wonderful time with the other attendees: Lauren Bacall, Kim Novak, Ben Gazzara, and Robert Mitchum. That same year, the Metropolitan Museum of Art in New York gave a salute to George with Robert Redford, Glenn Close, Kurt Vonnegut, John Irving, and William Goldman introducing his films. On opening night, a dinner was held across the street from the museum at the Irish Historical Society, and some of the seventy-five guests included Jessica Tandy, Hume Cronyn, Robin Williams, Glenn Close, and Swoozie Kurtz, along with his family, friends, and some of his old classmates from Yale. It was a night to remember.

In 2000, when I was about to retire and move back to New York City, I got the first dog I'd had in a long time, a darling little bundle of energy and love, Abby, named after my great-aunt Abigail. My dearest friend Margaret already owned Gracie, a Coton de Tulear, the same breed as my Abby. Abby helped me make the transition back to New York and into my retirement but left me far too early when she suddenly died of unknown causes in 2003. Biscuit, my current little love, is a Havanese and was found by Margaret on a website from the Havanese Rescue Organization. Biscuit has relocated splendidly from a foster home in North Carolina and has settled here in New York to become great company and comfort for me.

When I sold my house on Jacon Way in Pacific Palisades and made my way back to Manhattan, George invited me to live at his apartment on Fifth Avenue. By this time, his Parkinson's had progressed to the point where he was in need of 'round-the-clock care, and I thought it best to buy my own place.

At one time, I had stayed at Paul Mazursky's apartment at One Fifth Avenue down in Greenwich Village and loved that neighborhood. I enjoyed seeing all of the students from NYU as well as strolling through Washington Square Park. It was a lively neighborhood, much more exciting for me than the Upper East Side. I'd been looking for a place to buy and finally came across a sunny Greenwich Village prewar coop apartment at 26 East 10th Street. There were lots of good omens— probably the best one being the fact that George filmed the "Magic Gloves" scene from *The World According to Garp* directly in front of the building! Not too long afterward, Margaret got wind that the apartment adjacent to mine was for sale, and I was able to negotiate a deal to purchase that one too. Margaret helped me organize all the construction and design, and everything just turned out beautifully. I especially loved the two back-to-back wood-burning fireplaces!

Moving from a busy, thoroughly involving show business career to a life of leisure definitely has its pluses and minuses. It can be alarming to move from your telephone ringing every five minutes to it ringing every hour or so and then less. Writing this memoir, however, has reminded me that my career in casting spanned over some very special times and films. By the late 1990s, the film business had changed to such a degree that casting a film was not the pleasure it had once been for me.

I have nothing against youth. I was young once myself, and in many respects, I still am. It just saddens me that so much emphasis is put on it in films. It seems as though marvelous actors who still possess every bit of their faculties and talent cannot even get arrested these days. Yet young kids who look facially and physically terrific are handed leading roles in big-budget films and don't exhibit a clue about what to do once they are on screen, except to make sure their publicists get them into the tabloids every five seconds so as not to miss a twist or turn in their romantic pursuits and relationships.

If I'm going to pay twelve dollars to see a film in a Manhattan movie theater, I want to see an actor in a well-written screenplay directed by someone with an imagination and a knack for telling a story. I couldn't care less about seeing an "actor" when I know fifty things about their love life and nothing about their talent, particularly when it never shows up on the screen!

No matter how many millions and billions of dollars are being made on films today, I still would prefer to see the variety of films that were available when money and business weren't all what films were about. Thank God for independent films and the chance to see good actors emerge when many of them wouldn't stand a chance to break through in a big-studio film.

Throughout my many years of casting, the associates that I hired who worked alongside me eventually became known as my daughters and granddaughters, and most of them have gone on to successful casting careers of their own. Every year at Christmastime, we all try to get together for lunch in New York: Juliet Taylor, Wally Nicita, Nessa Hyams, Gretchen Rennell, Kathy Talbert, Bonnie Finnegan, Ellen Lewis, Laura Rosenthal, Patricia DiCerto, and Aleen Keshishian. Once in a while, we'll invite Howard Feuer, even though he's a boy.

My good friends Louis Zorich and Rocco Sisto usually come over to help celebrate my birthday, as we all share the same birthday week. I cook up my favorite Coq au Vin or Chicken Titties, along with my Heart-Attack Salad, and Rocco always argues with me about how to properly chop the onion! In California, I used to host an annual Super Bowl party with regulars like Manu, Charles Durning, M. Emmet Walsh, and other good friends.

Beyond that, when I'm not managing the Yankees from my couch or on an occasional visit to Yankee Stadium during the baseball season to see Mariano Rivera, Bernie Williams, and Derek Jeter, I've wrangled with a computer well enough to manage e-mails and some very basic stuff. I still attempt the treadmill for a couple of miles a week, but don't imagine I'll run in a marathon anytime soon. Another thing I thoroughly enjoy is my pilates with Barbara Allen over at Margaret's house. All this keeps the joints loosened up and gives me a little more energy.

Margaret and her husband, Warren Spector, get me out to the theater and dinner quite frequently. I've always been a fan of The Public Theater and Shakespeare in the Park, but now I've become an even bigger one! They also fill up many of my weekends with visits to their homes in Martha's Vineyard and Palm Beach, depending on the season. Probably what I love most these days is walking along the beach on Martha's Vineyard or helping Margaret tend to her many gardens.

In 1991, there was a campaign mounted to get the Academy of Motion Pictures Arts and Sciences to recognize my contribution to the film industry with a special Oscar. The decision came down to myself and

Satyajit Ray, the fine Indian director, who was finally chosen. Though the campaign was unsuccessful, it was heartening to read letters from Woody Allen, Chevy Chase, Paul Newman, Robert De Niro, Glenn Close, Louis Malle, George Roy Hill, Paul Mazursky, Jessica Tandy, Hume Cronyn, Juliet Taylor, Sydney Pollack, Clint Eastwood, David Picker, Robert Redford, and Mark Rosenberg and Paula Weinstein, who organized the campaign, extolling my virtues as a casting director.

Awards and recognition are lovely—I don't know anyone who doesn't enjoy them, but if it came to a choice between staring at an Oscar sitting on my mantel or being surprised by a phone call from one of my "discoveries" out of the clear blue to let me know they were thinking about me and grateful that I'd been a part in their lives, I know which I'd rather have.

I never had children of my own, but in an oddly parental way, each time I was able to give a young actor a chance to spread their wings and show their stuff on screen, it gave me a maternal pride. It has been lovely revisiting many of the films I cast in preparation for this memoir and realizing just how many good actors there are that have passed through my doors.

Later that same year, I was invited to be a judge at the Miss Universe Pageant in Thailand. Accompanying me was my elder sister Doris, and we left California just as riots were starting to break out in Los Angeles following the Rodney King trial verdict. Other judges included actor Estelle Getty, supermodel Kim Alexis, television personality Robin Leach, tennis player Vijay Amritraj, and a singer from Africa named Miriam Makeba, who was the most fascinating of all. Every evening, she was on the phone to her close friend, Nelson Mandela.

My last significant trip was with my dear friend and long-time associate Juliet Taylor and her husband Jim Walsh. We attended the Puerto Vallarta Film Festival in 2005, and I was treated like royalty.

Juliet and I gave a casting seminar to the Mexican film students, and each night, there was a fabulous event to attend. I met Roger Corman in Puerto Vallarta, and he was a very nice man who I wished I'd gotten to know earlier in my career.

As I reach the end of this memoir, I realize, having gone through so much of the material I had saved, and regretting not recording more information as I went along, that the life I had and continue to have is quite remarkable. I have honed a career that was also an art to a level of accomplishment that has kept me gainfully employed for over fifty years! My career allowed me to travel all over the world and to meet and work with some very rewarding and creative people.

Beyond my career, I have known love. I have known the joys of family and close friends. My life has been tempered with the loss and sadness of friends (both the two and four legged variety) that are no longer with me, but I do think my life has been balanced and rewarding.

It's hard to be "retired." I miss it all, especially the great souls that taught me so much and made my life so rich with their humor and love. To those wonderful friends . . . I thank them all for a grand life.

Appendix I

Personal File Index Cards

These are a mere sampling taken from my personal file 3 x 5 index cards which I'd write down these specific notes immediately after meeting with an actor for the first time.

Dustin Hoffman (August, 1957) Bob Duvall says is very good. Very good reading for SWEET PRINCE. 5/15/61 . . . use.

Martin Sheen (November, 1961) Very impressed by talking to him . . . is very well mannered. Soft voice, photos have a Jimmy Dean quality, but he's less "in." Nice looking, very interesting background (read the Bible in talent show contest).

Jon Voight (May, 1962) Appealing clean-cut American kid -- would see as very normal high school student -- maybe shy -- wouldn't think he'd be good for great emotion . . . only surly

Gene Hackman (June, 1962) Good type -- his reading was nothing but I believe he could be very good, especially as a gentle big dumb nice guy.

Michael Douglas (June, 1968) Nice young man . . . interesting face, less savage and more sensitive than father. O'Neill Foundation in Connecticut says he's very good.

Al Pacino (June, 1968) THE INDIAN WANTS THE BRONX -- excellent as flipped out punk . . . reminded me of Dustin Hoffman.

Robert De Niro (November, 1969) Good young character -- very funny. Speaks Italian and French. His pictures are fantastic as an Italian 45 year old man!

Don Johnson (January, 1970) Amazing boy . . . thoroughly lovable and bright as hell. Think he'll go very far -- I really dug him.

Christopher Guest (April, 1971) Liked this kid. Quite tall. Longish hair, quiet with sharp wry wit -- evidently is quite a musician too.

Richard Dreyfuss (January, 1973) Good stage experience. Smallish, but strong looking. Cold blue eyes, yet played very warm sweet boyish in AMERICAN GRAFFITI. Very intelligent.

Harrison Ford (January, 1973) Slow speech, sort of rugged Dirk Benedict. Summer stock - Chicago; has a humor; good strong quality; attractive.

Beverly D'Angelo (December, 1976) Divine reading. Very cute curly blond, an old-fashioned beauty look, a middle class quality -- funny girl.

Christopher Reeve (February, 1976) Very attractive Ivy League type, tall, rugged . . . he did very well, has nice humor. Someone thought his performance was surface, but it's a pretty nice surface!

Alec Baldwin (February, 1981) Really attractive. I liked him a lot. Was a student in politics and has just gotten started in acting.

Sean Penn (February, 1982) He is very good. Serious sort of classical face. Very shy at first and then sweet smile.

Rob Lowe (March, 1982) Hasn't studied yet . . . he is darling. No training, yet read very well and evidently does very well. Upper class look -- fresh, very handsome.

Helen Mirren (April, 1982) She'd rather play her own age. Blond, attractive - imagine she could be beautiful on screen . . . has class, but could probably play strumpet.

Ted Danson (January, 1983) 4 years Carnegie, then off-Broadway. More real and attractive in person - rugged.

Tim Robbins (April, 1983) Could be a slob or could do dumb upper class. Actually a bright guy -- not for romantic. Good studies and theatre work. I liked him. He did good improv with me.

Viggo Mortensen (August, 1983) Very soft spoken. Shy, but does have humor and read Tarzan with more understanding than others so far. USE this kid -- think he will be big.

Patricia Clarkson (May, 1985) Just graduated Yale. Sort of husky voice. Very nice open lady. Dark blond long hair. Good figure. She is a very funny lady.

Jennifer Connelly (October, 1985) She is lovely.

Johnny Depp (October, 1985) Obviously not much experience but perhaps a natural talent. Nice kid, sensible . . . Polaroid makes him handsomer than he is -- maybe the camera loves him.

Annette Bening (April, 1987) Excellent reading but not right -- too upscale. She had great humor -- now reminds me of Kathleen Turner. Sexy lady.

Ethan Hawke (June, 1987) Very good test for DEAD POETS SOCIETY . . . darling young man.

Julia Roberts (August, 1987) Can she act? Shyness that reminds me of the first time I saw Jessica Lange. Not good for this but she has something, a fawn . . . she really needs work but I bet she could do something.

Matthew Perry (October, 1987) Nice kid -- real boyish, best friend -- TV lead -- not movie lead. Cute preppy kid with a lot of energy, dark nice looks.

Joan Cusack (December, 1989) Red frizzy hair, long face, Betty Boop eyes. Very crazy, cute type. Talented.

Sandra Bullock (April, 1990) Very well adjusted. Normal, nice young lady. Quite attractive.

Julianne Moore (September, 1990) Chestnut long hair - beautiful. More or a TV person? 9/93 Saw a bit of her work in THE FUGITIVE and thought she did very well.

Adam Sandler (June, 1991) 4 years NYU . . . does stand up also. Very nice guy. Nice looking. "Recommends myself for serious stuff." Sort of a nasal voice.

Gwyneth Paltrow (March, 1992) Lovely quality - tall, string bean, looks like her mama and is doing a film for TV with her (she was cast first!)

Russell Crowe (June, 1992) Has done 8 good films in Australia . . . very attractive guy . . . sexy, manly.

Matt Damon (September, 1992) Nice kid, who is better looking than he was in SCHOOL TIES. He read okay but then didn't make an adjustment that he was given -- in fairness, he hadn't really studied the script so we will probably see him again in NY.

Selma Hayek (October, 1993) Built like a brick you know what. Very sexy and probably good. I'd like to read her in something good -- she could handle it. Lots of chutzpa.

Billy Bob Thorton (June, 1994) Darling, sturdy (doesn't seem 6') guy who is shy, sweet, but plays very bad in his own film and is a sleaze in INDECENT PROPOSAL. Sweet smile that could be dangerous. Soft twang. Not too much experience, but maybe he's very good.

Matthew McConaughey (January, 1995) This kid is gonna be a star. He's awfully good.

Ewan McGregor (January, 1995) I like him a lot. Scots but has good ear and can do a lot of accents. Seems much more mature than age and is very manly -- nice sense of humor, handsome.

Jude Law (July, 1995) He's an OK kid -- bright, serious about his work -- says he's pretty good at American accent. We had a nice talk. I chided him about being late.

Charlize Theron (August, 1996) Blond, very pretty -- not a bimbo at all. Put her on tape just to see if she could act -- it wasn't bad for an impromptu reading. She should study and might make it.

Aaron Eckart (March, 1997) Not interested in a charming leading man . . . would rather cry and be a character. Wants depth. He looks like an all American football hero and these are the parts he doesn't want. Instead of the boy next door he'd rather be the killer of that boy. Blond.

Freddie Prinze, Jr. (September, 1997) What a sweet young man. Quite serious and certainly a romantic type -- shy, with humor.

Uma Thurman (March, 1998) She's quite fascinating. Tall, thin, big eyes, blond. She's very bright and together -- imagine she can photograph beautifully.

Josh Hartnett (November, 1998) He's on a roll now. Darling looks . . . very manly.

Jennifer Lopez (June, 1999) Very attractive Latino; '98 OUT OF SIGHT with George Clooney -- she was very good.

Acknowledgments

The authors wish to acknowledge and thank Margaret Whitton, Warren Spector, David and Sally Bent, Steve Hoesly, Juliet Taylor, Wallis Nicita, Glenn Daniels, Johnny Brenden, Gretchen Rennell, Lara Kennedy, Bill Truesch, Thomas Olson, Helen Etnier, Fredrica Friedman, Robert Crawford, Jason Lisko, Rhea Hulear, Angela Vargas, Yvonne Kendall, Sandra Collins, Billy Monk, Barbara Allen and Maria Rubio.

We also wish to thank the Margaret Herrick Academy Library, the New York Public Library for the Performing Arts, Suzanne Finstad, Richard Schickel, Michael Feeney Callan, Lawrence Grobel and Andy Dougan for additional research material.

Photo credits: the cover image of James Dean is provided by CMG Worldwide. James Dean TM is a trademark of James Dean, Inc. www.JamesDean.com. The cover image of Robert Redford is courtesy of Universal Pictures. All other images and photographs in MY CASTING COUCH WAS TOO SHORT are provided by the personal collection of Marion Dougherty.

Marion Dougherty Safe Haven Fund

The Marion Dougherty Safe Haven Fund of the Mayor's Alliance for NYC's Animals will help transform the lives of domestic violence victims and their pets, and extend the legacy of this extraordinary woman.

A generous gift of $80,000 to be furnished over two years will provide support to the Alliance's Helping Pets and People in Crisis program, allowing NYC families to seek refuge from domestic violence without having to leave their animals behind. The fund will help the Alliance pay for pet vaccinations, spay/neuter surgery, and short-term boarding while families seek safety from abuse, ensuring that their pets can flee to safety as well. Marion Dougherty was forced to leave her pets behind when escaping a domestic violence situation in the 1970s.

ABOUT THE BOOK AND AUTHOR

Marion **Dougherty** shares her point of view as a casting executive who was there at the beginning of live television and then went on to cast many of the most important films of the 20th Century. It was Marion who had a gut instinct and took the risk to cast James Dean, Warren Beatty, Robert De Niro, Dustin Hoffman, Al Pacino, Paul Newman, Robert Redford, Mel Gibson, Danny Glover, Jon Voight, Robert Duvall, Martin Sheen, Matthew McConaughey, Gene Hackman, Bette Midler, Richard Gere, Glenn Close, Diane Lane, Christopher Walken, Woody Harrelson, Renee Russo, Lucy Lui, Wesley Snipes, Harry Connick Jr., Brooke Shields and countless other actors in some of their first major appearances either on live television or the motion picture screen.

Dougherty began her casting career in New York City during the Golden Age of Television, casting over 600 episodes of KRAFT TELEVISION THEATRE, NAKED CITY and ROUTE 66 which led to her successful career in the motion picture industry. She became the first female casting executive at Paramount Pictures in 1975 before securing the position of Vice President of Talent at Warner Brothers in 1979, a position she held up until her retirement in the year 2000.

Marion cast well over 125 films alongside film directors such as Stanley Kubrick, Richard Brooks, George Roy Hill, Richard Donner, Tim Burton, Woody Allen, Jonathan Demme, John Schlesinger, Clint

Eastwood, Arthur Hiller and so many others. A handful of the films she cast include: MIDNIGHT COWBOY, LENNY, HEAVEN CAN WAIT, REDS, AMERICAN GIGOLO, THE STING, PRETTY BABY, SLAUGHTERHOUSE FIVE, LETHAL WEAPON, BATMAN, BATMAN RETURNS, NATIONAL LAMPOON'S VACATION, FULL METAL JACKET, SLAPSHOT, MAVERICK, URBAN COWBOY, THE WORLD ACCORDING TO GARP, WILLY WONKA AND THE CHOCOLATE FACTORY, HONKYTONK MAN, THE HOSPITAL, LOOKING FOR MR. GOODBAR, THE KILLING FIELDS, ESCAPE FROM ALCATRAZ, SWING SHIFT, MEMPHIS BELLE and WHERE'S POPPA?

Marion Dougherty was a pioneer in the casting business with a career that spanned over 50 years, and most of her associates that she hired and trained throughout those years ended up becoming important casting professionals in their own right. The personal anecdotes that she shares in **MY CASTING COUCH WAS TOO SHORT** are a must read, and are an important part of television and film history, documenting the life and times of a Hollywood casting icon.

Made in the USA
Middletown, DE
30 December 2017